ROBERT WILLIAMS: CONVERSATIONS

Conversations with Comic Artists M. Thomas Inge, General Editor

Robert Williams: Conversations

Edited by Joseph R. Givens
and Darius A. Spieth

University Press of Mississippi / Jackson

The University Press of Mississippi is the scholarly publishing agency of
the Mississippi Institutions of Higher Learning: Alcorn State University,
Delta State University, Jackson State University, Mississippi State University,
Mississippi University for Women, Mississippi Valley State University,
University of Mississippi, and University of Southern Mississippi.

www.upress.state.ms.us

The University Press of Mississippi is a member
of the Association of University Presses.

First printing 2023
∞

Library of Congress Cataloging-in-Publication Data

Names: Givens, Joseph R., editor. | Spieth, Darius Alexander, 1970– editor.
Title: Robert Williams : conversations / Joseph R. Given, Darius A. Spieth.
Other titles: Conversations with comic artists.
Description: Jackson : University Press of Mississippi, 2023. | Series:
  Conversations with comic artists series | Includes bibliographical
  references and index.
Identifiers: LCCN 2023021785 (print) | LCCN 2023021786 (ebook) | ISBN
  9781496844026 (hardback) | ISBN 9781496844033 (trade paperback) | ISBN
  9781496850980 (epub) | ISBN 9781496850997 (epub) | ISBN 9781496851000
  (pdf) | ISBN 9781496851017 (pdf)
Subjects: LCSH: Williams, Robert, 1943–Interviews. | Cartoonists–United
  States–Interviews. | Underground comic books, strips, etc.–United States.
Classification: LCC PN6727.W55 Z46 2023 (print) | LCC PN6727.W55 (ebook)
  | DDC 741.5/973–dc23/eng/20230621
LC record available at https://lccn.loc.gov/2023021785
LC ebook record available at https://lccn.loc.gov/2023021786

British Library Cataloging-in-Publication Data available

Selected Major Works by Robert Williams

UNDERGROUND COMIX
Yellow Dog #7–10 (1968–69)
Zap Comix #4–16 (1969–2016)
Coochy Cooty Men's Comics #1 (1970)
San Francisco Comic Book #3, 5 (1970, 1979)
Tales from the Tube (1972)
Bijou Funnies #8 (1973)
Forbidden Knowledge #1 (1975)
Cocaine Comix #2, 3 (1980, 1981)
Yama Yama / Ugly Head (1981)
Go Naked #1 (1993)

ART EXHIBITIONS
Comix, Museum of Contemporary Art, Chicago (1972)
Zombie Mystery Paintings, Zomo Art Space, Los Angeles (1982)
Best of the West, Zero One Gallery, Los Angeles (1985)
Robert Williams, Psychedelic Solution, New York (1986)
American Pop Culture Show, Laforet Museum, Tokyo (1986)
Bad Influences, Parsons School of Design, New York (1988)
American Philistine, La Luz de Jesus, Los Angeles (1989)
Robert Williams, Tamara Bane Gallery, Los Angeles (1990)
Helter Skelter, Museum of Contemporary Art, Los Angeles (1992)
Kustom Kulture: Von Dutch, Ed "Big Daddy" Roth, Robert Williams, and Others, Center of
    Contemporary Art, Seattle, Washington; Laguna Art Museum, Laguna Beach, California;
    Maryland Institute College of Art, Baltimore (1993–94)
Psychopathia Aesthetica, Mambo Gallery, Sydney, Australia (1995)
Malicious Resplendence, Tony Shafrazi Gallery, New York (1997)
Best Intentions, Tony Shafrazi Gallery, New York; Copro Nason Gallery, Culver City, Califor-
    nia (2000)
Through Prehensile Eyes, Ben Maltz Gallery, Otis College of Art and Design, Los Angeles
    (2005)
Rene Magritte, Robert Williams and David LaChapelle, Tony Shafrazi Gallery, New York
    (2005)
L.A. Paint, Oakland Museum, Oakland, California (2008)
Robert Williams: Conceptual Realism, in the Service of the Hypothetical, Tony Shafrazi
    Gallery, New York (2009)
Biennial, Whitney Museum of American Art, New York (2010)

Robert Williams: Slang Aesthetics, Municipal Art Gallery, Los Angeles; Museum of Sonoma County, Sonoma, California; Santa Fe Museum of Contemporary Art, Santa Fe, New Mexico; Fort Wayne Museum of Art, Fort Wayne, Indiana; Louisiana State University Museum of Art, Baton Rouge (2015–18)

Visual Adventures of Robert Williams, Orange County Center for Contemporary Art, Santa Ana, California (2022)

ART BOOKS

The Lowbrow Art of Robert Williams (1979)
Zombie Mystery Paintings (1986)
Visual Addiction: The Art of Robert Williams (1989)
Views from a Tortured Libido (1993)
Malicious Resplendence (1997)
Hysteria in Remission (2003)
Through Prehensile Eyes (2005)
The Hot Rod World of Robert Williams (2006)
Conceptual Realism: In the Service of the Hypothetical (2009)
Slang Aesthetics (2015)
Robert Williams: The Father of Exponential Imagination (2019)
Ink, Blood, and Linseed Oil (2022)

CONTENTS

Courting Trouble: The Interviews of Robert Williams

> To create new values . . . , to gain freedom and a sacred refusal even of
> duty . . . , to claim the right to new values—that is the most terrifying
> claim for a burden-bearing, respectful spirit.
> —FRIEDRICH NIETZSCHE, *Thus Spoke Zarathustra*

Sitting down with Robert Williams for an interview is a memorable experience. The energy and dynamism that pervade his comics and canvases find a
direct equivalent in the rhetorical intensity of his enunciations as a witness
to his own life and the events that shaped it. After Joseph Givens and I spent
two days interviewing Robert Williams in 2015, his voice kept resonating in
my head for several days thereafter. For a while, I found myself inadvertently
speaking to others with the same panache, until the afterglow of the encounter
wore off. And even though the performative aspect of Robert Williams's skills
as a storyteller can only partially be captured by the transcribed interviews,
which this book assembles from an almost thirty-year period, much of their
visceral power has been preserved in the written form.

Robert Williams's significance as an icon of both underground comics and
"lowbrow" fine art during the late twentieth century and the early twenty-first
is by now well established, but his importance as a speaker, writer, art critic,
autobiographer, and sociological witness of the transformation of American
society from the postwar years to the digital age has been widely overlooked.
In this respect, the interview with Steve Ringgenberg is revealing. When
asked to describe his working process, from the idea stage to the finished
canvas, Williams replied: "I [first] sit down with drawing paper and a pencil

and a thesaurus and a dictionary and encyclopedias and all the books I need for reference. . . . I have my philosophy that art is a language. And it's a language that's more than thirty thousand years old."[1] The written word thus lingers above the pictorial execution as an ever-present subtext of Williams's creativity, a situation, which, of course, is also a defining characteristic of comics art in general. The literary dimension of William's art is furthermore borne out by his titles, which exist in three different forms: a short title by which the works are generally known; a scholastic designation, which could run the length of a paragraph; and a deliberately colloquial "remedial title." "The first title would be 'as you see it,' and the second would be as a pedantic art academic would phrase it, and the third title would be from the vulgar perspective of some low-brow slob who worked in a bowling alley or pool hall."[2] Behind this differentiation, therefore, lurks an informed commentary about the social and educational stratification of the art world. The intended effect is to be thoroughly satirical. The iconic *Exploration of the Subconscious on I-40*, a canvas once much coveted by the curator Walter Hopps for his private collection but owned by *Juxtapoz* cofounder Greg Escalante, boasts the following trinity of titles:

> *Exploration of the Subconscious on I-40*
> Scholastic designation: *Paris, South of Daggett, Where Sigmund Freud Is the Name of a Soothsayer's Parrot and Where the Wildest Revealed Dream of the Evening Is Posted over the Bar and the Best Dreamer Gets a Door Prize*
> Remedial title: *A Leotard Weekend for Tractor Jockeys on Their Way to the Louvre*[3]

The wordplay and the literary quality of long descriptive titles are not unique to Robert Williams. In late nineteenth-century France, the symbolist trailblazer Gustave Moreau, who, like Williams, stood squarely in the academic tradition of art, penned elaborate descriptions of his canvases, which were eventually published in book format as stand-alone literary works.[4]

But the literary contributions of Robert Williams do not end with his underground comics or the elaborate titles of his paintings. For example, over many years, from the 1990s through the early 2000s, he wrote editorials for *Juxtapoz* magazine, which he helped cofound as an alternative to the established art press. One of the hallmarks of *Juxtapoz* was that it featured underground comics, psychedelic posters, graffiti, tattoo and surf art, hot rods, et cetera, on the same footing as fine art. Robert Williams's collected writings were published in 2022 in a volume titled *Ink, Blood, and Linseed Oil*.[5]

Robert Williams, *Exploration of the Subconscious on I-40*, 1993. Oil on canvas, 76.2 × 91.4 cm. Darius A. Spieth collection.

The current volume complements and completes the (re)discovery of Robert Williams as a literary figure by assembling for the first time hard-to-find interviews, which appeared between 1987 and 2015 in various journals and newspapers, many of which are defunct by now.

Robert Williams's career bridges the gap between comics and fine art in a unique way. When the artist arrived in Los Angeles in 1963, his aspiration was to make his mark as a fine artist. His skills and ebullient imagination gave him a sense of self-assurance about his destiny as a figurative painter, which was soon dashed in art school at a time when abstract expressionism, and later conceptual art, reigned supreme. Robert Williams then switched gears—partly out of economic necessity, partly out of intellectual and artistic drive—to become, first, a commercial artist and graphic designer for Ed "Big Daddy" Roth's studios and then an independent comics artist, joining the *Zap* collective in 1969. Among the products of Roth's studios that Robert Williams helped develop and promote were comics and other printed matter, printed

T-shirts, and, of course, Kustom hot rods, a revolution in car and hot rod culture, because these four-wheeled fantasy creations prioritized aesthetics over speed. Although it was an after-hours job, the involvement with *Zap Comix* complemented William's career choice to work with Ed Roth. Founded by Robert Crumb in early 1968, *Zap Comix* published three issues in its first year; Robert Williams's debut as a contributor came with issue #4, in August 1969. He had finally arrived at the heart of the underground comics revolution.

Comics publications, at this point, fell into one of two categories: those approved by the Comics Code Authority (CCA), a self-regulating body of the industry established in 1954, and underground comics, which were peddled semilegally directly on the streets, since regular distribution channels, such as the mail system, were off-limits. As an underground comics artist, Williams was at the forefront of the struggle against censorship and legal persecutions of underground comics in the late 1960s and early 1970s. In many ways, whether one looks at his comics or his paintings, Williams's imagery is a catalog of all the themes that the CCA sought to ban: "Scenes of excessive violence shall be prohibited," "All scenes of horror, excessive bloodshed, gory or gruesome crimes, depravity, lust, sadism, masochism shall not be permitted," "Nudity in any form is prohibited, as is indecent or undue exposure," "Policemen, judges, government officials, and respected institutions shall never be presented in such a way as to create disrespect for established authority," among other, similar injunctions.[6]

In the 1980s and 1990s, Williams came full circle as a painter, eventually showing at Tony Shafrazi Gallery in New York and at the Art Basel Miami Beach fair by the early 2000s. It should be pointed out that all his canvases carry the stylistic and narrative imprint of comic art, evident, for instance, in the use of multiple panels recounting parallel narratives, which instill his compositions with a postmodern and deconstructive element. But beyond that, the canvases retain many of the hallmarks of traditional academic art, especially in the impeccable use of perspective and the anatomically correct rending of the human figure, evident in Williams's many depictions of the female nude set in deliberately trivial Pop settings, such as diners, roadside signage, or traffic accidents.

In his interviews and writings, Williams emerges as an art critic in the true, original sense of the word: he relentlessly criticizes established conventions of modern and contemporary art, and the "art world" that sustains them, by pointing out their contradictions and hypocritical nature.[7] By the same token, Williams never ceases to affirm that he "supports all art"—after all, how could an artist be against art? Comics, for him, are a corrective for the perceived wrongs of the institutionalized, "official" art world, which scorned him and his works for so many years. Williams's argument that there are two "art worlds," one "official"—shown in museums and galleries, reviewed by "art professionals," and looked upon kindly by the press, but excluding almost all materials that do not obey its unwritten rules (narrative content is passé; conspicuous skills are to be derided, etc.)—and that of the artistic "underground"—sustained by collectors and "private" enthusiasts, cherishing innovation and originality, valuing risk-taking, skills, and effort, and not bending to the moral codes of the mainstream—has now been validated by other, powerful critical voices, such as that of Marc Fumaroli in France or that of Vittorio Sgarbi in Italy.[8]

Needless to say, comic art largely lives in the latter, underground space. Comic art provides an escape from the closed circuits and narrow-mindedness of the "official" art world. Because comics are drawing based, they also revalidate the academic idea of the primacy of draftsmanship. Being in the underground, however, means perpetual struggles but also offers, by way of reward, a reenchantment with the romantic idea of what it means to be an artist. One of the underlying arguments that drives Williams's rhetoric is endurance. While so much slapdash high-modernist and conceptual contemporary art is praised to the skies by a chorus of art professionals, most of it will be forgotten in a few years' time. The art of comics, like rock 'n' roll, by contrast, is here to stay and will find its readers and viewers in the future just as it does in the present.

Undoubtedly, Robert Williams, in his interviews, writings, and art, seeks to shock the reader or the observer. A recurrent trope throughout his work is the artistic bohemia, whose lifestyle patterns, summarized by the term *peintre maudit*—a "cursed painter"—were established largely in France at the turn of the twentieth century. Itself derived from the French expression for "cursed poets" (*poètes maudits*), the label was applied to painters ranging from Caravaggio to Paul Gauguin, Vincent van Gogh, and Balthus. Like the original poets and writers from the symbolist literary movement of the late nineteenth century—Charles Baudelaire, Paul Verlaine, Oscar Wilde, and Arthur Rimbaud—the *peintres maudits* shared a reputation for flouting social norms, sexual transgressions, and abuses of alcohol and drugs, excesses that, to varying degrees, fueled their artistic genius. Williams enjoys being at once a Dionysian and a Nietzschean figure, an *artiste maudit* and a *poète maudit* combined in one person. Even if some of the statements found in this book run the gamut from the questionable to the inexcusable—and this is particularly true for some of the earlier interviews—they nevertheless need to be interpreted in their original context of radical and polemically heated attacks against Williams during the late 1980s and early 1990s.

Two events defined this key stage of his career, which, for better or worse, catapulted him to the rank of a figure of public notoriety. In 1987, a then little-known rock band named Guns N' Roses licensed, for a few hundred dollars, a Robert Williams painting for the cover of *Appetite for Destruction*, which became the best-selling debut album of all time in the United States. Williams's namesake *Zap*-styled painting, *Appetite for Destruction*, also inspired the title of the band's debut album, which eventually sold more than thirty million copies worldwide; eighteen million copies were bought in the United States alone. Williams had already been licensing his artwork to rock bands for decades when the album was released. The record cover licensing business provided a steady, if minor, source of income, and Williams typically conducted such business without great formality in his own house. Most of the bands he had dealt with previously vanished from sight just as quickly as their members had appeared on his doorstep. Axl Rose and his crew promised not to be much different. Williams laid out a number of cover options for the band members, but Rose had already made up his mind: he wanted *Appetite for Destruction*. Williams tried to dissuade him. Rose would be asking for all sorts of trouble: difficulties in exporting the album to Canada; difficulties with self-appointed moral authorities or even political rabble-rousers. Rose could have any other image, but not this one.

Appetite for Destruction could possibly be interpreted as a secret rape fantasy: a blonde itinerant saleswoman of miniature toy robots is apparently being assaulted by an adult robot, equipped with metal claws, metal jaws filed to a point, and telescope lenses for a brain; he is dressed in a tacky brown trench coat, shoes, and hat. The victim is about to be avenged by a fire-red demon in shiny, chrome-plated body armor, matched by a metal helmet and knives for teeth, who manages to levitate himself from behind a palisade.

In the end, Williams backed down and agreed to license the image, which was already close to a decade old by then. Both he and Guns N' Roses did not have to wait long for the backlash. *Appetite for Destruction* appeared as cover art for the namesake album, but after a wave of controversy and protest, the record company replaced it with a more symbolic Celtic cross, studded with the skulls of the band members and their iconic hairdos. The original cover design, however, had not vanished entirely, since Williams's image was moved to an inside sleeve of the album, an ingenious solution and perhaps an unprecedented example of compromise censorship.

Robert Williams, *Appetite for Destruction*, 1979. Oil on canvas, 71 x 38 cm. Private collection.

Williams had certainly already established a reputation for scandal as a *Zap* cartoonist. But the lascivious nature of these comics was known to only a small group of individuals; the Guns N' Roses scandal in 1987 was the kind of material that found its way into the mainstream media. Oddly enough, several important aspects of the episode were readily overlooked. While all attention focused on the visual content of the *Appetite for Destruction* image, the title of the album from which it derived remained unchanged. It was Robert Williams who had coined the title, and no matter the censorship

Robert Williams, *Oscar Wilde in Leadville, April 13, 1882*, 1991. Oil on canvas, 144.78 × 262.26 cm. Los Angeles County Museum of Art, gift of Stuart and Judy Spence in memory of Greg Escalante (M.2019.403.8).

controversy surrounding the image, its title proliferated globally, emblazoned as it was on the best-selling album cover in the United States. Much of the criticism focused on the alleged immorality of the music industry, which sought to seduce its youthful audience with corrupting and sinful imagery and lyrics. The public outcry therefore largely bypassed the artist—or even the band, for that matter—but things turned out differently a few years later in a museum context.

The second defining event was Williams's participation, in 1992, in the *Helter Skelter* exhibition at the Museum of Contemporary Art (MOCA), Los Angeles, where a room was given over to his art, and protests ensued. The centerpiece of the *Helter Skelter* exhibition was a large canvas titled *Oscar Wilde in Leadville, April 13, 1882*. Williams had conceived it as an homage to the Irish symbolist writer, whose work Williams genuinely admires. The picture's narrative was inspired by a historical event in 1882 when Wilde, during a lecture tour on aestheticism across the United States, made a stop in the mining town of Leadville, Colorado.[9] By this time, Wilde had acquired an international reputation as a "dandy," who sported on such occasions an outfit decorated with sunflowers and lilies. Rumor had it that some local youths planned to interrupt the lecture with pranks and that they would wear costumes mocking the floral outfit of the famous visitor. In fact, no interference happened, and Wilde charmed the audience of this rough-and-tumble mining town with his direct yet sophisticated talk on Renaissance art and the nature of beauty. Williams's picture therefore represents more of a speculation about what could have been than what really happened on April 13, 1882—a strategy that is typical of the notion of "conceptual realism," which Williams prefers over the now-prevalent term "lowbrow" to describe his art.

But the humiliation that Wilde was spared on April 13, 1882, now, in 1992, descended on Williams, albeit in a somewhat different form. In keeping with Williams's method, the Wilde painting also bore a "scholastic designation" and a "remedial title," which contained a pseudo-colloquial but nevertheless mild allusion to Wilde's homosexuality, as it could have been phrased by the Leadville miners: *A Fairy's Kiss for a Syphilitic Lily Sniffer.* Nevertheless, the expression proved to be insidious. As Williams recalled subsequent events:

> Some people were unwilling to comprehend the purpose of the title. They were imagi-
> nationless, politically correct, and shallow people, who mobilized the gay community
> against me, and then the feminists came out against my female nudes. I became the
> target. So, the night of the opening, they picketed me, and I was the "bad fella," and
> everyone was mad at me that night. There were one hundred and fifty write-ups
> around the United States, and I was the villain in *all* of them. I was the artist who had
> the realism and the startling visual content. [MOCA chief curator Paul] Schimmel said
> that I drew more than half the crowd, but he would never show me again as long as he
> lived. There were people coming to my room and handing out pamphlets about what
> a jerk I was in *my* space. One of the most famous shows in the history of Los Angeles,
> and I was the criminal. I felt so low.[10]

A critic writing from the judgment seat of avant-garde aesthetics, the periodical *Artforum*, had already set the tone for this type of criticism in the year preceding *Helter Skelter* when he wrote about Williams's art that "since the obscene rears its head everywhere in these psychotic nightmares, it's beside the point to try to sort out the 'gratuitous sex and violence' from the more artistically purposive carnage. . . . It would seem virtually impossible to accommodate this material without a certain distance."[11] In fact, Williams would never be asked again to show his pictures at the Museum of Contemporary Art during Schimmel's tenure, and it would only be under Schimmel's successor, Jeffrey Deitch, that Williams would be invited to present a documentary movie on his life and work at the museum.[12] In 2015, however, the Los Angeles Municipal Art Gallery at Barnsdall Park dedicated a comprehensive retrospective to Williams, which was warmly received in the press. Chris Campion, for example, writing for the British *Guardian*, remarked on this occasion that "the work of once-fashionable artists inevitably fades from view but, decades on, Williams and his dirty, funky, kitschy pictures still feel vital and remain very much in vogue."[13] Since 2019, *Oscar Wilde in Leadville, April 13, 1882* has been part of the permanent collections of the Los Angeles County Museum of Art—a donation of Stuart and Judy Spence in memory of Greg Escalante—but while accepting the gift, the museum still prefers not to put the canvas on display or publish it on the internet. The rehabilitation thus remains only partial.

A careful reading of the interviews, presented here in chronological order, shows that Williams's statements became more measured and moderate over time. The same development can also be observed with respect to the evolution of his art's iconography. Many of the more recent interviews reflect the wisdom that comes with a retrospective distance on an eventful life and a destiny out of the ordinary. But even underlying the more radical opinions, one finds ideas that have extremely "classical" roots and would hardly raise eyebrows if presented in a different context. One can think of the professions that art is based on the observation of nature and the use of one's imagination, that art's ultimate purpose is to convey notions of beauty that are wrapped up in sexuality, or the centrist political position to not cater to either conservatives or progressives.

Hidden in these pages are jewels of sociological observations that teach audiences of the twenty-first century how phenomena and mentalities taken for granted or seen as trivial today may have been revolutionary not too long ago. One can think of how the act of riding a motorcycle in a leather outfit, in the 1950s and 1960s, was interpreted as an invitation to gang retribution and violence, if it could not be backed up by the bravado of real street power. Or about the observation that the Vietnam War changed the aspirations of a younger generation from operating and moving machinery to becoming college-educated brain workers.

The interviews are furthermore a testimonial to the genuineness of the struggle to gain acceptance with an art form and a talent that did not fit in with the mainstream—neither in the 1960s nor today. Above all, there is much information here to absorb about the relationship between comics and the world of fine art, with its museums, galleries, fairs, auctions, snobbery, and claims of artistic freedom, which hardened into new orthodoxies, imposing new rules and limitations on creativity. Nevertheless, the world of comics can also learn from that of art, as the latter provides a vocabulary and an intellectual framework for thinking and talking about visual information and its relationship to language and history, aspects that are frequently overlooked in the analysis of comics. Robert Williams's place, straddling these two extremes, makes him an ideal figure to begin such conversations.

This book is the result of years of interaction with the many levels of Robert Williams's work and ideas. The editors would like to extend a special thank-you to those whose contributions made this publication possible: first and foremost, Robert and Suzanne Williams, who were unwavering in their support and kindly introduced the editors to many of the authors who appear in the pages that follow; Gwynn Vitello, who generously offered the republication of content from *Juxtapoz* magazine and *Thrasher* magazine, which makes up a significant portion of this volume; and Williams's archivist, Steve "Sketch" Vallino, who introduced the editors to even the most obscure and long-forgotten interviews. Blue Trimarchi helped with providing many of the images featured here. Without the late Greg Escalante, who established the first contact with Robert Williams in 2011 and tirelessly defended the artist and his contemporary "lowbrow" creators, this book would likely never have become a reality. Finally, we would like to express our gratitude to the staff of the University Press of Mississippi, especially Lisa McMurtray and Mary Heath, who recognized the significance of these interviews and their place within the Conversations with Comic Artists Series early on. Any publication is a teamwork effort, and we very much appreciate the contributions of Joey Brown, Pete Halverson, Todd Lape, Michael Martella, and Jordan Nettles at various stages in the creation and launch of this book.

Darius A. Spieth, PhD
San Diego Alumni Association Chapter Alumni Professor of Art History
School of Art
Louisiana State University

Notes

1. Steve Ringgenberg, "Robert Williams Interview," *Comics Journal* 161 (August 1993): 42–70, reprinted as the seventh interview in this volume.
2. Robert Williams, interview with the editors, Chatsworth, CA, April 7, 2015.
3. *Malicious Resplendence: The Paintings of Robert Williams*, ed. Gary G. Groth (Seattle, WA: Fantagraphics Books, 1997), 230. The volume contains many more examples of artworks with a similarly structured triad of literary titles.
4. Gustave Moreau, Écrits sur *l'art: I. Sur les œuvres et sur lui-même* (Fontfroide: Fata Morgana, 2002).

5. Robert Williams, with contributions by Gwynned Vitello and Darius A. Spieth, *Ink, Blood, and Linseed Oil: The Collective Writings of Artist Robert Williams* (San Francisco: Last Gasp, 2022).

6. Cited after "Code of the Comics Magazine Association of America, Inc., Adopted October 26, 1954," in Senate Committee on the Judiciary, *Comic Books and Juvenile Delinquency, Interim Report, 1955* (Washington, DC: United States Government Printing Office, 1955).

7. The term "art[-]world" was coined by the philosopher, critic, and Columbia professor Arthur Danto, who published an article on the subject in 1964, "The Artworld," Conference Proceedings of the American Philosophical Association Eastern Division Sixty—First Annual Meeting, *Journal of Philosophy* 61, no. 19 (October 15, 1964): 571–84, which contained marvels of insight, such as "to mistake an artwork for a real object is no great feat when an artwork is the real object one mistakes it for" (575). Danto also repeatedly defended the role of "an authority in philosophy and an expert in aesthetics" like himself "to determine the importance or the significance of such and such an artist, such and such installation or performance, in such and such gallery, along the actual art context. But I am also a private person, with his personal taste, and I can assure you that in this capacity, I prefer by far . . . Chardin [an eighteenth-century realist painter of still lifes]!" Cited in Marc Fumaroli, *Ut Pictora Poesis: What Language to Say the Arts? French Rhetoric and German Aesthetics in the Eighteenth Century*, trans. Darius A. Spieth (Baton Rouge: LSU Press, 2016), 14. The same text by Marc Fumaroli contains an extensive analysis of Danto's aesthetic philosophies as they pertain to the notion of a class of "professional artworld authorities," which echoes, from a historical and academic point of view, many points of art institutional criticism that Robert Williams made in his writings and interviews.

8. See Darius A. Spieth, postface to *Ink, Blood, and Linseed Oil*.

9. Lloyd Lewis and Henry Justin Smith, *Oscar Wilde Discovers America: 1882* (New York: Harcourt, Brace, 1936), 308–18.

10. Editors' interview with Robert Williams, Chatsworth, CA, April 7, 2015.

11. Benjamin Weissman, "Robert Williams: Tamara Bane Gallery," *Artforum* 29, no. 8 (April 8, 1991): 133.

12. See also Jeffrey Deitch's interview with Robert Williams, "Robert Williams: The Master of the Slang Aesthetic," *Juxtapoz* 22, no. 3 (March 2015): 49–61, reproduced as the fourteenth interview of this volume.

13. Chris Campion, "Robert Williams: 'My Stuff Is Way Kitsch—to an Abstract Level,'" *The Guardian*, April 1, 2015, online, reproduced as the fifteenth interview in this volume, http://www.theguardian.com/artanddesign/2015/apr/01/artist-robert-williams -appetite-for-destruction-slang-aesthetics (accessed September 5, 2022).

CHRONOLOGY

1943   Robert Williams is born on March 2, 1943, in Albuquerque, New Mexico, to Robert W. Williams and Betty Jane Spink-Williams.

1947   Williams's parents have a tumultuous relationship. Betty Spink-Williams remains in Albuquerque with her mother, and Robert W. Williams moves to Montgomery, Alabama, and opens the Parkmore Drive-In. They share custody, and Robert spends his childhood traveling between Albuquerque and Montgomery.

1954   Williams discovers EC horror comics and *Mad* magazine, both of which profoundly influence his creative aspirations.

1955   Williams's father gives him a 1934 Ford coupe. During the same year, he visits family in Los Angeles. These events spark Williams's fascination with hot rod culture.

1956   Williams's parents separate for the final time, and he chooses to live with his mother in Albuquerque.

1958   Williams joins a traveling carnival and begins to experiment with alcohol and other recreational substances.

1960   Williams develops an interest in progressive jazz and the beatnik culture that surrounded it. He frequents the Purple Turk coffee shop in Albuquerque.

1961   Williams is expelled from Albuquerque High School for truancy and misbehavior.

1963   Williams moves to Los Angeles and enrolls in Los Angeles City College (LACC).

1964   Williams meets Suzanne Chorna in April and marries her in June after a brief courtship. Williams produces several editorial cartoons for the LACC newspaper, *The Collegian*, and is awarded second place for editorial cartoons at the National Convention of Junior Colleges.

1965   Williams withdraws from LACC and enrolls in Chouinard Art Institute (CalArts). He works a brief stint as an illustrator for *Black Belt* magazine before taking the job of art director for the Kustom Kulture icon

Ed "Big Daddy" Roth. He withdraws from college, frustrated with the elitism of the academic institution.

1967   Williams attends the Monterey Pop Festival, where he sees a psychedelic pop-up art fair that inspires him to start work on the painting *In the Land of Retinal Delights*.

1968   Williams is introduced to underground comix with *Zap Comix* #2. He completes work on *In the Land of Retinal Delights* and approaches underground comic publisher Print Mint with the request to distribute prints of the painting. Print Mint counters the offer with an opportunity to contribute to *Yellow Dog* #7; Williams agrees, and it is the first time he is published as an underground comic artist.

1969   Williams is the cover artist for *Yellow Dog* #8. He joins the *Zap* collective as a seventh member and contributes to *Zap Comix* #4.

1970   Roth Studios closes, marking the end of Williams's commercial career. Williams is commissioned to produce ten paintings for Brucker's Movie World. Williams collaborates with other *Zap Comix* artists to publish issue #5, and he releases a solo effort as an artist and writer of *Coochy Cooty Men's Comics* #1.

1972   The Chicago Museum of Contemporary Art features Williams and other *Zap* artists in the *Comix* exhibition.

1973   Williams and other *Zap* artists publish issues #6 and #7 of *Zap Comix*, and Williams contributes to *Bijou Funnies* #8.

1974   Williams introduces the "cartoon" line in his painting *Rooster's Lament*. It is the first of a series of paintings produced during this time that he describes as "supercartoons."

1975   Williams is featured in *Zap Comix* #8 and *Forbidden Knowledge* #1.

1978   Williams is featured in *Zap Comix* #9.

1979   Williams paints *Appetite for Destruction*, which will become the cover and namesake of the debut album for Guns N' Roses. The underground comic publisher Print Mint publishes Williams's first art book, *The Lowbrow Art of Robert Williams*.

1980   Williams's first one-person exhibition, *Rabid with Sophistication*, is shown at California Alternative Gallery. Williams contributes a short story to *Cocaine Comix* #2.

1981   Inspired by the expressive alternative style of Gary Panter and S. Clay Wilson, Williams publishes the indie comic *Yama Yama / The Ugly Head*. The expressive, slapdash style is a marked departure from the precision of Williams's trademark style. Williams's iconic smiling devil is featured on the cover of *Cocaine Comix* #3.

1982   Williams responds to the burgeoning Los Angeles punk scene with an expressive series of paintings, *Zombie Mystery Paintings*. They are featured at an exhibition at Zomo Art Space, which skyrockets Williams's popularity in the Los Angeles underground art scene. Williams continues to work as a comic artist, and his work is included in *Zap Comix* #10.

1984   Williams cocurates the *Art Boys Open Class Public Exhibition* at Graffiti Gallery.

1985   Slash from Guns N' Roses sees Williams's art in the *Best of the West* at Zero One Gallery, an encounter that leads to the band approaching Williams for an album cover. Williams is featured in *Zap Comix* #11.

1986   Williams's art is shown in New York for the first time at the sold-out show at Psychedelic Solution Gallery. His work is shown abroad for the first time at the *American Pop Culture Show*, Laforet Museum, Tokyo. He releases his second art book, which collects the *Zombie Mystery Paintings* and includes a foreword by Robert Crumb.

1987   Williams's painting *Appetite for Destruction* is selected by Gun N' Roses for their debut album. The suggestive nature of the cover causes public outcry, resulting in controversy, bans, and the eventual redesign of the album cover. Williams is given his first public art commission and paints abstract murals inspired by cartoons and graffiti in MacArthur Park in Los Angeles.

1988   Williams is featured in *Bad Influences* exhibitions at the Parsons School of Design in New York and Los Angeles. Williams contributes to *Zap Comix* #12.

1989   Williams is featured in a one-person exhibition at La Luz de Jesus, a venue that would become a mainstay of Los Angeles underground art. Williams befriends the underground art patron and collector Greg Escalante, who begins distributing archival prints of Williams's paintings. Last Gasp publishes *Visual Addition: The Art of Robert Williams*, a book that collects over sixty paintings and includes a foreword by the feminist punk icon Lydia Lunch.

1990   Williams is featured in a one-person exhibition at Tamara Bane Gallery in Los Angeles.

1992   Williams's art is prominently featured in the seminal *Helter Skelter* exhibition at the Los Angeles Museum of Contemporary Art. The controversial exhibition sparks protests that were covered by national media. His work draws the attention of the prominent New York "blue chip" art dealer Tony Shafrazi, who includes Williams in *The Other Side* exhibition at Shafrazi's New York art gallery.

1993 Williams is one of the key personalities in *The Kustom Kulture: Von Dutch, Ed "Big Daddy" Roth, Robert Williams and Others* exhibition at Laguna Beach Museum in California and Maryland Institute College of Art in Baltimore. Timothy Leary, an icon of 1960s counterculture, writes the foreword for Williams's fourth art book, *Views from a Tortured Libido*. Williams contributes a short story to the "Art Brut" comics anthology *Go Naked* #1.

1994 Williams cofounds the underground art magazine *Juxtapoz*, which would become the number one art magazine in America. Williams contributes to *Zap Comix* #13.

1995 Williams is featured in the one-person exhibition *Psychopathia Aesthetica* at the Mambo Gallery in Sydney, Australia.

1997 Williams receives widespread acclaim with the high-profile one-person exhibition at Tony Shafrazi Gallery, *Malicious Resplendence*, which is accompanied by a career-spanning catalog.

1998 Williams contributes to *Zap Comix* #14.

2000 Williams showcases eighteen artworks in *Best Intentions*, his second one-person exhibition at Tony Shafrazi Gallery in New York. Williams's art is included in the Los Angeles County Museum of Art's *Made in California* exhibition, the first time since the *Helter Skelter* controversy that Williams's art is displayed in a museum space.

2003 Williams is a keynote speaker at the University of Florida Conference on Comics, *Underground(s)*. Fantagraphics publishes *Hysteria in Remission*, an anthology of Williams's comic art, which featured comic art from *Zap, Snatch, Arcade, Cocaine Comix*, and *Coochy Cooty Men's Comics*.

2005 Williams is invited to teach classes as an artist in residence at the Otis College of Art and Design in Los Angeles. His recent paintings are shown in an exhibition, *Through Prehensile Eyes*, hosted by Ben Maltz Gallery and Otis. Williams contributes to *Zap Comix* #15. Last Gasp releases the art book *Through Prehensile Eyes*, which includes fifty-eight of Williams's recent paintings.

2006 Williams produces an illustrated autobiography of his experiences in hot rod culture, *The Hot Rod World of Robert Williams*.

2008 Williams's art is part of the *L.A. Paint* exhibition at the Oakland Museum of California.

2009 Williams partners with Gentle Giant Studios and creates large, free-standing sculptures, which are featured in the *Conceptual Realism: In the Service of the Hypothetical* exhibition at Tony Shafrazi Gallery in New York and at California State University Northridge. In his artist statement, Williams describes himself as leading a new wave of post-modern figurative artists, a movement he names "conceptual realism."

2010   Williams is included in the *Biennial* at the Whitney Museum of American Art in New York. *Mr. Bitch'n*, a documentary about the life and art of Williams, is released. Williams is honored with a Lifetime Achievement Award at the Beyond Eden Art Fair in Hollywood, California. Williams's sculptures and paintings are the centerpieces of Tony Shafrazi's booth at the Miami Art Basel.

2012   Williams is honored as Louisiana State University Art and Design Paula G. Manship Distinguished Lecturer. His talk is accompanied by the biographical exhibition *Poison for the Impressionable*.

2014   Fantagraphics publishes the collected *Zap Comix* in an archival boxed set.

2015   Williams's first major one-person exhibition in a museum space, *Slang Aesthetics*, is shown at the Los Angeles Municipal Art Gallery. It is accompanied by a group show of artists who cite Williams as a key influence. The exhibition sets a museum attendance record. *Slang Aesthetics* travels the country and is shown at the Museum of Sonoma County, Santa Fe Museum of Contemporary Art, Fort Wayne Museum of Art, and the Louisiana State University Museum of Art in Baton Rouge.

2016   The *Los Angeles Art Show* awards Williams with the first Lifetime Achievement Award.

2019   Fantagraphics releases a comprehensive, career-spanning retrospective book, *Robert Williams: The Father of Exponential Imagination*.

2022   Williams releases an anthology of his collective writings, *Ink, Blood, and Linseed Oil*.

ROBERT WILLIAMS: CONVERSATIONS

Psychopathia Aesthetica

PAUL GRAVETT / 1987

From *Escape: The Modern Guide to Comics and More*, no. 10 (1987): 40–43. Reprinted by permission of Paul Gravett.

England is my ancestral homeland, and this is my first visit. Since I was a child, I've been filled with Arthurian legends. My mother wanted me to be a cowboy, but I wanted to be a knight. Friends tell me this is the land of "fuddy-duddies," but I can't make a statement like that. I've only been here two days, but you got a real problem here studying art history, because you can only point to maybe three or four really wild artists, like Turner, Beardsley, Blake, and Bacon. Otherwise, England seems pretty constipated.

I grew up in Albuquerque, New Mexico, and in the early fifties, I was a hot-rodder. I'd been raised in a family that had always been around race cars. I got my first hot rod at eleven years old, a '34 Ford Sedan. I worked for three years on this roadster, and every cent I got went into this car, putting in the chrome and parts, and I had a beautiful blonde fiancée, and we spent a lot of time out in this car.

Then my fiancée left me and I failed school. I was thrown out of a lot of schools and had a lot of police trouble. I inherited a little money, and I thought, "Forget this hot rod, I'm going to Los Angeles and get an art education." Now, for the last seventy years, art schools have been de-emphasizing craftsmanship in drawing, so I had a lot of problems there because the teacher wanted me to paint sloppy and expressionist, and to think in planes, but I wanted to draw tight modeled shapes. That blew my mind. I ran across Suzanne on campus, and we got married. I had the responsibility of taking care of her, so I really had to go to work. I finally got a job as the art director for *Black Belt* magazine. After about six months, they fired me because I worked too slow. I got a job as a container designer, but I had to wear a tie because it was an uptight business. I was a funky dude, so it didn't take long to see through that.

After the container job, I went to the unemployment agency and they said, "We got nothing for an artist, but this one job no one will take. There's this guy named Ed Roth and everybody we send down there says the place is too filthy and they don't want the job." I showed my stuff to Roth, who hired me right there. That was in '65, and I was making twice what I made before, and I could dress any way I wanted. I could come and go totally free. It was like heaven. Actually, it saved my life!

I was Ed "Big Daddy" Roth's art director for five years. I had to do four lushly illustrated ads a month. Roth doesn't do much drawing himself. What you think of as a Roth drawing was actually done by a guy named Ed Newton. I picked up his chrome technique and learned to put it on other things than car bodies and parts. That was in '65, and now you see it everywhere. But it all started with me and "Newt." Roth wanted to be a bohemian, and his idol was Von Dutch, a true madman who brought pinstriping to hot rods, a real master machinist, cartoonist, and painter. He thought Roth was a real hack. Roth's best work was in '65 and '66, but quality was never the deciding factor because when you are on the crest of a fad, you can shit and it's great! Ed Roth's probably one of the most faithful Americans there is, but somehow, he got it into his head that the Hells Angels were some mistreated group of people. He always attracted bohemian types because he saw romance in them.

Before Roth's studio, in the late fifties, I'd worked with a traveling carnival in the Southwest, and that was my first exposure to real outlaw underground jerks. They rattled off in carny talk, a kind of pig Latin with Zs between the syllables. I got familiar with it, and when I left the carnival, I'd run across degenerates in the streets who spoke it, too. It was a language of decadence and drugs. This was the origin of hippies.

As for the underground comics, I'd read the EC comics when I was a kid, but I'd had no dealings with comics for a long time. I remember in '64, me and Suzanne were in LA and some hippie from San Francisco pulled up in this '51 Chevy full of comic books. This was the first comic collector I'd met. Soon after there was a giant craze over Marvel Comics, like *Doctor Strange*. With that, comics were back in my life.

The draft board was on me the whole time to draft me into the Vietnam War. Before the war, the United States was a real repressive place. The police had a license to mess with you, especially if you were young. In Hollywood, they said if you get pulled over, have the cop arrest you right there because if he pulls you around the corner, he's gonna beat the shit out of you. I tell

Robert Williams, advertisement for Roth Studios, Maywood, California, 1967–68.

people today who think they're cool with mohawks and stuff that they don't know what terror was.

The only bulwark against the police were some underground newspapers, some leftist inspired, maybe a little Communist, with cartoons and graphics. As much as I hated the police, I wasn't a Socialist or Communist. I liked tits 'n' ass, and as much as I tried, the underground papers would never put me in. The psychedelic posters came along, with Moscoso and Griffin, but I was a painter and I'd developed a tremendous animosity to commercial art. I hated to be told what to do.

When the underground comics came out in '67, I was primed for them from the minute they started. I did some stuff for *Yellow Dog*, and Gilbert Shelton rang me up. I'd known him from the hot rod days. I drew for *Zap* when the underground was a small community. You could stand them on a porch and piss on all of them. All of a sudden, we were little princes. We had art historians following us around and picking up our remarks, and we thought this is just the beginning. It got real big, but about '73 it got too watered down. There were two thousand people trying to do undergrounds. The print costs started to shoot up, and the movement petered out. Today you've got thousands of young artists dying to do something, and they can't do nothing but minicomics and small press stuff. The strongest will survive that.

One disturbing thing about these young artists is that they've got little concept of the tremendous amount of groundwork that's been laid for them at the expense of a lot of other people. When we were doing underground comics in the late sixties, our asses were up for grabs. We knew that if the government had swung any more to the right, then they would have rounded us up.

As for the new guys, like Gary Panter and Bob Zoell, they're in Willem de Kooning's world. I'm somewhere in the Bosch, Dalí, and Mickey Mouse worlds. Gary was getting such energy out of this work, and I'd always known that when you do tight stuff, your devices for energy and movement are really muffled. Gary helped me loosen up in these new "over-expressionist" paintings. For my book, I took these "Zombie Mystery Paintings" to psychiatrists to have them analyzed, but they just started justifying them. What I wanted was some provocative butchery, so I got a psychiatrist to sit down with me and help with terms so I could write my own. Each oil painting has three titles, and alongside are three paragraphs. The first is a verbatim description of exactly what you're looking at. The second is a wimpy liberal look at the picture that doesn't even deal with the violence and vulgarity of it, just the design and color play. The last is written by a behavioralist that minces no

Robert Williams, cover for *Yellow Dog* #8, 1970.

words. They've been to two shows in Los Angeles; one show is all my paint-ings, and the other is *Western Exterminators*, with me, Roth, Panter, Zoell, and Georganne Deen.

I'll never give up doing comics, because they have the element of the fourth dimension, Time. A painting doesn't have that. Roth, he got religion. That happened after he lost the business over those Hells Angels. The wife left him and his whole life fell apart. He got so low that he went back to being a truck mechanic. Finally, somebody from a right-wing kind of Disneyland attraction called Knott's Berry Farm picked him up and put him in charge of all their signage. It was perfect for him, and he's still selling his T-shirts, decals, and other stuff. But I hope when I become an old man, I don't start referring to the Bible all the time. Maybe that happens when you get old, but somehow I don't think that's going to happen to me.

The Sublime and Ubiquitous Robert Williams

MARK DANCEY / 1988

From *Motorbooty*, Fall 1988. Reprinted by permission of Robert Williams.

Mark Dancey: The motto on your business card is "Fouling the Art World's Nest since 1957."

Robert Williams: Nineteen fifty-seven was the first time I ever did an oil painting. I was a young student at the time, probably in eighth grade.

Dancey: What was the painting of?

Williams: God, I don't remember. I think it was some abstract stuff—some pathetic attempt, I guess. That first shit I did is comparable to the stuff I see around today.

Dancey: So why foul the art world's nest?

Williams: I'm a counter-aesthetician. I don't pretend to interior decorate with my work. I don't do art that will very well fit into the scheme of most people's living rooms. I do art that goes against interior decorator aesthetics. I come from a school of art that's very big in this country right now: artists that were influenced, or poisoned, by cartoons.

Dancey: Like EC Comics?

Williams: EC comics and cartoons in general—it's something I can't get away from. I made attempts when I was younger to be a snob artist and sophisticate up my technique, but I can't—it just ends up looking like a cartoon. I first went to formal art school in 1963, out here in California. I had come from Albuquerque, New Mexico, and was kind of backward—I had all these ideals in my head about what I wanted to do, how I wanted to be a good draftsman and really develop a good language in art. But when I came out here and got into art school, I discovered that the worst thing I could do was actually be a capable draftsman. I was discouraged at every turn about this—my work would be "too introspective" or show too much work to warrant much attention. But if I'd just slop the shit on there and go for the abstract,

9

I'd get along well with my teachers, my fellow students would like me because I offered them almost no competition, and then there'd be no problems anywhere. I'd be one of a million abstract artists. But as a child, I'd already seen this fantastic draftsmanship in EC comics, early Max Fleischer animated movies—all the stuff that I'd been drawn to. And I couldn't get away from it. So I didn't do well academically.

I got straight As in all my art classes, but I didn't get along with my fellow students—I was referred to as "the illustrator." I hate that term—it's like a handle of prostitution or something. Unfortunately, we live in a time where everyone who's capable and talented at drawing has gone into illustration or comic books, but they can't get into fine art shows because those shows are owned and dominated by people with only vague ideas about what art is. When I was younger, I hated this school of art domination, but I've come to a point where I've realized that I can't enter their world, and I hold nothing against them. To hold something against them would be wrong. Let them sell their interior decoration for eons to come. I have pretty much established my own following. All I can do now is build a bigger audience.

Dancey: Yet you say you come from a school of art that's very big in this country right now—what does that say about the art world?

Williams: Well, let me give you this comparison: I got this really thick book from the 1890s, and it had all the top artists in the world at that time, as judged by the English Academy of Arts. I went through that book, and except for Auguste Rodin, there wasn't one fucking name in there that I could recognize. Hundreds of top artists from 1890s—and I know art history. The same thing's happening now. You've got all these fuckin' flash geniuses, but they're not going to hold up posthumously. There again, I'm not interested in posthumous success. I want to live now, and after that, I really just don't give a shit. I just drew that comparison to you to answer your question.

Dancey: What is your biggest dislike of the art world?

Williams: The art world is like a locked matrix of economics and people trying to get involved. My artwork sells like crazy, but I cannot get into galleries. Not because my artwork will not sell in a gallery, but because it offends the paying underwriters—the people who sponsor the galleries I try to get into. In other words, my creative ability can be no further out than the small group that runs the money to control the venues. Which is probably the way it's always been.

Dancey: That must lead to a lot of frustration.

Williams: Well, yeah, sure it does. But being involved in underground comics and working for Ed "Big Daddy" Roth, I generated a pretty good audience, and I got a really good mailing list. I depend on these people who've been following me for two decades—that's what's really kept me going. Things were pretty coarse when I started working for Roth back in 1965. Roth was interested in selling decals and T-shirts to kids: monsters and nebbishes with beer cans and bumps, the kind of stuff kids wanted. Stuff with honest, basic appeal, the way art actually should be. I picked up a bunch of people from Roth in the mid-sixties, and in the late sixties I picked up a lot more from underground comics. We thought that underground comics were going to be just the biggest thing in the world—in '69, '70, and '71. We thought the way the thing was mushrooming, we were all going to be farting through silk here pretty quick. But it just pooped out.

Dancey: What happened?

Williams: The Vietnam War ended, and people were no longer interested in being involved in the subculture and following what was hip and what wasn't. Another problem was that there were so many underground cartoonists trying to get on the bandwagon, it couldn't take it, like too many people getting on a boat and sinking it. The same thing happened a few years before the comics with the psychedelic posters. There were a few good poster artists, and then every idiot who could buy a rapidograph was doing psychedelic posters. I think if you look at the price guide for underground comics, you'll see like two thousand names, and, believe me, I've been involved at the core of the motherfucker all these years, and I don't think five people made a fuckin' living off it.

Dancey: What happened to the original *Zap Comix* artists?

Williams: Well, we're still working on *Zap*—we've got a new *Zap* coming out. We just had our twentieth anniversary *Zap* party up in the Gallery in San Francisco—had a big party and all the artists got together, did a lot of character assassination, and stayed up for three days fighting each other just like we were young hippies again . . . incredible. We don't make any fuckin' money off *Zap*. I think it's the challenge of doing it that keeps us together. You might not agree, but I think the quality of the stories has still kept up.

Dancey: Well, we're wondering why your style—in oil paintings as well as cartoons—has changed from the tight and elaborate stuff you were doing in the 1960s and '70s to the much looser stuff you've done recently?

Williams: It's a lot more breezy . . .

Dancey: Yeah—how come?

Williams: There are some very good reasons for this. I used to do very fine oil painting, very detailed oil painting. I was young and naive, and I used to believe that to be a master painter, you just did a masterpiece. I didn't realize

Robert Williams, *In the Land of Retinal Delights*, 1968. Oil on canvas, 138 x 110.5 cm.
Private collection.

you didn't have to paint at all—you just have to know politics, know how to
suck ass and wrangle your way, and you don't have to do artwork at all. But
over the course of a decade and a half of doing fine painting, I learned to
paint, and I could get away with it. I used to paint with no peers or cohorts;
I was just by myself trying to be a master painter, and everyone I knew had
painted from abstract expressionism and referred to me as "the illustrator"

and hated my guts. Now I was doing the comics and still painting, and I was selling these time-consuming paintings for top fucking dollar—I was getting ten or twelve thousand dollars for these paintings, and this was fifteen, twenty years ago.

So I've always done well. Even when the comics wouldn't support me, the oil paintings would, so I always made a living as a painter. But I could not get into galleries, and I could not get any promotion, and could not get into any movement at all because the paintings were so unlike anything else.

Now, there was a guy named Gary Panter who came along and started doing very fast paintings, and he was from an underground school of art. Gary was like the king of LA. Gary is a friend of mine, but I could not get in at any of the venues that Gary was in, because my work was too sophisticated and tight. He was in these bohemian fuckin' punk rock places, and I couldn't show my stuff there. So I had to start hammering out very quick oil paintings that looked like they were just shitted and secreted, to get in the underground shows with Gary. So I did forty paintings called *Zombie Mystery Paintings*, and that was the only way I could get shown. The paintings were sold sight unseen, and they were all sold before they were even painted. I took orders for them. I had a list of buyers, and I told them, I'm coming out with a really nice set of paintings, one thousand dollars each, just put your name on the list. I did forty of them in just under two years. Since then, my new paintings have got a lot more detail; they're a combination of what I used to do a long time ago and the *Zombie* paintings.

Dancey: In the *Zombie Mystery Paintings* book, each painting is accompanied by pro and con pseudo-intellectual comments . . .

Williams: It's a joke—I mean, how serious is fuckin' art? When you start getting serious about art, you make a religion out of it.

Dancey: . . . but what was the actual reaction when the paintings were shown?

Williams: I had a show downtown here in LA at a gallery called LACE, and there are a lot of feminists there, and I just upset people to the point of being a villain. It was a group show—the only way I got in was that it was a group show and I just kind of slipped in there. But boy! when I started bringing these paintings in, it started dawning on these women exactly what they'd be having to deal with for a month. This is a really famous gallery, and they just fuckin' flipped. They've got a bookstore there, and they wouldn't take my book—wouldn't handle it.

You know, in the sixties I had to put up with right-wing fundamentalists, but now I have to put up with left-wing feminists. I'm very sympathetic to the women's rights movement because I think women have gotten a rough deal all through time. I'm glad to see women starting to get a fair shake, but I think they're like fucking going overboard. I've got women who want to shoot me and castrate me. Seriously, there is one fucking town I don't think I'll ever want to go to because the women there want to kill me. The situation is ridiculous, fucking ridiculous. It's like they don't have anything better to do.

I was in a group show in Japan, and I put the *Zombie* paintings there. I could never do a show in a big gallery or big public art museum here, but I did that in Tokyo. Man! They loved those fucking paintings, but I don't know what to think about that. I get that *Zombie* book and look through it, and I think, "Jesus Christ!—I'm trying to pass this stuff off as art or something!" It makes my hairline recede when I look at that stuff.

Dancey: We started talking about women . . .

Williams: Yeah, women are the basic beginning measurements of aesthetics, and all judgments of beauty begin with women. That's where aesthetics come from. Different textures and everything else is all in contrast to women. You know that sounds very sexist, but if you think society is going to get rid of it, then you are crazy. If you think you're going to get all men to stop thinking of women as objects, and vice versa, to get women to stop thinking of men as objects, you're fucking crazy. Because the key ingredient in sex is perplexing . . . the question, the mystery—your mind is continually trying to resolve an unresolvable puzzle. Actually, there's really nothing to sex except the existence of the mystery of it.

Dancey: How did you start doing album covers?

Williams: I did a whole bunch of bootleg album covers a long time ago, and I think every major record company has called me up or made some feelers to get me to do stuff. It started with the chrome stuff. I'm the first guy in history to do all this chrome psychedelic stuff. Everyone else got credit for it—Peter Lloyd got wealthy off of it, and some other English character got well known, but I'm the asshole that started all of it. There was a guy that I took the job from at Roth's named Ed Newton, and he taught me how to do chrome, but he couldn't do it on any surface other than cars. Immediately it registered, Man! I could put this stuff on women and wooden fence posts, and everything. I learned the key of how to make everything follow the laws of reflection and started doing this in about '66. In '68 that came out in *Zap Comix*. One thing about *Zap* is that it was the cutting edge of graphics, so all these other people without imaginations had to buy this thing to copy and ease their imagination impediments. I think 99 percent of artists today have imagination impediments, and that's the problem with the entire art world.

That's why art is so fuckin' boring today: they're trying to make art sophisticated by being boring.

Anyway, I tried doing some album covers, but they would reject them or have some kind of problem with 'em, because they were too underground or controversial. I did a lot of stuff for the Grateful Dead that they never used and an awful lot of stuff that none of these record companies used. They'd pay me off with kill fees and that was it. So I got to the point where I really avoided commercial art and record people—and movie people.

There's not too much difference between movie executives and record executives, except I think record people are just a little more arrogant. You know, the swift characters that are going to pull off a fast deal, they're alive for the fast deal, and you're an expedient part of the hardware to do it with. I just fuckin' cringe. Then these Guns N' Roses people got in touch with me after hunting me down. I heard from San Francisco that they were looking for me, so I avoided the fuck out of them. But somehow they got my home number and called me up, so I said all right, give me a grand and we'll do it. And I told them, this is pretty rough subject material—this was like a year ago, and I was really fighting these fuckin' women. I told them, you're going to get in a lot of trouble with this, why don't you come over to my house and go through what I've got and pick something that could be a little more palatable for the general public. Because I remembered from working with the Grateful Dead, and this is a statement on the whole fuckin' record industry, the bottom line is that whatever you do with that album cover, it's got to be geared for a fourteen-year-old girl.

Dancey: So Guns N' Roses came over . . .

Williams: And they said, "No, we just want this one thing." Well, okay, sure. Then their agent said, "Send a 4 × 5 inch color transparency over to Warner Bros.," so I sent that over there, and after I sent it over, I talked to a friend who's an agent for commercial artists, and I told him about it. "You sent that to Warner Bros.? You know that's an all-women art department?" I thought, "Oh, fuck!" So I call up the next day and said, "Well, did you get that 4 × 5?" And the woman was really cool; she said, "I got it, but are you sure you want to go through with this, because we're not touching it at all. We feel that it's very offensive." I said, "Does this mean that the situation's over, that you're not going to use it?" She said, "Oh, no, it's going to be done by an out-of-house studio." It didn't surprise me when the cover was finally changed. I don't know, the Guns N' Roses music is good heavy metal, if you like that stuff, but I like punk rock music.

Dancey: Whom do you like?

Williams: A whole fuckin' bunch of people. I like Fear and Black Flag and that bunch, but I also like people like the Swans. One of the early bands I really liked was X-Ray Spex; I liked them a lot. That's my favorite kind of music. I listen to classical music, and then I listen to punk music. I hate jazz, though, and I'll tell you why. I listened to rock 'n' roll when it first came out. Before rock 'n' roll, it used to be called bop; I really liked bop. Then it was rock 'n' roll, and I really liked rock. About 1958 rock 'n' roll just went fuckin' stale or something, it just fuckin' died, and I was right at that age when I needed it the most. I was entering my beatnik phase in life, so I started listening to a lot of fuckin' jazz, 'cause rock 'n' roll had gone down the toilet. It was like Dave Brubeck and a lot of good jazz relative to what rock 'n' roll were around. And then rock 'n' roll started a marvelous comeback—the music was like a renaissance in rock 'n' roll, and after I got the good life back in me from rock 'n' roll, I could never go back to the morose fuckin' Greek tragedies of jazz. Off and on, I've tried to go back and listen to jazz, but it's too fuckin' morose for me. It affects me the same way as listening to country western music. It's full of simpleminded people with tragedies anyone could avoid. I had so many friends that were on heroin and laid out on their backs listening to jazz. So anytime I hear any jazz, I think of my dumbass friends sloped out somewhere, just absorbing time from their lives.

Dancey: What do you listen to when you work?

Williams: If I do real tight stuff, I listen to classical music, but I generally just like to listen to real rough punk rock music. It keeps me fuckin' generated and charged like a fuckin' wild ox.

Dancey: You said earlier that the punk artists lost a lot of ground that your original underground cartoonists gained.

Williams: Yeah, that's hard for me to explain. You see, in the sixties, we started doing some pretty rough material. We started getting rougher and rougher, and when comics would get busted, we just kept fighting it by pumping out more fuckin' filthy comics. The more people would get busted, the more we'd do, so that the government would get the feeling that this was an open floodgate—they weren't even going to start to stop it. This was during the Vietnam War, and we just had a tremendous amount of resentment for any form of authority. *Zap* #4 got busted tremendously in New York, San Francisco, and LA. I think something like 150 newsdealers got popped in New York, another 75 in San Francisco, and 75 in LA. There were an awful lot of people busted, and court cases went on for a long time over the different stories in there. So that's when we really started pushing stuff like *Snatch* and *Jiz*, and those little comics. The ultimate filthiest one of all was one called *Felch*.

Dancey: Who came up with that one?

Williams: Well, [S. Clay] Wilson got it from Ken Weaver of the Fugs, and I heard the word and I said, "Man! We're doing a book on that." I was the editor of the *Felch*. I'm the one who rounded up all the artwork and got it to the publisher. So, time went by. There's a comic distributor here in town named George DiCaprio, and he distributes all underground comics and books in Southern California. George had a store down here in Long Beach that got busted on account of the comics, so all the rest of his shops that he distributes to refused to take any more comics until they saw the outcome of that trial. So George went down with a lawyer and the store owner and the clerk, and they were sitting outside the judge's place there. Apparently, the prosecution had an example of each one of the comics there, and they were going to base the entire case on *Felch*, which was undisputedly the filthiest in the world. And apparently someone hanging around the prosecutor's office dug through there and stole that little comic book, figuring no one would miss it. Anyway, George stood outside there, and all he could hear was the judge and prosecutor yelling, "Where's the *Felch* comic?" They couldn't find the comic, and the case was dropped, and all the stores went back to buying George's comics.

We had an awful lot of worry, right up 'til about 1972. We honestly thought this with the greatest sincerity, and thousands of people that were in the underground and bohemians thought this, too: if the Vietnam War was going to turn any more sour than it was, they were going to start rounding up dissidents. We heard they already started reconditioning the Japanese internment camps out there in the desert. I had already dodged the draft and put up a big stink because I wasn't going to fight in the fuckin' war, so my ass was up for grabs.

I worked for Roth, and the FBI was watching him, so I was on the list for that. I was doing underground comics, so I was on the list for that. My ass was like really fuckin' up for grabs. We all felt that we were going to an internment camp if something bad happened, so it was like a fight. We were scared, we were cutting ground, and we were like fuckin' partisans fighting a cold war in our country. I mean we were like fucking nervous. I can't express enough how scared we were. It was a conscious thing—that we were fighting a front and putting out these dirty fuckin' comics was just like bullets and guns to us. We made territory and we beat back the law.

Okay, time goes by, and the Vietnam War is over, we get to be a little older and not important anymore, and the young generation comes up on the same groundwork that we broke, giving us no fucking credit, walking on the stepping-stones that we laid, thinking that they're fucking inventing the wheel anew. It's okay if the younger generation steals our credit, but when they don't keep the situation pushed back like we did—and that's what we did, we kept the fuckin' doors open and the laws liberal. Well, you get Gary Panter and these other people that came in there, and the oppression just was not there, because we pushed it back. But they didn't know why it wasn't there because they'd never faced it. I mean all these punk rockers had never thought about ever being rounded up and shot, taken out in the desert, and disappearing. They'd never had to worry about that. They just knew they weren't going to get a home and a television like they wanted, so they had to revolt and worry about their own personal suicide. So, in that respect, the punk rock movement, as far as cartooning goes, was really kind of pathetic. But the comics and cartoons of the punk rockers turned cartoons closer into art than the undergrounds were.

Dancey: Yeah?

Williams: I used to be involved with people who did posters and album covers in the sixties, and even exalted as we were, we were no more than the asshole who drew the label on a bottle—a commercial hack. The rock 'n' rollers were like the fuckin' gods, and we could be friends with them and everything, but we had no chance of ever being equals to them. But this isn't true, come along Gary Panter. Gary Panter got more famous than most of the goddamn punk rockers. Gary is one of the pioneers and really deserves a lot of credit, and exactly like Crumb, when he did something, a thousand people followed him. But none of them figured that you have to get out there and fight to do stories the way you want to do them. The people who were doing punk rock comics would not fight to do what the hell they wanted. *Raw* is a perfect example. *Raw* is a very censored, trendy publication; it's the backbone of modern trendy new wave art, and it's as conservative as it could be.

Dancey: Anything else we need to know?

Williams: I'm currently involved with a group of artists—Mark Mothersbaugh, Georganne Deen, Byron Werner, Neon Park, and Gary Panter. We've got a form of an art school. It's formalized, but it's not a closed thing where you have to be Mr. Hip to be in it. We're just trying to get enough momentum going where we can make a living and other people can too.

Robert Williams: Fouling the Art World's Nest since 1957

CHRISTINE NATANAEL / 1990

From *Rage*, May 1990. Reprinted by permission of Robert Williams.

While brainstorming over what to include in this premier issue, my editor and I were discussing things that just sort of seem to jump up, slap you in the face, grab you by the neck and rattle your head until you see stars or some type of a neo-psychedelic-nuclear revelation. You know the kind of shit that I mean, something outside the music parameters yet somehow still relevant to a music audience. The perfect solution to this seemingly complex subject matter problem appeared before our faces in the form of the Guns N' Roses album *Appetite for Destruction*. Yep, what a better topic than graphic painter extraordinaire Robert Williams, who has been alternately called "the most culturally adept and metamorphically hip artist of the last quarter century" by *Forced Exposure* magazine and "a guru of the countercultural underground . . . and maverick disregarded by the prevailing power elite" by *Artforum International Magazine*. All the while, still managing to keep it all from going to his head.

Almost twenty years after his self-exportation from Albuquerque by way of Alabama, finally resting in the hell-den of North Hollywood, Robert is getting much of the recognition that his brand of twisted genius deserves. So, it may have taken a long time to get around to him, but that's all right. My phone line connects to his just as he is finishing up his long grueling day. Yeah, I know it's only 7 p.m. California time, but for a man who gets up at 4:45 a.m. every day of his life, it's almost past his bedtime. He's not the acid casualty crazed madman which many envision behind the hyper-kinetic brush of doom, porn, and gore. But then again, what does a man have to look like in order to create such underground classics as *Coochy Cooty's Men's Comix* and *Felch Comix* or any one of the number of issues of *Zap Comix* done alongside

Robert Crumb and Rick Griffin and S. Clay Wilson, stuff that tested the lim-
its of freedom of the press and spawned an entire degenerate youth culture
(including later "punk" artists such as Gary Panter, Condom, et al.)? But I'm
jumping ahead of the story. It really all began back when he got his first hot
rods and first got the feel of a red-hot engine under a heavy low-slung ride
with some body-slamming torque. "Yeah, well, it's been an indulgence with
me," he admits. "At one time I tried to get away from it, and I did, for a few
years, but I wandered back into it. You know, socially, hot rodding is kind of
a creep thing. The mentality level isn't too high in hot rodding. But there's an
adventure and thrill coefficient there that I've always enjoyed. There's a little
romance in it. I was raised down South, and my father used to own stock
cars. I'd always been around souped-up automobiles and motorcycles and one
thing or another."

It was the love of cars and the love of painting that put him in the rather
peculiar position of painting vehicles for one of the leading figures of car cus-
tomizing on the West Coast. "I was working for Ed 'Big Daddy' Roth," says
Williams reminiscently. "I worked for Roth from 1965 to 1970, and I had had
hot rods all my life. I got my first hot rod when I was about twelve years old.
My dad had bought me a '34 Ford coupe, and I was in a rural town so I could
drive it out in the country without a driver's license. So I had, all through
the years, owned hot rods, and I had gotten kicked out of high school, and
I was still messing around with hot rods. Every cent I could get would get
dumped into hot rods. My fiancée didn't like it. She dumped me because of
the cars, and my life was looking pretty peaked, and this was about 1963. And
I had the draft hanging over my head. I had lost my job, my girlfriend/fian-
cée had kicked me out, and I was starting to run around with a lot of people
taking a lot of drugs, and it was obvious that a lot of trouble was coming my
way. I tried to get into college to take art classes, but you had to have a high
school diploma, and that didn't work out. But a friend of mine told me that
there was a junior college in Los Angeles, called Los Angeles City College, that
would take you without a high school diploma for $6.50 a semester in tuition.
So I got my Ford and drove out here, and it saved my life. Inside of two or
three months, I was on the Dean's List."

Actually, his aptitude for drawing and painting was recognized at a very
early age. Like many other kids across the United States, he mutilated many
a school textbook out of boredom, slowly but surely creating and perfecting
his own style. "I'd be putting little people walking down there, and some little soldiers marching—stuff like that," laughs Robert. "Then I kept at it. I
remember being in school and being known as the kid that could draw really

well. I wasn't good at anything else because I was dyslexic, and I couldn't read very well. I couldn't concentrate. I had no concentration, so this kind of compensated for the fact. They thought I was pretty bright because I could draw. I remember that all the kids in my class, they were all drawing on this big mural out in the hall. And they'd all get up there and they'd put their little contribution on this big piece of paper, but I was like the only mother fucker who could get up there and draw the background and tie all their bullshit together. It was my job to go up there and make a composition of their nonsense. One would draw a cow here and the other one would draw an airplane here, and this here, you know, and I would have to like, figure out how to make the airplane that's lower than the pig down in a gulch and shit like that. I would complement it for them and I was the miracle man."

Being a man who tended to live on the dangerous edge of society where the nights were a little blacker, the women a little wilder, and the bad-asses a whole lot badder, Williams somehow got himself associated with the music world and its lot of flotsamesque characters. When I point it out to him, he chuckles before commenting, "Isn't that funny? You know, there's a statement there, and you know, I spent my whole life studying art and I just don't get along very well with other artists. I have to rub elbows with a lot of other artists, but I've got this natural attraction to people in the music industry. They hang around me and I hang around them, and this next coming week I'll be running around with Chris Stein and Debbie Harry all week. They're coming out here. And I'm just more comfortable with people in the music industry. I think they like me because they're looking for that kind of artistic romance. It's like the same situation happened a hundred years ago when Wagner used to dress like Rembrandt.

"There's a lot of romance in being an artist that actually isn't there. If I was in the rock industry, I would refer to myself as a musician before I would refer to myself as an artist, but musicians insist on being referred to as artists, and it's kind of funny. It's semantics, I guess," he continues. "But you know, it is funny how there is this cheesy romance that is associated with being an artist and suffering or something. People really put a lot of stock in this fact . . . of course, art rates next to religion. They see definite values in it which aren't there, so I don't know. I know a lot of artists, and many have real bad personalities. They see themselves as celebrities, and they don't know how to deal with themselves in crowds. You know, I was like that when I was younger. When I was in my early twenties, I experienced a certain amount of success, and I got real big-headed and hard to deal with. I thought, 'Well, this is just the start of it. From here I'm gonna go to Napoleon.' Then I came down to earth, and I got older and realized that nothing big is gonna happen in my life, and I'm gonna do a lot of goddamn work. When I was young, I took on a lot of training thinking success is right around the corner, and then it wasn't. But consequently, the training paid off over a real long period of time. If I had known when I was young that things wouldn't work out instantaneously, I don't know if I would have spent my life being an artist. But you're a prisoner of your compulsions and you're a prisoner of your metabolism. You can rationalize out all these virtues but you're gonna do what your metabolism tells you to do, and what compulsion guides you to do."

Williams's paintings are the kind of thing that you either love or you hate. There's not really much ground in between. The man likes it that way. Along with the bold, vibrant, almost apocalyptic flashes of color, he incorporates the mundane, adding fast food, deserts, and women—always women. "Aren't you gonna get around to the part about how I always draw women in the nude?" he asks, as if he is shocked that I'm not violently offended. The man does tend to use some of the sluttiest, pornographic chicks in his paintings, but it doesn't offend me. I can see the beauty of a nude, even if she is swilling beer and lounging in stockings and heels. "It seems to bother all women in one way or another," explains Robert. "Men can be quite a problem to women. I think it's that women have the problem of being just a sexual notion to men. That's a big problem. Women, intelligent women, certainly know how to use it. I think sometimes I do it in bad taste and I do it to the detriment of womankind. I think that all beauty and the measurement of beauty starts off—woman, as the point of origin for beauty, I think that's the starting point to measure all beauty, is a woman. And that's only relative to me being a male. You know, it's so surprising, all these artists today and then so damn few of them can actually draw women. It's just obvious as hell that women are like the very beginning point of, the beginning orientation of what beauty is, the starting point of where you would go from beauty would be a woman. A woman's ass will stand up against anything, beautiful mountain ranges, the dynamics of the universe, a woman's ass will put it all to shame. To be some kind of a fucking person who makes a living off aesthetics and not being able to draw a woman is like a hypocrisy, you know what I mean? I just naturally go to drawing women. Now, men are much harder to draw than women. They are much harder to draw. There's a lot more angularity in them and there is a dramatic sense that you have to instill in a picture of a man. It's hard to keep a male from looking cartoonish. You want a certain amount of drama in a male, so a man is a little more difficult."

Williams's penchant for the beauty of a woman and his often-shocking interpretation of the world around him have been the cause of much controversy, not only among the feminists but with the general public and even the Parents Music Resource Center (PMRC), since Mr. Axl Rose, an underground comics fan, chose *Appetite for Destruction* from the *Zombie Mystery Paintings* series of 1979 to grace his debut album cover. "This kid, Axl Rose, had seen that piece on the cover of my book *Zombie Mystery Paintings*. And they were just a little nothing band that nobody had ever even heard of in their town. And they had contacted someone up in San Francisco to get in touch with me. Somehow their manager, Alan Niven, had gotten my number and called me up. I knew from the beginning what was gonna happen with this whole thing because I had been through it all before with the record companies. So, I told them to come over here to the house and look through all of my stuff to see if there was something that they maybe would like better. So they all came over here and looked through everything, and after all that looking, he said he still wanted *Appetite for Destruction*. So I said all right, but I warned them what was going to happen with a cover like that. All of a sudden, the band started catching flak. Well, actually they [the authorities] didn't want much to do with me. They weren't too concerned with me. It wasn't like the artists that had a lot to do with the underground bands, like the Grateful Dead. They were always real appreciative of their artists, but Guns N' Roses didn't have any fucking interest in me one fucking way or the other. You know, so I was just like out of the picture, except there started to be a lot of write-ups about the album and about the cover. And I had someone over at Geffen call me and say, 'Well, these guys, they are not too articulate, would there be a chance of verbally defending the piece?' And I said, 'Damn right. I fucking painted it, I'll fucking defend it.'

"So this got me on MTV a bunch of times and one thing or another, and then the PMRC, I guess is, well, I mean, that is bordering on witchcraft persecution or something, you know, but the PMRC got on this thing, and then I heard a couple of religious groups got on this goddamn album cover, and then finally, it took some while, but the feminists finally hit this thing. And there are about six or seven groups in Northern California that hit this thing with both claws, both talons, and they started in Santa Cruz and they picketed all the record stores that carried it and forced them all to not carry it except Tower Records. Tower Records refused to pull it, and then they moved to Berkeley. They did the same thing to Berkeley. They took their thing to Berkeley and all the rest of the record stores took it right off the shelf, except for Tower Records. Then Tower Records called me and got a statement from me, and it got really ugly. These fucking women's things got this thing looking really ugly, and they got real petty about it, and they started using pressure at the Berkeley school and the school at Santa Cruz and the paper and got a real movement going. In the end, it was other women who would come to my fucking defense. These gals would just tear them apart verbally in the papers. I really felt for these gals that had come to my defense. They were intelligent, articulate women and realized that these were just a bunch of fucking broads that had complexes or something that fucking needed a hobby or something.

"So then they dropped the Guns N' Roses thing and started attacking this pornographic video game thing. That got them off the hook. But they caused a number of papers to call me up to get my explanation on this thing. You know, I defended it. I think as good as probably could be defended on the obvious. The goddamn picture—I don't know. My defense was that I can't be responsible for it being a fucking monkey-see-monkey-do world, you know. That was my defense. My only other defense is that I tend to do pictures like this, and if I'm a bad person, well, I just happen to be a bad fucking person. Now, I've just copped to the fact that I'm a bad person in this respect. And it might not have been the discreetest thing in the fucking world for Guns N' Roses to use as a fucking album cover, but you know, I don't think it is a crime that they did this. The picture does create anxieties and it was designed to create anxieties and that's my defense. But the people that didn't like it still didn't like it and the people that were supportive of it—it still didn't change anybody's mind. You know, everyone had already had their own conclusions drawn.

"Now, in my town, in LA, there is a large faction that I didn't rub elbows with that are feminists. A lot of them I get along with, and a lot of them hate my fucking guts. And, uh, you know, I don't know what to tell you, you know? Of course, it's a sensitive situation to me that I make certain women unhappy, but on the other hand, goddamn, you know, if you have to kowtow to everyone who has some fucking little anxiety over something, then, you know, it's—they refuse to let my book down in Laith, the most liberal fucking place in the world, Laith's Art Gallery and Bookstore, they refuse to, it's run by a feminist, she refused to have my books in there. And she didn't have a legal ground to not have my books in there. She kept coming up with reasons, you know, and just puttin' it off week by week not letting my books get in the fucking bookstore. It was a situation I face a lot. I don't know what to tell ya."

And that situation may or may not be one that Williams will have to face again with the release of his new book titled *Visual Addiction*. It is a hundred-page book on the art of Robert Williams complete with thirty-two full-color reproductions and a "scorching" introduction by the one and only Lydia Lunch. It will be available from Last Gasp, 2180 Bryant Street, San Francisco, California 94110 for $19.95 (so save those nickels, dimes, and quarters, kiddies). For those who would like to see more of his work, Robert wants you to know that both his books, *The Lowbrow Art of Robert Williams* and *Zombie Mystery Paintings* are being reprinted at the same time.

Robert Williams: More Than Meets the Eye

JONATHAN SHAW / 1991

From *Tattoo Revue* 4, no. 13 (Jan. 1991): 11–13. Reprinted by permission of Robert Williams.

Jonathan Shaw: Recently there's been a big explosion of interest in your work, and like anything else that's out there, this has worked its way into the general tattoo lore. Consequently there's a lot of Robert Williams tattoos being inked. What do you attribute all this to?

Robert Williams: As far as the popularity of the images go, I think that could be said of a lot of underground cartoonist's work, especially Crumb, Rick Griffin . . .

Shaw: Why do you say especially Rick Griffin? I don't remember having seen any of Rick's stuff done as tattoos.

Williams: Well, I remember seeing a lot of little Rick Griffin sort of things on some flash sheets.

Shaw: Oh, sure, like the eyeballs, the flying eyeballs with the swords.

Williams: So it seems like all the underground cartoonists from the late sixties and early seventies are a favorite with people who are into Americana and simple design. Especially design that's kind of questionable.

Shaw: The stuff that's always interested me the most in American art has been comic book art, all the way from the EC stuff to the underground stuff to your stuff. And those comic book designs sure do look good on the skin.

Williams: I have been seeing my work appear as tattoos from about 1965. The first real large public exposure I had where people could actually get ahold of the images was when I was working as Ed "Big Daddy" Roth's art director in Maywood, California. I was doing some of his ads and T-shirt designs and a lot of real basic, strong, bold, emblematic imagery. Roth also put out a publication in 1967 or '68 called *Choppers Magazine*. It was the forerunner of all outlaw bike magazines.

Roth really went against the grain when he came out with *Choppers*, and no newsstand would carry it. Harley-Davidson was even opposed to it at first but later changed their minds. When *Choppers* came out there were only two or three motorcycle magazines. Every once in a while they'd feature something that was suggestive of the chopper scene, but they were real careful because they were into portraying this real straight image of a motorcycle person. But Roth dared to come out with an outlaw motorcycle magazine. Consequently, he had to face all the storms of protest, and the only way he could sell this magazine was to advertise it through the hot rod and car magazines. After a while, even they denied him advertising space.

All the problems with *Choppers* were part of the reason Roth fell into very bad financial times. He had tied all his money up into this motorcycle magazine, and he couldn't sell it. It was the beginning of the end for him, and he went out of business in 1970. Later, other people picked up the *Choppers* format, and since the groundwork had already been laid, they did well with it. But anyway, I had a section called "Tattoos of the Month" in *Choppers Magazine* where I did these real basic, banal sort of designs, like devils holding Harleys and bikers busting through skulls on choppers, and thousands of people had this stuff tattooed on them. They just went nuts over these designs. People started sending photographs of this stuff after it'd been tattooed on them, so I know there are thousands of people walking around with my images on their skin.

Shaw: You've been hanging around the tattoo world for a while, and I know you're acquainted with some of the more notorious people in the tattoo world. So did you ever think about getting a tattoo yourself?

Williams: Bob Roberts and Ed Hardy asked me that and even offered to put a tattoo on me. But I have a real graphic problem. Imagery is more than an occupation for me; it's almost a psychosis. I get really involved in the imagery I'm confronted with. I guess you could say, "Well, here's this guy, and he exploits these tattooed people, and he runs around with them and enjoys their company and their parties, but when it comes to actually making the mark on himself, well, he turns a little shy there!" But that's not the case at all; I appreciate tattooing as a form of vanity and as a sexual thing, and I certainly have those two qualities.

The problem with getting a tattoo is that I make a living dealing with imagery. I'm very cognizant about what I do, and I get very emotionally wrapped up with what I do. At one time I would spend a year or a year and a half working on one painting, just noodling it and trying to get it as perfect as I could, trying to emotionally adjust to an idealism that would be impossible to reach.

To be a more practical person, I've had to learn to live with a lot of things I produce that aren't perfect, that fall far short of perfection. I discovered that if I did a painting really quick, and the painting looked fairly good and I sold it, that the best thing for me to do was to get the thing out of my sight because certain things in me would just keep driving me to keep working on this thing, just noodling away at it to try to correct the things that I didn't like about it. And I also found that if I come across paintings that I've done and haven't seen for ten years or so, I will immediately spot things that I don't like in the painting. The viewer sees the painting one way, and they perceive it through their optimistic perceptions, but when I look at my paintings, I see all my shortcomings. I see that I did this hand wrong, I got the foreshortening wrong, I could have staged this better, should have used a darker shading here, but it becomes a situation of "look, I've got to get this thing done in a week, and it's got to be good and I've got to let the damn thing out of here because I've got another painting to do after this and another one to do after that and I've got to be intelligent about this."

I'm very confident in the quality of my paintings. Compared to the other work I see out there, I'm very satisfied with what I do, but I'm not happy being where my work is stuck in my face. I'm always in a growing process, learning and forcing discipline out of myself. And I know that, of *course*, it's not as important as I make it out to be, of *course*, it's not the big deal that I'm building it up to be in my mind, but it's a situation that drives me fucking nuts! So, if I went to Ed Hardy, or Bob Roberts, or yourself, or any real quality tattoo artist, and said, "Look, I've been working on this thing, put it on me," I'd have this thing on me for about two weeks and then I'd start seeing things like, hey, I don't like this area right here, well, it would just drive me nuts. I have got to be able to get away from my stuff.

Shaw: What about if it wasn't your artwork? Maybe you could just pick something off some sheet of pre–World War II flash, something like the "Who Me" duck?

Williams: I thought about that, but then it would be almost the same situation. If I picked it, no matter how much it was faithful to the original design, it would be on me, so I'm still stuck right there with the original problem. If I had an exact copy of Popeye on my arm, then I just know that two weeks later I'd be looking at it and saying, "Well, that ain't exactly right, because of that one little hand." It would just be a point of neurosis to me.

Shaw: So would you describe yourself as a perfectionist?

Williams: Well, that's the easy way out. Anyone else would say, "Oh, I'm such a perfectionist, I can't have this thing on me," but with me, it's more of a case of neurosis. If I get a little bump on my face, it drives me nuts.

I think of tattoo designs on myself all the time. For ten years I've been thinking about getting the perfect Coochy Cooty on my arm. I thought, "Oh, man, if I just had the perfect Coochy Cooty on my arm, and a little suntan, I could show the chicks, man, I'd roll my sleeve up and show the chicks my Coochy Cooty." But, you know, there are like five or six different Coochy Cooty designs that changed from 1960 until now, so which one would it be? There's the first one, the 1930s-style retro Coochy Cooty, then there's the later one that was updated, then there's the last one, the punk rock Coochy Cooty. Which one am I going to get?

Shaw: Get 'em all! Get a chorus line of Coochy Cootys.

Williams: So that's why I can't get a tattoo. That's my defense.

Shaw: Sounds like it's more your dilemma.

Williams: I gravitate to tattooed people because when you have a tattoo, it's going to be there forever, so it's got to be really strong. It's going to be something that you're going to stand behind. You get a tattoo, and even if it's some old crude thing, you're still going to stand behind it because it's there forever.

Shaw: You're stuck with it.

Williams: You're stuck with it, so there's definitely some kind of dramatic strength in having a tattoo.

Shaw: You've depicted tattoos in a lot of your paintings, for example in *Op Tattoo*, and *The Man with the Wooden Nose* . . .

Williams: Well, I'm attracted to tattoos. They're anthropomorphic and they deal with human beings. You can't get any more personal than tattoos. What I was attempting to do with *Op Tattoo* was to find an intelligent and sophisticated way to transcend from one plane to another in graphic explanation. I was attempting to depict a tattoo that becomes real in a way that wasn't silly, and I still haven't found a really good solution or a good way of doing that. I saw a really well-rendered picture that Boris [Vallejo] did where the tattoo is becoming real, and I just didn't *get* it. So in *Op Tattoo* I tried to break the thing down graphically into two dimensions. First, you see the three-dimensional stuff and you see it as real, and then you see an obviously two-dimensional thing and you have to force your mind to make that transition into two dimensions, and then I wanted to make that two-dimension graphic carry off into the picture and make you believe something else. I tried that again in that painting with the girl with the butterfly tattoo on her ass, tried to break it down two-dimensionally with cartoon explanations. You see the butterfly in another picture, and it's actually the head of a Siamese monster. And the Siamese monster has a thought bubble, and it is incorporated into some two-dimensional form along with the woman with the butterfly.

Robert Williams, *Op Tattoo*, 1987. Oil on canvas, 50.8 x 61 cm. Private collection.

Tattoos hold a tremendous amount of magic. I don't believe in magic, but I'm fascinated with attempts to create the *illusion* of magic. And tattoos, being that they are on human beings, are an emotional thing. When I was growing up in New Mexico in the fifties, the Latino groups were called Pachucos, and they had a very distinctive cross design that they had tattooed right on the crux of their index finger and thumb. I was told later that in Cuba this cross design was a really serious thing; it was like a prison code that defined your criminal actions. I later did a painting called the *Pachuco Cross*, which I showed at the Otis Parsons gallery. It was an expensive painting, about a ten-thousand-dollar painting. Anyway, I had that painting hanging on the wall, and some guy came up and just hit it as hard as he could. He really fucked the painting up! He was a Latino, and he just went nuts over that Pachuco cross. His feelings were so strong that he had to express them by damaging the painting. It's amazing the kind of reactions that images can evoke.

Shaw: Maybe the Pachuco cross would be the tattoo for you?

Williams: No, I don't think so. [*Laughs*]

Robert Williams, *Pachuco Cross*, 1979. Oil on canvas, 48.3 x 61 cm. Private collection.

Shaw: You said before that sometimes you have to churn out one of these paintings in a week. When you're working on one painting, do you already know what the next one is going to be?

Williams: I have a pool of ideas; I have a pool of notions, and I have a pool of emotional impressions. The ideas are pretty solid, the notions are kind of what I'd like to do, and the emotional impressions are things that just attract me. So then I get all this research material out, and I scribble down things, slogans, pieces of poetry, whatever comes to my head. So I get all this down, this mulligan stew of crap that has no relation to anything, and then I start figuring out how I can work all this into a painting. Maybe I'll hang up a card with one word or idea on it, get a thesaurus out and check out the eighteen different variations on that word. Will anything change or add to this idea? What I do is take a simple concept, like making candles, and I'll research the hell out of candle making until I get some actual feeling for the subject. I'm looking for something that's intrinsic to the subject, like what was it like to live in the 1700s and make candles for your family. I immerse myself in the subject until I've gotten in so deep, until it's so esoteric that I know I've gotten in too far. I'll never be able to explain to people this log cabin existence of a candlemaker in the 1700s. But I can bring back a mood, and I can depict and explain that mood to people through my paintings So when you see one of my pictures, man, there's so fucking much thought in it.

Shaw: More than meets the eye.

Williams: Oh, yeah, and not only that, but there's fragments and scraps of ideas from years back. Every painting I just keep pushing along the scraps from the last painting . . . and the one before that. Hopefully, somewhere down the line, all the scraps will fall into place.

Shaw: A lot of people are really affected by your paintings, but they don't exactly know why. They just know the work moves them. Is there some kind of collective unconscious exploitation going on in your work?

Williams: I paint what people want to see. I paint women's asses and tits and a beautiful woman's smile and nice sunsets. You can't beat those things. But instead of just stagnating with three-dimensional representations, I incorporate two-dimensional art. Two-dimensional art is very strong; it's simple and it cuts. If you can incorporate its strength into these more subtle things, then you can get the energy of both in one painting.

Shaw: I think that's why some of your stuff works so well as tattoos. It's that billboard kind of thing where the work just punches you right in the eye. You don't have to look too hard to appreciate it. It's right there, right in your face.

Williams: The greatest problem is design overkill. For example, I'm the first person who started to use chrome. Working with Roth, I had to learn how to illustrate and render automobiles, and the hardest part of that was learning how to depict shiny surfaces. So I had to learn how to use chrome. But then I took it beyond cars; I used it on lettering, fence posts and clouds, and human beings. I even came out with a thing in *Zap Comix*, the Psychedelic Centerspread, where everything was chrome. But what also happened was I laid down the fucking Rosetta stone for every two-bit fucking ad agency in the world who wanted to learn how to chrome anything. A lot of people used that technique and made tremendous incomes with it, but there was actually no way to give me any recognition for pioneering the technique.

If you don't understand the philosophy behind a piece of art, then you won't be able to copy it. That's the way I pretty much approach all of my art. I try to find something in it that I alone understand. It's a way of trying to fend off the copycats because, man, I am plagued by fucking copycats.

Shaw: I know that feeling.

Williams: What the copycats do is they overkill stuff. The chrome thing got overkilled immediately. Inside five years the ad agencies had made everything chrome, and it just got cheap. They never used it to any real advantage other than commercial use. So I know that all the upstarts and copycats are going to be ripping off the work I do now. They'll be painting nekkid women on things with barnyard scenes in the background and all that kinda stuff. They'll put a two-dimensional background in it and think they'll have my formula down, but they don't.

Shaw: Speaking of your formulas, lately you've been having some problems with the feminists. What brought that on—was it a classic case of misunderstanding, or are you as bad as they say?

Williams: I guess you're talking about that Guns N' Roses *Appetite for Destruction* album cover, the one that was boycotted in record stores. But since Jesse Helms has been expressing himself about what he thinks is art and what isn't, it seems that these women's groups are getting more careful about what they attack.

Shaw: Between that album cover and doing a lot of new books and shows, you've gotten a lot of good publicity lately. You've got a waiting list of about 150 people who want to buy your paintings.

Williams: Well, the main reason you're here interviewing me is because I have a small following of people who really like my work. My work deals in anxiety and sensationalism and drama. A lot of people refer to it as "lowbrow" or "uncultured" art, and possibly it is, but it is still pop art and it is as American as hell.

Shaw: Just like tattooing.

Williams: I have a really interesting story about tattooing. About three years ago, this gentleman confronted me while I was in the company of Ed Hardy and said that he would like to commission me to design a back piece for him and then have Ed do the actual tattooing. Ed said yes, and the guy said he'd follow up with me later. So I got a letter from him, and he said that although he'd like to get me to do this big design, he didn't have any money to pay for it. He then went on to cite instances of Japanese men selling their heavily tattooed skins to art collectors and offered to leave me *his* skin after he died. I laughed it off at first, but then I thought that this could be a good promotional thing. But the guy was a lot younger than me, so I figured he might outlive me, and I'd never get the skin. On the other hand, the guy was a biker, and he might *not* outlive me. On yet the other hand, if he did die on his bike, he'd probably tear up the tattoo. So what to do?

I went to a friend of mine who's a top pathologist and told him the story, and he said, "Well, what in the hell are you going to do, Bob . . . skin this guy in your garage?" [*Laughs*]

It turns out that it's against the law in California to own even a small piece of human flesh. He said that even in his line of work, when he wants to get rid of a kidney or something, he has to bottle it up and document it and send it to a special place to be incinerated. He said it would be impossible to save this guy's skin. I guess I could have snuck the cadaver into Japan to have the skinning done, but the more I thought about it, the more complicated it got. So I wrote to him and said I couldn't think of a way that I could collect that skin from him and that he should think of some way to just pay me for the work.

Shaw: Do you get a lot of people asking you about tattoo designs?

Williams: Yeah, but I really don't have the time to sit down and deal with people. When I have taken the time, I discovered how finicky people that want tattoos are! I have a great deal of sympathy for tattoo artists because you must deal with people all the time who aren't sure of themselves.

People have begged me to do designs for them, and when I've stopped my work, they say "that isn't what I wanted." After doing revision after revision, I realized that people don't know what they want. Now, I just tell them to find something they like in one of my paintings or drawings and just deal with it themselves.

Shaw: It's a challenge to tattoo your stuff exactly the way you painted it. Even though it's big and bold and really readable, the original image is done in oil paints, and so it's hard to duplicate exactly. Have you ever thought of doing a set of flash?

Williams: At one point I did have a set of xeroxed flash, and I've thought about doing another set, but since I don't have any tattoos myself and I've never pushed a tattoo needle, I feel that it would be an impropriety for me to do flash. But if someone sees a design that they like, I'd be willing to send them a simplified black-and-white xerox of it for a small charge.

Shaw: Have you ever thought about taking up tattooing yourself?

Williams: Yeah, I've thought about it. But I'm really occupied with what I do. I've got so many irons in the fire already. And if I get into tattooing, I'll also have to start learning how to do that, and that would be time taken away from doing what I've already learned how to do. Eight years might go by before I was any good at tattooing, and I could do a lot of paintings in that time. There's a limit to what you can do in your life if you want to do it well.

Shaw: I'd still like to get a little piece by you the next time you wander into my studio. I'd just like to set a machine in your hand and see what happens.

Williams: I guess I could tattoo some potatoes for you.

Shaw: No, you could tattoo my fucking leg. You could do a Pachuco cross on there. That'd be hard to fuck up. [*Laughs*]

Williams: Yeah, I would do that. But you might end up with a Pachuco cross right up your ass. Once I got that needle going, I wouldn't know where to stop.

Shaw: Have you ever held a tattoo machine in your hand and let it run?

Williams: Never in my life.

Shaw: Sometimes when I do something that's really cool, something that's a little beyond the reach of my abilities, I get the feeling that it's not me doing these things. I get the feeling that there's something out there that I'm in touch with when I'm creating something. Do you feel like you're in a battle to get closer and closer to the source of whatever that might be?

Williams: Well, there's a tremendous occult thing to art. There's actually nothing to art except the techniques and the thought that goes into creating a piece, but people have a tendency to make a big deal out of things. Art is caught between religion and philosophy. And it's to the advantage of the people in the art world to pull the wool over everybody's eyes. You buy this very expensive piece that's maybe just some cloth with a few slashes in it, and it has this very complicated manifesto that comes with it, explaining why this thing is so great and the whole complex evolution that the artist went through to be able to get to the point where he could create this thing. But without the manifesto and the explanations of overtrained people and all the propaganda, you'd have nothing but a rag with some slashes in it. My interest is to usurp that completely and have a painting that generates its own energy, so I don't have to be standing there with it. It should be able to sell itself and entertain people all on its own and take care of you and be a self-sufficient and self-generating form of mental energy. I don't want to create some goddamn thing where you have to take a prep class before you understand what it is. So this goes against the grain of things. Abstract art has ruled for twenty years with hundreds of thousands of artists just copying each other's styles and chasing their tails. I always point out to young artists the need for them to come up with something completely different. Copy nobody or your chances of making it will be really negligible.

Shaw: Anything else you want to say?

Williams: Yeah, let's go out and get a pizza or something.

The Robert Williams Interview

DONALD M. BAILEY AND LONG GONE JOHN / 1992

From *Friction*, Summer–Winter 1992. Reprinted by permission of Robert Williams.

He's been called the Bizarro World's equivalent to Norman Rockwell. He is the creator of the insane comix character Coochy Cooty. He's believed to be the first artist to use chrome-style lettering and is known for such lowbrow sayings as "if it commands attention, it's culture; if it matches the couch, it's art."

Robert Williams is certainly no stranger to that oozing chasm known as contemporary art. Indeed, the average citizen, curious onlooker, devout artist, or persistent craftsperson may find it very difficult to enjoy a piece of work from that insulated, seemingly difficult-to-understand community.

For all it's worth, Williams's works are even more obscure. But, interestingly enough, unlike the run-of-the-mill contemporary artist, his art is hyperexperimental, challenging, beautiful, and tasteless—all at once. Best of all, it shatters even the most remote chance of anyone using any preconceived notions while trying to figure it out. That's why it's so entertaining.

His work can be very controversial and hard to pin down for closed-minded folks and, arguably, the greatest visual fix for the more adventurous. That's why even the best-educated critic, exasperated patron, or pissed-off media addict has trouble understanding his lowbrow appeal. You have to approach this stuff with an open mind, which, more than anyone realizes, is a necessary attitude to enjoy the future of fine art.

Williams (to use a disgusting reference) is a true pioneer of the arts. Onlookers can admire, worship, criticize, or just plain hate his work because, just like his chief artistic influences—Spanish surrealist Antoni Gaudí (1852–1926) or Dutch visionary Hieronymus Bosch (1462–1516)—each piece has lots going on in it, even when taken in detail.

It's hard to imagine Williams's paintings evoking less than a torrent of feelings from any viewer. That's what makes his stuff so special, so much more engaging than the average one-dimensional contemporary art piece.

The same artist who paints those insanely realistic tan lines on his female subjects, the same hot-rodder who first used the chrome look in lettering as we know it today, the same underground cartoonist who created a slew of bizarre, convoluted, and entertaining comix stories in the 1960s, '70s, and '80s for *Zap* and other publications, the same guy who created the classic character Coochy Cooty, is the same man who has been the target of feminist criticism.

Williams is not afraid to shock. Probably his most controversial work is a painting called *Appetite for Destruction*, which Guns N' Roses, the incredibly popular Los Angeles rock band, purchased to use as the cover for their best-selling debut album of the same name. Shortly after it was released, the cover art was changed due to ill feelings from the general public. Subsequently, copies of the initial print run have been valued in amounts often exceeding one hundred dollars. That's not surprising—Williams's original paintings routinely sell for thousands of dollars to appreciative patrons of the art-collecting world. He currently has a waiting list of over one hundred people ready to purchase his paintings.

His work reflects his life and his interests—the kind of entertaining culture some modern artists only dream of experiencing. Williams's world is loaded with what he calls the "lowbrow and oddball"—art, hot rods, and comix. Holding back is not a part of his style. The one element that makes Robert Williams so admirable—there are two, but let's discount the fact that he's still living—is that he's upfront with his audience, honestly spilling his crafty psyche for all to see. He's not afraid to paint whatever comes to his mind. It seems nothing is hidden from the canvas except what he does not have time to show us.

He's been plugging away for the better part of forty years, painting, penciling, drafting, inking, studying, inventing . . . and we've only glimpsed the outskirts of his undeniably unique vision. Due to his fine-quality work and powerful persistence, Williams is treading the fine line of exploding into infinite importance in the art world, or teeter-tottering on the brink of cult-art obscurity forever, for whatever reasons: allegations of sexism in his pieces, his rebellious youth, the fact that he collects German war helmets.

For the definitive history of this important California artist, read the interview below, along with the profusely illustrated *The Lowbrow Art of Robert Williams* (Rip Off Press, 1982) and his latest in a line of arcane texts, *Visual Addiction* (Last Gasp, 1989). Both books showcase some mighty fine, entertaining writing by Williams and Gilbert Shelton, creator of the Freak Brothers.

In March 1991, I wrote a number of questions and sent them to "Long Gone John" Mermis, an entrepreneurial California record mogul and publisher of

Corpsemeat Comics. He in turn conducted the following interview, with fine embellishments, at Williams's home in southern California's San Fernando Valley. Present were Williams, his wife Suzanne, and good old John. Here is a part of what transpired:

Long Gone John: Let's go back to where it all began for you.

Robert Williams: The first conscious thing that I can remember, and I get kind of a masculine shot off of it, was being at a military gathering in a reviewing stand in a horrible dust storm with my mother and father. My father was in the Army Air Force in the Second World War, and I was born in '43, so this was probably at the very end of the war, so I'm like two and a half years old at the time. There were large fighter planes revving their radial engines, exacerbating the dust that was already blowing. Airplanes don't have mufflers, and these engines were roaring like hell. There were ten or twelve of them all revving their engines and taking off in sets, causing this dust to pick up in this already horrible wind. I was crying my eyes out and wishing I was somewhere else. My first horrible experience, other than my birth trauma, was in this reviewing stand.

Suzanne Williams: Yet it was probably fabulous to witness.

RW: It would have been fabulous to witness for anyone who was mature.

LGJ: Well, to have that vivid of an imagination, to remember an experience at two and a half years of age, is pretty amazing. A lot of your paintings come from early experiences, don't they, from childhood experiences?

RW: Well, maybe so. Other than what I told you, the only things I can remember from that far back were real basic things your parents teach you. Like they parrot your name to you again and again and again, so you'll know it when you go out and get lost. And they parrot your address to you. It was that far back that I was apparently starting to talk. Anyway, I don't want to delve that far back. The fifties? Is that where to begin?

LGJ: Yeah, the beginning of your interest in art and when you began to draw.

RW: Well, I've always drawn—I have a propensity for it. I remember getting attached and getting involved in drawings for hours and hours. Getting off in my own little escaped world and feeling safe drawing. I must have been four or five when I got a large piece of butcher paper and I got a red crayon out and I drew a big skeleton, bone by bone, on this giant piece of butcher paper. It was so big I had to crawl around to draw this skeleton. And, of course, it was Red Skeleton [after the popular comedian and radio and television host Red Skelton].

LGJ: Where were you drawing that image of the skeleton from?

RW: Well, you know, Halloween skeletons and stuff like that. I always had an interest in bones and death and macabre things like that. Dinosaurs . . . my grandparents had an old, old set of Compton's encyclopedias, and out of boredom, I started going through them. I came across the dinosaurs, and it was a real revelation to see all those Charles Knight illustrations of dinosaurs. By the time I got to the fifth or sixth grade (I was in Alabama at that time), I had quite a reputation with the teachers as an artist. I remember one incident where they were painting a mural at the end of the hall in school. All of the artistically proficient children were chosen for this. Each child would take a little section and paint something on the wall, and I was the person who would put in backgrounds and take all the stuff that was painted on the wall and tie it all together to make some kind of intelligent thing out of it. I was the only one who could handle composition. I would have roads going up to a guy's house and so forth. It wasn't necessarily what I wanted to do, but I was the only one who could tie all those idiot things together.

I went to a military school when I was in first and second grade. I'd come from a very military family that had pushed discipline on me, and I responded to it. I did very good in military school (I made it to corporal), but I was in a state of terror. I had to get up real early in the morning, polish my shoes, get my little uniform on, and it was, like, serious military.

There was no PE [physical education] or recess, but in the middle of the day, you would go out and drill. We drilled in the hot sun or the cold weather. We had to be out early in the morning for inspection. My unit would have to be lined up, and I was responsible for six or eight other kids' shoes being shined because I was a corporal. It was okay when I was young when it could be forced on me and drilled into me, but then around the third grade, I'd started developing characteristics that were obviously not those of a conformist. I convinced my parents I couldn't handle this anymore.

LGJ: Was that as a result of being told what to do every hour of the day?

RW: Well, I was not an emotionally strong person to deal with discipline and doing things in thoughtless situations. Later, I did pretty well until about the seventh grade, and then I started failing all my subjects and having a lot of trouble in school. I think I was probably a little dyslexic; I had a little trouble reading, and I fell way behind the other students, and, being left-handed, I just could not keep up. The outward appearance was that I was kind of an idiot or something. I was just not as mentally fast as the other kids. To an English teacher, I would appear to be an idiot, to a math teacher I would appear to be an idiot. To an art teacher, I was preparing to be an Einstein, a

Picasso! So, from the seventh grade on, my success in school was just so hard in coming that by the time I got to the tenth and eleventh grades, I was failing so badly—while still trying to hang in there—I just got kicked out of school. There is a point that comes up in those later grades when they think, "Well this individual is just better off in the labor force than he is here," and got run out of school.

The 1950s I remember well. I spent some time in Alabama, Florida, and California and a lot of time in New Mexico. It was such a modern time, full of promise, but there was so much bigotry. It was taken for granted that everyone was of one mind, and that way it was right up until the Vietnam War, so 1956 was very much like 1963. I remember the beatnik movement coming in. I remember personally being involved in gang problems and a number of gang rumbles. I remember being in one that had hundreds of people in it. It took place in the back of a bowling alley and later migrated into the bowling alley itself. People were bowling balls around and stuff, and some ended up in the hospital.

LGJ: So the beginning of the beatniks was the beginning of the anti-establishment movement—people questioning everything and making outward statements that weren't too favorable to mainstream society?

RW: Yeah. There were an awful lot of criminals who were beatniks. It was an excuse to be a nonconformist, and I ran around with a lot of these people—some were gang leaders and others were college students. There was a romance about the beatniks.

Prior to 1963, drugs were so socially condemned you didn't even talk about them. It's like what they're trying to do now, to get us back to the 1950s. I remember smoking marijuana very openly, even though it was a tremendous crime, but almost no one could identify it. It smelled like Bull Durham tobacco. I remember coffee shops opening up in 1957, '58, and '59, and that is where the college kids would be. There would be these fishnets and globe floats and corks, women in leotards, and people sitting around on the floor on pillows with little tables drinking espresso. Me and a friend would ditch school all the time and go to the coffee shops, and we got extremely good at playing chess—to where we could judge maybe ten to twelve moves ahead on the board. We were about fourteen years old. We would go to these places and play chess for money against these twenty-three- or twenty-four-year-old college kids and just wipe their asses. It was really fun.

I started noticing social change when I started seeing interracial couples for the first time. There was this kid who lived around the corner from me in a nice house. He had this real mild-mannered American dad with a tie, and a real American mom. I knew this kid for a while, and he wasn't an extrovert or anything. He didn't run around with our gang, but I ended up at his house a few times. One day, someone said, "Let's go over to his house." We go over there, and the furniture is gone, there are fishnets hanging from the ceiling, and it looks like a coffee shop. Everyone's sitting around on the floor, and we said, "Well, what's going on around here?" The mom comes back with a girl-friend, they both got dates, and they're both Black! Whoa! This is like 1959! I was really shocked, I was just kind of set back, like "this isn't the America I know—we got us a change going here."

From that point on, and seeing what I had seen in coffee shops, I realized that this was a situation that was going to be expanded upon. This wasn't the kind of lifestyle that I particularly cared for, but it was the first lifestyle I'd ever seen that was a diversion from what I'd always been forced into.

LGJ: Were things starting to go in a different direction?

RW: Yeah, and since this was happening in Albuquerque, it didn't take Einstein to realize this had been going on heavily somewhere else before it got there.

LGJ: At what point did your fascination with art turn into a more serious part of your lifestyle? When did you start working towards becoming a full-time artist?

RW: It was obvious in elementary school that my predilection for this kind of deal was great. I just stood out in all my classes. I came from a military, agricultural family with a very tight Puritan ethic, save your money and so forth. I didn't like driving a tractor, and I sure as hell didn't like the military. I just realized I don't exceed at that, and from that point, I knew I was going to be an artist. I noticed that in about 1954 I really got hung up on style, personal style, and fashion. I remember 1949, '50, and '51, the beboppers and the bobby-soxers, and how they dressed, and there was a tremendous amount of interest in cars and hot rods.

I was into music. My father owned a drive-in restaurant on the Atlanta Highway in Montgomery, Alabama—the Parkmore. It made my father wealthy. It was gigantic—it serviced one hundred cars at a time. It had movie screens at each end and had its own radio station, and my dad had a nightly radio program of rock 'n' roll and popular music. He was friends with Hank Williams and Gene Krupa . . . people like that. So being in this music situation all through the early 1950s, I was always conscious of what was hip. There were always hip people hanging around the place. I watched the metamorphosis of bop—now it's called rock 'n' roll, but back then it was called bop.

I knew guys that had flame-painted Harleys and stuff. I started running around with hot-rodders and some people of the criminal nature, bohemian nature. I realize that the people I emulated were on the fringes of society . . . I was of an artistic ilk, and I really couldn't find a peer group. I'd read car magazines, and I knew that some hot-rodders were kind of artists, like Von Dutch. So Von Dutch became my immediate hero. I was versed in Salvador Dalí and some art. I'd always studied all I could learn about art, even when I was young. I learned about Calder, Matisse, Van Gogh, Monet, Manet, Toulouse-Lautrec, and Cézanne. The impressionist school was once this revolutionary school but [is] now so accepted. It was the kind of art that everybody's mother liked, and she would gather sensitive sons to be art students, and the mom would bombard them with this Cézanne-Monet-Matisse bullshit, which to me had no graphic interest whatsoever. It just appeared to me that they weren't any better than what they revolted against.

LGJ: You moved to California, on your own, to go to art school?

RW: Right, on my own, to a place near Los Angeles City College (LACC) in 1963. Things just picked up for me instantly.

LGJ: Did you find a groove, a peer group to fit in with out here?

RW: Well, I went to art school at LACC, and I got along with everyone fairly well. Prior to that, my art education was comic books and those Walt Foster how-to-do-its, lettering books, circus banners, books on Dalí, and anything that I could copy that interested me. I had known about De Kooning and Pollock and people like that, but when I got to LA and went to school, that was it! De Kooning, Rothko, and Pollock were simply the rule, the thing, ya know. A lot of stuff like that had made itself official, and I was a nobody, and this was the official program. The stuff I had learned before then was questionable, very questionable. Later, when I got into the psychedelic stuff, that's when I met a lot of my brethren, see? But I was running around in 1963, '64, and '65 with painters that were trying to get New York shows.

LGJ: Did you ever try to be a part of that abstract movement, or did you just completely step aside?

RW: I tried, but my personality . . . I was so good at what I did, I couldn't bring myself to join the abstract movement. When I'd sit down to do a painting, when I'd get up from the painting, I'd want something I could look at, and they would do a blurred, shitty thing. Instead of correcting it or making changes to it, they would just get another canvas and do another thing, and get *another* canvas and do *another* thing, and then you'd have a hundred canvases. You'd go into these artists' studios, and there'd be a hundred canvases all over the fuckin' place. And I hated every one of them.

There was this artist—I should not mention his name—he was living on top of a launderers with his wife, and he was pumping out paintings like crazy. He was like all the rest of them, trying to go for the party line on proper art, and he tried to go through all the proper motions to join the Los Angeles

Art League. He submitted one or two drawings and paintings, and he worked really hard on them to get in there. I was digging through his shit, and he had all this abstract expression shit that was really fuckin' boring, and at the time I was being really open-minded. I was trying to say, "Oh, I like the way you did this purple, and this color . . ." I was trying to really be receptive.

Then I found these two paintings that looked like they were inspired by covers from the weird science fiction of the 1940s or something, real way-out good draftsmanship and stuff. And I said, "Whoa, what are these?" And he goes, "Oh, that's just garbage, that's garbage!" I said, "Well, no—what do you mean? This is great!" He said, "I did those two months ago trying to get into the Art League building—I should have known better with shit like this. They took one look at them and said it was crap, and they wouldn't let me in."

A couple of years later I went to a surrealist show over at the Art League or some snobby fucking organization. You can put this in print—I slander these people with a great deal of pleasure. Me and Suzanne crossed the street in some heavy traffic and went over there to see some surrealist show. We were looking at each other, wondering why we came from the Valley and crossed a dangerous street to look at this.

LGJ: They had no conception of what surrealist art was, or were they just trying to pass that off as surrealist?

RW: Well, there is a vague area of surrealism that goes into blurry abstraction, that overlapped into their hopeless fuckin' abilities. So that was the situation that existed then, and to a great extent now—to a real great extent now.

In 1964, Roy Lichtenstein and Andy Warhol came out with pop art. It was like sending an electric charge through this fuckin' shitty art world. Jasper Johns and Roy Lichtenstein and Andy Warhol had hit the situation with such a glancing blow that it slid in. They didn't try a T-bone attack on the art world—they hit kind of a New York angle through high society. So they got in and it was accepted. It went over in New York, so they got to take in LA, and they got to take in Paris. It went through all the points where it had to be accepted. Immediately, I saw it as 'Image Is Back!'

Before it was called "pop art," it was called "neorealism." Because it was the new realism with new things there. For a brief period of time, I thought it fit in very well. Then it was labeled "pop art" and it took off. You never hear "neorealism" anymore, but that's what it was called, for a while. Anyway, that had been the exception that broke through, and after that, a bunch more shit came in.

The situation seems to be: art will always be what the mass of the ability of the idiots can do. If the majority of people can only stick their thumb up their ass, then that is what art is going to be. They're going to sell this to the wealthy people—sitting around with your thumb up your ass is what's going to be sold. It's not going to be who's the best at a certain thing, like it used to be 150 or 200 years ago. So the only thing that makes you a master is how well you can manipulate yourself into promotion and politics.

LGJ: And somehow, somewhere along the line, it's down to a few people's opinions about the buyers that the public seems to respect, for whatever reason. They give something their personal okay, and all of the sudden it becomes the desirable or acceptable format. Who's at fault? Who's to blame for that situation?

RW: You can put your thumb on the problem in several places. I used to put it on the schools, and the schools are partly to blame, but the schools only respond to what the students want. The school will teach you how to cut your own throat if you'll pay tuition for it. In that way, they're flexible enough. But there are so many painters and so few chances of making a living at it that art schools everywhere are stuck full of people trying to be teachers, because they can't make a living being a painter, see?

So you have this glut. You've got thirty years now of abstract expressionist teachers that never were painters, and could never make it as painters, and they've ended up recycling the same shit that they couldn't do, passing on their own inabilities. And nobody is getting off at a distance and saying, "Hey, ya know, this isn't functioning." The reason no one can do that is because it isn't like mathematics or literature—there is no ill effect from cause and effect. If they teach mathematics badly, then suddenly you have a generation of people who can't do anything. Or you've got a generation of people who can't read or write. But in art, this observation never comes up, so you've got three or four generations of this fuckin' horseshit. There are no checks and balances of what's good and what's bad because you've opened all the doors—it's total freedom.

LGJ: You say you consider yourself to be self-taught, but I wonder how important a part your schooling played in your success.

RW: Oh, formal art training did help quite a bit. It made me realize that you deal with certain media, and you deal with people, and you deal with an attitude, and you deal in a direction called Art, and you deal with the formalization of art.

LGJ: As far as somebody teaching you technique . . .

RW: Well, I did take lettering classes and things like that, and I did learn from that. I'm an advocate of art school.

Then you get into painting class. If you've got thirty people in a class, there are three of them who can draw well, and the other twenty-seven aren't so good at it. So you have to do what the twenty-seven of them can do. You can't make them paint something that only the three can do, so you have to adjust yourself to that.

LGJ: Can you remember when you first started to paint?

RW: I did my first painting in eighth grade; it was in 1957.

LGJ: What was the subject?

RW: Some abstract blobby thing.

LGJ: Does it exist today?

RW: No.

SW: The earliest existing painting that he did is in the *Lowbrow Art of Robert Williams* book. I think it's that apple, that skull/upside-down apple. Isn't that the earliest?

RW: Just one of the earlier ones.

LGJ: We've sort of covered some of your personal art interests; can you talk more about Roth and those sorts of things?

RW: Yeah, it's pretty much what was in the pages of *Visual Addiction*. Roth Studios . . . should I explain who Roth was?

LGJ: Go ahead.

RW: Roth comes out of American hot rod culture. In the early 1950s, when it got fashionable to paint hot rods really wild, there was a guy named Von Dutch who distinguished himself in it. Von Dutch did pinstriping—line paintings—and in the process, he revived an art that went back to the last century, when they used to paint wagons and expensive automobiles before the First World War. That had pretty much fallen out of favor for years, and Von Dutch learned it and brought it back and did some real wild pinstriping. It became a giant vogue overnight.

Ed "Big Daddy" Roth was a hot-rodder, and he picked it up and was a little more of a promoter than Von Dutch was. Roth made a financial empire out of doing hot rod T-shirts with an airbrush. He drew monsters and pinstriping. He made custom cars that toured the United States. His business got really big, and he had such a following from young people. I was heavily influenced by him and Von Dutch. I later went to work for Roth.

LGJ: In what capacity?

RW: I was in charge of his advertising program. I was one of his idea men, and I was pretty much his art director and troubleshooter. I was the guy who had the tightest hand and could sit there and . . . and I had a rich imagination. That's the kind of people who worked there. It was an early hot rod bohemian think tank. Kind of a wild RAND Corporation or something. Nobody in the overground would accept it, but everybody knew about it.

LGJ: What about *Zap*?

RW: Okay, now *Zap Comix* is an underground comic book that belonged to the family of underground comic books that was started in late 1967, early 1968. The first was started by Robert Crumb, but they obviously evolved out of psychedelic posters, of which some were broken into comic strips. Some say they were all heavily influenced by *Mad* magazine, but I think it was the old, early EC comics that everyone was more interested in. And they dealt with extreme left-wing commentary and antiwar sentiments and bohemian, artsy things.

LGJ: Let's go into the origin of Coochy Cooty, since that's one of your strongest characters.

RW: Coochy Cooty was designed to look like a 1930s cartoon character, which was the high point in cartoons, the classic cartoon period. I wanted a cartoon character that looked cute, like Felix the Cat or Mickey Mouse, in that easy-to-animate style. But instead of having him in simplistic situations, like old cartoons used to do, I wanted to have him in horrible, difficult situations that were common in underground comics.

LGJ: What do you think of underground comics today, or are they not much in existence anymore?

RW: Well, I think it's in existence, but I think that when underground comics lost their thrill, they never really got back on their feet—not since 1972 or '73. I think even good comics today have an obstacle to face—not having that spark of romance that the first ones did.

LGJ: What other obstacles are hindering underground comics today? No new directions to go in?

RW: Well, for the very first *Zap* comics and the other early underground comics, there were no set formats. So you had all these styles, and it had not been determined what was going to dominate, see. There was wild stuff and stupid stuff and a bunch of different stuff. In 1972 and '73, a formula set in, and a group following it had to have a certain kind of graphic story in control. Me and Rick Griffin and S. Clay Wilson and maybe Moscoso, we were on the graphic, arty side. Crumb, Gilbert Shelton, Justin Green, and a few other people were more for the literary side and not so much interested in the visual thing. So you had two schools right at the very beginning. The literary school kind of won out.

Everybody was telling me how my stuff had no story ability. Rick got it really bad. Rick didn't tend to get involved in stories, so he caught a lot of flak.

LGJ: Do you follow any comics today?

RW: New, not really. Some of them are okay. There are a lot of them I can't stand. They just keep pecking at it like they've got some kind of future or something. I'm not going to mention names.

SW: It's basically just not your world anymore.

RW: No, it's just not my world anymore. After a while, it came to an impasse. I can't do the kind of color work I want to do. I like writing stories, but on the other hand, you can't do the visual things you want because you're encumbered by the story.

LGJ: Now you've got an audience that pretty much demands a rational story, which isn't a bad thing.

RW: Coming up with stories is a lot cheaper than doing movies. But I'm much more comfortable doing paintings. I think that paint represents, like, the false figurehead called Art. That's like an old romantic-classic thing that I'd like to whip the shit out of. Anyone who is intelligent can see that art is bullshit. I like being successful enough to challenge these already established assholes with their really boring crap. The art world is really boring— it's a formula for boredom. All this money is changing hands, and the whole empire is based on boredom. And people get behind this boredom, and they think it's chic and hip and it's going to change the future. It's so restricted and constipated and controlled, and there's so much lack of ability and craftsmanship. I just immediately react against art.

LGJ: There is a California-unique style of art.

RW: You're damn right there is. There's West Coast art here that's soon to ignite the entire Pacific Rim, and when it does, then New York's going to be over here, see. It's obvious. These guys know this is going to happen, and they're trying to hang on to their little cards of what they've been copying. They're little pop art copies.

I'm not going to mention any names, but it ain't going to take you too long to figure out who the fuck I'm talkin' about. You know the LA County Museum is full of the shit. I'm not going to lock horns with these people, ever. I'm just going to make my living and hope what I do rises like cream, see.

LGJ: Is this beginning to happen?

RW: I've done well for myself. I've gone as far as I can go right now, for a long time. I've beaten Los Angeles to death.

LGJ: How did you feel selling every piece that went into one of your recent shows, and having another hundred people waiting in line for your work?

RW: Well, that makes me feel real good. I'm very indebted to the people that have supported my work.

LGJ: When was your first sellout art show?

RW: The first show I sold out was at Psychedelic Solutions. My ignition point—when I started doing good—occurred at this *Western Exterminators* show at the Zero One in 1985; that's when things started turning my way. There were five or six artists showing, and I got a lot of recognition there.

LGJ: Something that seems apparent to me is that as the paintings become a little bit more expensive, you seem really determined to give people more for their money.

RW: Yeah, you have to be rational about the sales of my paintings. I'm trying to get a good solid market in the prints. It would relieve a lot of pressure in my life if I could get the print sales up.

LGJ: What about your books?

RW: The books and prints would really make my life easy. The books are selling real good, but the prints are still in the growing stage.

LGJ: Will the paintings in your latest show pave the way for a second show to come together as another book?

RW: Yeah, I'd like forty to sixty paintings in a book. Well, I tried to form a coalition with Georganne Deen, Gary Panter, Joe Coleman, and several people to get an intelligent school going that would be beneficial to everybody, but there were a lot of ups and downs in that. It didn't work out as well as you think it would.

SW: You mean a manifesto school of art?

RW: No, not a manifesto school of art, not as tight as a manifesto, but at least a group.

LGJ: You have a very strong vocabulary and a very keen ear for vernacular. This is clearly shown in your writing. Where did you hone or develop these skills, and how did you come up with some of the more unusual titles for your pieces? And maybe mention your habit of giving them not only one name but at least three different names.

RW: Well, I can't stand a painting that's just a bunch of scratches on the canvas and then you look at the title and the title is *Untitled Number 15*. Now, you not only have nothing to look at, but you've got nothing to think about. And being involved in the comic book world where you're responsible for entertaining people, you have this obligation and responsibility that another human being is going to look at this.

I would do these paintings and have some flowery names for them. Then someone would call and want to talk about the painting or something, and they'd go, "Well, what about the red turkey, you know, the painting like the red turkey," and they would give the painting this name . . . fuckin' name had nothing to do with what I gave it.

Then I realized when you're in a pinch, your mind will come up with a descriptive thing. I adopted these names, and I started figuring, well, I should come up with my own common name, but I also liked the flowery name. I liked the pedantic nonsense. After giving a painting a couple of names, I realized if you come up with a name that you're going to call it, then a real pedantic name that overdescribes it, and then some goofy quick name that someone's just trying to say really quick—"y'know, the one with the eye," or something—by the time someone reads the three titles, they've formed all these different divisions of observation on this painting which really enhances it, so it was natural.

LGJ: At what point do the titles come in? While you're working on your initial sketches, or what?

RW: When I sit down and do the idea, I sit down with a thesaurus and lots of research material, and dictionaries. Sometimes before I will paint a painting, before I'll do a sketch, I will verbally describe the painting in words. The titles of almost all of them are very early in the concept of the paintings. You'd think it was something I'd pasted on later, you know, like "the carrot was in the shape of a nose," call it the "Nose Carrot," or something like that. No, it's not like that at all. I would think of the nose carrot that made the carrot look like the nose, see.

LGJ: What books, magazines, or publications do you enjoy?

RW: I am fascinated with the past and present because I think I should be fascinated with the future. But the future just seems like a bunch of shit to me, so I can hide in the false romance of the past. The future just looks like an overpopulated world where everyone has to be watched very carefully because there's so little space, everything's accounted for. The future seems so oppressive to me. This is very wrong and very pessimistic, and I don't like this thing in myself. When I revert to the past, I feel bad for doing it, but I get a great deal of research material out of the past. When I come up with an idea for a painting, if it's a hobby horse, I'll read everything I can on a hobby horse, what kind of people it originated from, and what kind of social status the hobby horse was in, just to have a little small hobby horse in the corner of a painting.

LGJ: So this is just one little incidental thing in a painting?

RW: This will separate me from other artists. I'll tell you what I do when I'm learning to draw. Drawing is always a state of learning. I would go out and I would buy all the bad art books on drawing. I would not only get the good ones, but I'd also get all the bad ones. And I would find stylizations and different positions and things, and where this bad artist is teaching to draw this thing . . . would do some awkward thing. So I would do an impression of this thing. If I drew something, I'd want to see what a bad drawing of it looked like, because it was someone's imagination that drew it. Where he fell short, maybe I should fall short there too, or maybe I should make it better there.

I like hot rod books, and I like historical books. I've currently been reading about Mata Hari. I read everything I can on Mata Hari—this is the most fascinating thing in the world.

LGJ: So, at some point, she'll no doubt surface in one of your paintings?

RW: She has before. That style . . . there's a style that she lived in, that I use in my paintings all the time, see. This phony "Oriental" dancer by the name of Little Egypt, prior to the First World War. France, Paris, this obsession with Orientalism.

LGJ: There's a lot of sexual imagery, body parts, nudes, violent depictions, and earth-shattering weird scenarios in your work, why?

RW: Because my stock-in-trade is imagination, and if not the pilot, the copilot to the imagination is the libido. When your imagination runs around in its own kingdom, it searches out things that interest it, and usually it's sexually related.

LGJ: Briefly detail how the *Zombie Mystery Paintings* came about.

RW: I used to do oil paintings, done in the very tight academic style of the 1830s. And a few guys named Gary Panter, Bob Zoell, and a few other underground punk rock artists were showing up in clubs around LA. They were after-hours clubs, styled after the clubs in New York popping up in the early 1980s. And these guys were doing this real slapdash quick art, Day-Glo and marker pens and stuff, and it was an obvious punk rock style that had just been invented, specifically by Gary Panter.

Now me being part of the underground, or the alternative cultural world, I felt very left out by not being invited to these galleries, or even allowed to get in these galleries for these shows. My work was just too fine, and the stuff they were doing was slapdash. When May Zone would show at these places, she wouldn't do the work until the day of the show. She'd stop by garbage cans and alleys and stuff and pick the work up on the way to the show, get it there and put some Day-Glo on it and call it her show, see.

I would have to compete, with my finer paintings, with the stuff that was done instantly. I decided, well, I could whip this stuff out, too! And I started on a series of really quickly done oil paintings called *Zombie Mystery Paintings*.

I figured with my ability in anatomy and composition, even me at a high clip, I might have an advantage. I started doing a bunch of these paintings, and after I got two or three of them done, I started getting a lot of immediate orders from people. So many people wanted them instantly that I made a list of people, and I allowed some of these people to pay me off on time. I made the stipulation that, well, I've got so many wanting these things, and I am taking time payments, that when your name comes up on the list, you'll just have to buy the one that comes up. In other words, you'll buy the thing sight unseen, since the painting is only six hundred bucks or nine hundred bucks. And if your turn comes up and you don't like the painting, your name's going to go to the back of the list. So this group of people said, "Well, yeah, sure, no problem." And the paintings just started selling like crazy. Now a couple of people did get paintings they didn't like and mailed them back to me, and said, "Well, we're just disappointed."

LGJ: They couldn't display them for whatever reason.

RW: See, I use this subject matter that's so raunchy, and so full of gratuitous sex and violence, that it would have a tremendous energy impact at these after-hours clubs that were frequented by people that were dissipaters and indulgers. They were usually on drugs or drunk. [With] this kind of stimuli, these kinds of paintings were just electrifying, and people really enjoyed it. I did well in competing with Gary Panter, Bob Zoell, and May Zone and sold out this whole bunch. I named this form of sales "blind subscription." And that's all there is on the *Zombie Mystery Paintings*.

SW: Let me add something. What motivated you to publish a book about them? As I recall, the whole point was you were working towards a book, and that's why you weren't letting people pick and choose and give descriptions of what they wanted to be painted.

RW: She brought up another point; there is another situation here. I already had my first book out, *The Lowbrow Art of Robert Williams*, and it sold well. As I was working on this bunch of paintings, it was natural, for me, to see the second book coming around. I made a book called *Zombie Mystery Paintings*. This was the very first book to come out of the underground on oil paintings.

LGJ: How about a little background about the Guns N' Roses cover, and maybe now in retrospect, if there're any feelings about it. Did that bring a whole new world of people into what Robert Williams is all about? Was it something other than money that made you license this artwork?

RW: Some people think it was. It got me something. My adversaries were very careful to not use my name. The six or seven feminist groups that were

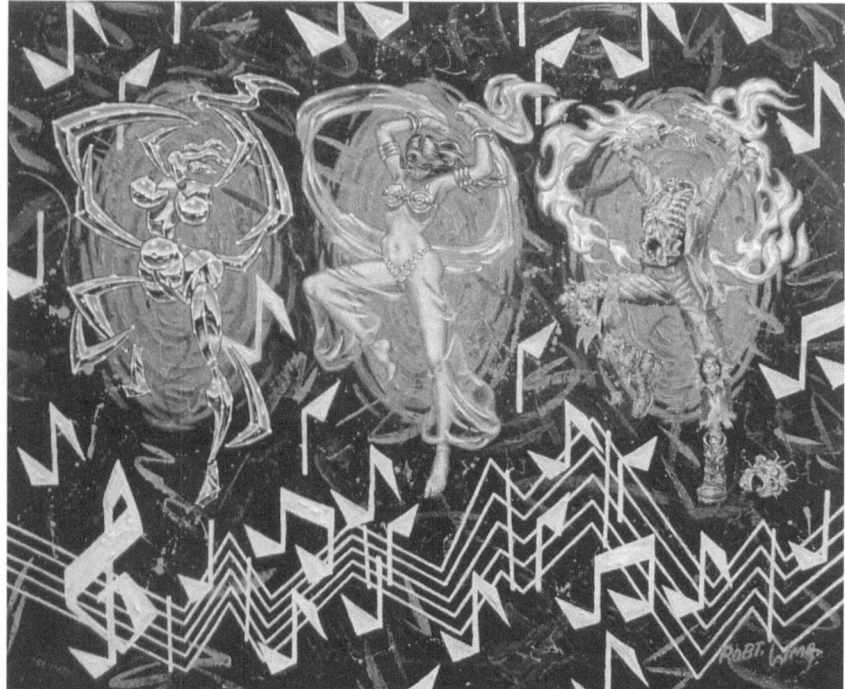

Robert Williams, *Salome Being Mocked by Personifications of the Future and the Past*, 1987. Oil on canvas, 76.2 x 91.4 cm. Private collection.

attacking me because of that album cover were very careful never to use my name because they knew that was what I wanted. So I got a lot of write-ups, and I was on television a lot. There was a lot of publicity.

The feminists that attacked the album cover would not attack me, would not directly confront me about it. It was always the record company. Even when I would have phone calls with the newspapers from Santa Cruz and Berkeley, I would never get a direct response from the feminists. They wouldn't say, "This artist has got a problem"; they would say, "This record company has a problem, this band has a problem." They had the intelligence to know that you don't attack art.

LGJ: Did the whole incident accomplish something for you?

RW: Yeah, it did, it really did. That piece of artwork was one of my "super cartoons" and was done in a very banal way. I painted it to academic standards, but the subjects were banal and simpleminded. It would appeal to your lower component of society. It is an orange monster jumping a fence with a robot attacking a woman. It was a perfect design for a tattoo and was no higher elevation in culture than a tattoo, but here it was an oil painting, selling for ten thousand dollars. And to verify this, to verify the success of this thing, not only did I paint it, but I also appreciated what I painted, and I sold the son of a bitch.

Then along comes a banal band and divvies it for their emblem, their album cover. And when I talked to Axl, he wasn't giving me great intellectual reasons for choosing it. He just liked the monster that attacked girls. It was exactly the appeal that you'd want on this thing. This picture was validated, and when the feminists bitched about it, they validated it even more.

LGJ: And putting out an alternative cover as well, because some stores would not stock it.

RW: Yeah, this is shit, this picture is shitty, this is questionable.

LGJ: And they've never replaced your thing up there with the original cover, did they? That's funny. The fact that they asked you to create a different album cover, whether it was commissioning you, or using yet another piece of art . . . did you immediately turn them down, and not talk about the money or anything?

RW: Well, I like Guns N' Roses, and I like their music, it's okay. I like punk rock music better than I like Guns N' Roses, but I like those guys. And if I was going to do an album cover for anybody, I'd do it for them. But there were a couple of things . . . I was painting a lot of oil paintings that had to be done, and I didn't have time. Another thing was they wanted to dictate what I should paint. Y'know, if I was going to break my schedule, it sure as hell wouldn't be to do what they wanted.

LGJ: So you're very focused.

RW: Yeah. If I'm going to be a nobody, I'll be my nobody.

LGJ: You're pretty involved with music, aren't you?

RW: I listen to classical music, some grand opera, and I listen to a lot of punk rock. I like a lot of punk rock. When I listen to classical music when I paint, I get too introspective and too tight. And when I listen to punk rock music, it makes my metabolism jump—and more open to whipping the workout. I'm much better at listening to real harsh punk music. Like Big Black, Kerosene, and stuff like that.

LGJ: Real powerful, noisy, and overpowering stuff. Do you have some favorites right now, I mean you like Big Black a lot, Lydia Lunch is a favorite, Jim Foetus?

RW: There's so damn many of them. Flesh Eaters is one of my favorites, Babes in Toyland, Hole, and L-7.

LGJ: Where do you paint? When? I know you get up real early in the morning. Do you just paint until you drop the brush or what?

RW: Yeah, about seven or eight. A twelve-hour day.

LGJ: Have you worked in any other artistic medium, film, video, or posters?

RW: Sculpture, what else? Let's see I've done storyboards, a few attempts at writing movies, and a few things like that.

LGJ: In *Gauntlet* magazine, you mentioned how artists have to worry about being censored by the political Left. How does this tie in with how you present your work?

RW: The left wing of politics is very idealistic, and things must be very politically proper with the left wing of politics. And I search for freedom, and I want to do what the hell I want to do. Sometimes it's done in very, very bad taste. And, of course, I'm conscious that I don't hurt people, but sometimes I do. If you're a stickler for political correctness, you'll find a lot of questionable things in my work. I have more trouble with the political left publications, like the *LA Weekly* and the *Village Voice*, than I do with any other publications. The other ones won't pay attention to me at all; if they do, they'll just glaze over me. But the important publications that I need exposure in . . . you know, I just don't fit in their parameters of what would make them comfortable.

Esthetician of the Preposterous

MICHELLE DELIO / 1992

From *Art? Alternatives*, April 1992. Reprinted by permission of Robert Williams.

He's been called hero and heretic, womanizer and woman hater, genius, and jerk. Disgruntled gallery goers have destroyed his paintings and threatened his life at the same time as rabid Robert fans line up to buy one of his paintings. His work is sold years in advance of his ever laying brush to canvas (there's currently a 150-person waiting list to purchase a Williams painting), but until very recently, he could not get mainstream galleries to show his work.

The idea for *Art? Alternatives* magazine came from a conversation Robert and I had about a year ago when he mentioned that he couldn't get a gallery to show his work. I was amazed that this man, whose paintings are so sought after that an elaborate waiting list scheme had to be constructed to deal with the demand, was still not accepted by the "art world." So the idea for a magazine showcasing outsider art was born. I first worked with Robert Williams while editing an interview with him for *Tattoo Revue* magazine. I'd been a longtime fan of his work, but during the several weeks we worked on that interview, I also came to admire and like Robert Williams the man. He's refreshing.

Robert does not deal well with bullshit, false pretension, or foolishness. He can spot a liar in two seconds and will quickly cut him (or her) down to size. He's both an obsessive, compulsive, driven workaholic and a caring friend who is generous with his time and support.

This interview was a long time in the making. Originally the plan was for me to fly to California and interview Robert there. The untimely death of Rick Griffin caused us to move on to plan two, sending another interviewer out several months later. The interview was done, and the tape was promptly lost somewhere between New York and Los Angeles. Plan three was then put into effect, and I set up a date to interview Robert over the phone. The appointed hour arrived, and my tape recorder died. But we finally got it together, and *Art? Alternatives* is proud to present this portfolio of Robert Williams's work.

Michelle Delio: Want to start from the very beginning?

Robert Williams: I was born in Albuquerque, New Mexico, in Saint Joseph's Hospital, on a cold and rainy Tuesday morning in 1943.

MD: And then what happened? [*Laughs*]

RW: Well, my parents got married and divorced about four or five times . . .

MD: They kept marrying and divorcing each other?

RW: Yeah.

MD: Were they artists?

RW: No, no, no!!!

MD: You're being very adamant.

RW: Well, my father is totally opposite from an artist. He was a military man and an oil man.

MD: What about your mom?

RW: My mom was just a good ol' gal from Indiana. They met in New Mexico during World War II.

MD: What was your very first memory?

RW: I have this vague memory of a horrible event, way in the back of my mind, which I assume is a memory of being born. I just didn't want to come out of the womb.

MD: Why?

RW: Well, I was prematurely born. It just wasn't time.

MD: So nobody in your family had any artistic talent, huh? I guess that blows the hereditary theory.

RW: Yeah. I'm left-handed too.

MD: And dyslexic, right?

RW: Yeah. They think that something happens to people to make them left-handed. I had an odd birth, so that's what probably caused it.

MD: Being dyslexic, was it hard for you to learn to paint?

RW: No, that wasn't a problem for me. It's always hard to learn to paint, but it wasn't any harder than anything else I did. Anyway, I was twelve years old when my parents finally separated for the last time. I ended up in Albuquerque. My father was well-to-do, and I was supposed to be brought up as a southern gentleman. So I was brought up like a little military aristocrat. And then, when my parents got separated for the last time in 1955, there I was, out on the streets of Albuquerque. My mom could barely support us; she worked as a saleslady, and women didn't get paid much in those days. So I was just this little hoodlum on the streets. I got my ass kicked on a daily basis, but I got street savvy real quick.

MD: When did you realize you had artistic talent?

RW: I'd always known that. When I was a little baby, they did this thing they used to do to kids back then. They take a little baby and they put him on the floor, and at the other end of the room they put a bottle of whiskey, a Bible, and a dollar bill. Then they see which one he crawls to. That's supposed to predict his future.

MD: Which one did you crawl to?

RW: The dollar bill. Anyway, I always had a propensity toward paper and crayons.

MD: Did you go to art school?

RW: My first school was a military school that had no art classes. I had to be in school real early in the morning and pretend to be a little corporal. I hated it. But, being young, I didn't realize that other little kids had it differently. By the time I got into third grade, though, it had become really apparent that I didn't have the character to be a military person. So my parents took me out of that school and put me into public school. I did really well there, but the thing I liked about this school was that there were girls in my classes. That just excited the living piss out of me! The opposite sex was so alien to me.

MD: In between checking out the girls, did you still manage to draw?

RW: They had this mural in the hall, and the kids that the teachers thought were the brightest got to work on the mural. So these little idiots would express their little selves in shaky little patches all over the wall, and I was the guy that had to design a landscape to accommodate their little ideas. I'd have a road going over to this guy's little idea connecting it to someone else's idea, and if one patch was bigger than the other patch, I'd have the one patch be in the foreground.

MD: Just tie it all together, right? Sounds like editing.

RW: Yeah. Then when I started getting into the seventh grade, my reading and math abilities stopped growing, and it started to look like I had a problem, and in 1954 there was no such thing as dyslexia.

MD: Just that you weren't working up to your potential.

RW: Right. And at the same time, I'd started to develop this real fascination for girls and social life. So I failed class after class, until I finally got kicked out.

MD: How old were you?

RW: Sixteen.

MD: Well, you did better than I did. I left school at the end of the eighth grade. I used to cut out a lot and spend the day in our local library. I was convinced that school was interfering with my education.

RW: That's about the way I looked at it too. I would ditch school and just hang around reading books or playing chess.

MD: When did you start seriously thinking about art as a career?

RW: Well, in the fifties, when I was involved with gangs, I would ingratiate myself with the gang leaders by doing artwork for them. I could draw naked ladies, cars, and things that would actually appeal to these guys. This knack for drawing that I have literally saved my life. I was also into hot rods, which were sapping my money . . .

MD: You had motorcycles too, right?

RW: Yeah, Indians. They were my motorcycle of choice. I spent a lot of time between hospital sheets because of Indian motorcycles.

MD: Yeah, they do tend to throw you.

RW: There's a large mortality rate with motorcycles. You can only hope that Dame Fate is on your side.

MD: I always figured that if you ride, you're gonna go down. It's a given. You can only hope you don't land too hard.

RW: Yeah, you gotta be lucky and super alert. Anyway, I got into a lot of trouble with the police over the motorcycles and my involvement with gangs. The thing was that I had kind of an odd personality. I had absolutely no social skills whatsoever. The only folks I was at all comfortable with were criminals. The rest of the student body was into sports and such, and they seemed like such fucking numbnuts to me. A conformist bunch of idiots. The people that interested me were the real hardened criminals, who were always dragging me into trouble. But they had style. There was another factor to my fascination with outlaws, too, and that was girls. The average girl in the 1950s did not put out. She was not sexually malleable. And the girls of lesser morals would get you into tremendous trouble, because if you were fucking them, then everyone else was, too. So all these males fought over the girls who would piece out, and the rest of the time was devoted to trying to convince the good girls to put out.

MD: That's horrible.

RW: And it was really hard for me because I was socially inept and didn't have the greatest chance of scoring with the girls. The smart thing would have been to give up, but I'm kind of a driven person. I'd be running around with these scraggy gals, and then I'd end up having to fight somebody over them.

MD: Weren't you working at a carnival around this time period?

RW: Yeah, I was a concessionaire; I made the change for the game where you pitched in the nickels and won a prize.

MD: It's interesting because carnivals are set up to play off people's subconscious wants. And your paintings do the same thing. Is there a tie-in there?

RW: Yeah, I guess. I've always liked pushing people's buttons. And there is a dazzle to the carnival.

MD: How did you hook up with Big Daddy Roth?

RW: One of my major influences was hot rod magazines. And there was a fella named Von Dutch that was like this master pinstriper and hot rod artist. An offshoot or copy of Von Dutch was this guy named Ed "Big Daddy" Roth. He hit the scene about 1959. He made a series of really wild show cars. I'd run into him at a couple of car shows. Anyway, I eventually moved out to California, where I had art job after art job and failure after failure . . .

MD: Why "failure after failure"?

RW: Well, all I could seem to paint were monsters and naked ladies.

MD: Was that all you could do or all you wanted to do?

RW: I guess it was all I wanted to do. I could be a practical illustrator, but it really didn't interest me. My first real important job was being the art director for *Black Belt* magazine, a karate magazine. They bounced me after six months. Then, in desperation, I took a job as a container designer at a fascist fucking cardboard box factory. It didn't take them long to realize, especially since I was doing a lot of acid at the time, that I wasn't the executive type. So then I went to the unemployment agency, and they said, "No, we don't have anything for you. . . . Well, we do have one thing, but nobody will take this job, it's kind of dirty." I said, "What is it?" and they said that this guy Roth down in Maywood needed an artist. I went down, did some shirt designs for Roth, and he hired me. I was making three times more than I made at the box factory, coming and going whenever the hell I wanted. The job was made for me. Going to work at Roth's was unbelievable; the place was like a surrealist factory. All of a sudden, I was surrounded by all these odd, incredible, and wonderful people that worked for Roth. Their stock-in-trade was wild ideas and building hot rods.

MD: Sounds wonderful.

RW: It was. The feds were in there all the time. It was a real colorful place to work. I was his art director for five years.

MD: What happened after you left Roth?

RW: Roth had a competitor named Stanley Mouse, who became "Mouse" of psychedelic poster fame in the sixties. It was Alton Kelley and Stanley Mouse, Rick Griffin, Victor Moscoso, and Wes Wilson who made up the big five in the psychedelic poster movement. I knew these guys and hung around with them some, but every free moment I had was devoted to painting, because painting wasn't a commercial thing like those psychedelic posters were. I still had some grand illusions that there was some great surrealist movement coming. So all those years I stayed home and noodled away on these fucking paintings.

MD: Were these paintings the same kind of stuff that you're turning out now?

RW: Yeah, I had this blind dream that there'd be some revival of a surrealist movement, of representational fantasy art. Then I found out about this guy called Robert Crumb, who was doing these underground comics. He did one called *Zap*. I saw it and I said, "This is what I want in on. This is as close as I'm going to get to what I'm after." I got in touch with the *Zap* people, who were Gilbert Shelton, who did the *Fabulous Furry Freak Brothers*, Rick Griffin, S. Clay Wilson, Spain Rodriguez, and Victor Moscoso. In the beginning, there was them, me, and maybe one or two other underground artists, and that was it. Then *Zap* got popular, and within a year there were two thousand underground cartoonists.

MD: You guys who were doing *Zap* didn't all work together in one office, did you?

RW: No, I was down in Los Angeles, and sometimes Rick was down here too, and the rest of the guys lived up north in San Francisco.

MD: Did everybody just work on their own stuff and mail it in?

RW: Yes, that's exactly the way we did it, and we took turns doing the covers. When you see an underground comic now, you don't think much about it. But, if you can, try to picture what America was like in 1963. It was starting to loosen up a little bit, but not much. America in 1963 was just like America was in 1943. Morally, there was almost no change. But in 1967, the resistance and rebellion against the Vietnam War were just starting to cause a lot of change. There was a giant move in the porno market, and underground comics just started spurting out, but this didn't happen without tremendous resistance. When the first *Zap* that I was in, *Zap* #4, came out, 150 newsdealers got arrested for selling it.

MD: Busted for selling *Zap*?

RW: Yep, and seventy-five were busted in San Francisco, and another seventy-five in Los Angeles, because *Zap* showed sucking and fucking and penetration.

MD: Was this a financially lucrative thing in spite of the busts?

RW: We thought it was going to be, but then the market got flooded with underground comics, most of which weren't worth a shit. It was diluted fairly quickly, but *Zap* was still the flagship of the whole movement, and sales were okay until the Vietnam War ended in '73 and the movement to go against established thought just about ended with it.

MD: *Zap* isn't being published anymore?

RW: I guess it is, but we just haven't decided to do another one. The last *Zap* was printed in 1989.

MD: Is there going to be another one soon?

RW: I kinda doubt it. You know Rick Griffin went off and got himself killed, and he was supposed to be doing the next cover. So maybe we'll just lay the thing to rest now.

MD: That's a shame, because people still buy *Zap*. The cool thing is that even the very first issues don't seem dated.

RW: Yeah, there's a lot of good reading in them.

MD: Anyway, meanwhile you're still at home, noodling away on your paintings.

RW: That's right. Eventually the paintings saved me. Going back a bit, to the Roth days, when his life fell apart, he sold the business to this millionaire, James Brucker. He bought all of Roth's cars, and he bought a bunch of my work, too. So it seemed like the perfect time for me to try and sail on my own, to attempt to make a living from painting.

MD: Obviously it worked out okay.

RW: I haven't had to take a commercial commission since 1970.

MD: In your book *Visual Addiction*, you said about your paintings, "I'm passing this shit off as art." What did you mean by that?

RW: Art is caught between philosophy and religion. Some people like to think of art as an unquestionable sacred thing. It's like religion: you just don't question it. It's the true spirit of man, and it's one of the sacred grounds that you just don't violate. The other theory is that art is philosophy. It's the deeper side of man in his moments of contemplation. Both of those theories are true, and both of them are bullshit. In times of starvation, war, and famine, the first things to go are the artists. Art is just not a very practical thing. And I think an artist has to come to grips with the fact of just how very fucking useless he really is, and when he comes to the absolute understanding of what his position really is in the world and grasps the fact that he's dealing in gossamer fairy tales, then he can be strong.

MD: But people make such a fuss over artists.

RW: Yeah, it's not the artist who makes himself, it's the people around him, the people who champion artists, who make him. There's a lot of artists who are helpless that have been made into giants. And then there are fantastic artists, great masters, who never got anywhere because they just didn't know how to synchronize what they did with society and people.

MD: Yeah, it's that whole business side of the art world that kind of leaves lots of talented people in the dust.

RW: Yeah, that's it. You can look at the career of Peter Max, who never did anything for bands or anything, he was always on the outside, but he was one of the most famous psychedelic poster artists. He made all the money while the big five hardly made shit.

MD: You've got to be a really strong person to be able to merchandise yourself, to be able to drag your portfolio around and deal with constant rejection.

RW: Well, that's only if you're commercial. If you're in fine arts, your ass is really negligible. I got this figure from the Guggenheim a while back that said there are over one hundred thousand artists involved in the fine arts on the island of Manhattan alone.

MD: Most of them are working as waiters.

RW: Yeah, and their religious hope in life is that they'll be picked next. That their little fart will be the next golden fart.

MD: But most of them are just ripping off what other people did. There's very little being produced that's original.

RW: I agree with what you're saying, but if you look at it through their eyes, they're doing like Andy Warhol and recycling things into pop usage. They think they're deifying things by recognizing them.

MD: I think that when people first started doing that, it was interesting. But now it's gotten to the point where people are recycling already recycled work. So where does it stop?

RW: I'm like you. I'm as critical of it as you are, probably more. But the thing that has to be established is that art has to be absolutely free, and everybody can do whatever the hell they want. So you just have to live with the fact that you've got umpteen hundred idiots that can't do a fucking thing.

MD: The other thing that pisses me off is this new school of "shock value" art. I guess you do that to a certain extent . . .

RW: I'm part of that, sure.

MD: Well, you did say at one point that you paint for reaction and not approval. But I'm not sure if you really mean that, or if it's just a way of covering your ass if you don't get the approval.

RW: Probably I do want approval. I might think I don't want it, but maybe I do. It's like sex: you can't really define it. I do this artwork for attention, I'm sure, and I might have these great philosophies, and I might write pages and pages of manifestos describing what I do, but the bottom line is, I'm just compulsive. My compulsion is the master; I just come along and paint it and put some kind of name to it. I get up way too early in the morning, seven days a week, and work like a driven idiot, to produce this product. I try to take a vacation, but I can't because I'm being driven by this compulsion.

MD: If you had to put a name to this compulsion, what would it be?

RW: Anxiety, which I can pacify by telling myself I'm going to be this great artist if I face and defeat certain obstacles.

MD: What are the obstacles?

RW: Getting the work done. Setting goals for myself that are real tough and getting them done. An exact example of this is the pyramids. Historians now say that the pyramids were not built by slaves, they were built by paid craftsmen, so the pyramids were built by compulsion. The whole society had the compulsion to build these edifices. Just like the pyramids down in Mexico. Now, why the hell did people do those things? Compulsion. So when I cry about my sufferings in doing these paintings, actually that's bullshit, because I'm driving myself to do them.

MD: When you say that you paint for reaction, you don't specifically sit down and say, "Now, what's going to piss people off?"

RW: I don't paint an open wound to shock people, but I would paint something similar to an open wound to get someone's attention, whether they like it or not. Then I'd put other elements in the painting that associate it with an open wound, to put enough story there to get their brain cells to wonder about it. After they look at this thing of mine that they didn't really like, but had to look at, it would hold in their memory banks for a while. If I can get that to happen, I consider myself successful. But I don't consider its sheer shock value; that would be too obvious a way to say it.

MD: But that's what pisses me off with the shock value school. It's so premeditated. It's like the artists sit down and think about it and figure, "Okay, dead fetuses always gross people out," so that's what they paint.

RW: I know what you're saying, but there's another way to look at it. It's not so much about how gross someone can be, but it's about taking a taboo subject and rendering it in a rhythm and style that's never been seen before. Joe Coleman does it to a certain extent, and someone who does it to a really fine extent is S. Clay Wilson. He does it to the point that it's almost a symphony of beautiful grossness.

MD: But I don't get the feeling that Wilson is sitting down and trying to be insane. I get the feeling that he is and he's enjoying the fact. Maybe that's the difference. I think Wilson whistles while he works.

RW: What you're talking about is something that must be looked into and analyzed, because more and more artists are doing it now, and there is, or should be, more to it than sheer shock value. But shock value was the first wave of it.

MD: Well, I've come to the end of my prepared questions. Anything else we should talk about?

RW: Let's discuss women's asses a little bit.

MD: I figured we'd get to this eventually.

RW: I've always had this fascination with women's lower backs.

MD: I know. And I guess all men do, to some extent or another.

RW: Well, women do too, right? You're a woman, what's your opinion on that?

MD: About other women's asses or just asses in general?

RW: No, no, men's asses. Have you ever developed a real appreciation for men's asses?

MD: Depends on the ass in question. Now, this is the scientific appreciation we're talking about, right? The wonder of life and the mysteries of the human body and all that?

RW: No, I think it's legitimate aesthetics, I really do. Is a woman's ass a temple of God or merely an object of beauty? I could contemplate something like this until I'm blue in the face. I have this theory that sexual attraction is based on one's search for the opposite end of the pole, because all living things have a polarity. So your base instincts are caused by simple magnetic fields. That doesn't sound real plausible [*laughs*], but hey, it's something to think about.

MD: What got you thinking about this?

RW: Well, it's probably an attempt to rationalize that a large part of a man's life is based on chasing another creature so he can catch it, stick his wee-wee in it, and shoot fluid into it. Afterward, you have to wonder just why you did this. What does it all mean?

MD: You're such a romantic.

RW: I am! The other day I was thinking about what exactly beauty is. And I think that, classically, the perfect woman is the perfect average. The face isn't too thin, or too fat, the nose isn't too long, and the mouth isn't too wide. So the thing is that when you have sex with this perfect woman, you are vicariously fucking every woman in the world, because this woman is the sum average of all women.

MD: Robert, your mind wanders down some strange paths. Listen, is there anything else you want to say to the world, or at least to the readers of this magazine?

RW: Yes, I am now involved in a large group show at MOCA, the Museum of Contemporary Art in Los Angeles, with fifteen other artists. This is my first serious museum show. I am facing some real problems with a couple of women's groups. You must understand that I am a supporter of the women's movement and the struggle against oppression for more than half the world's population, but nevertheless I reserve the right to worship woman as a three-dimensional deity, and I do not believe that my representation of females aids in their oppression. It is my artistic right to render the images of women as my imagination sees fit. Remember, I will gladly accept the title "bad person" to continue my expression. In other words, nothing short of death will stop me from painting naked ladies. Anyway, the MOCA show is called *Helter Skelter*, and it is curated by a man with guts, Paul Schimmel. The show runs through April 26. My second big deal is my New York show at the Bess Cutler gallery in Soho, in the fall of '92 (possibly September). Bess dares to show thirty of my new oil paintings in an even more sensitive environment, the New York City art world.

Robert Williams Interview

STEVE RINGGENBERG / 1993

From *Comics Journal*, no. 161 (Aug. 1993): 42–70. Reprinted by permission of Fantagraphics Books and Gary Groth.

Robert Williams may not be the world's most politically correct painter, at least not in the opinion of some feminists, gay activists, and hidebound conservatives. But he has produced some of the most shocking, searingly weird, and densely layered images of the postmodern era, and despite the mountains of abuse heaped on him by the above-mentioned sectors of the populace, and the concerted opprobrium of mainstream art critics, Williams has carved out a niche for himself in the art world by dint of sheer, unvarnished talent, and his own creative fearlessness.

There is literally almost nothing Robert Williams won't tackle in a painting, and despite the currently moribund state of modern art, he has continued to enjoy great success selling his paintings. He has a waiting list of 250 people who've plunked down deposits for an original Williams, as well as limited-edition prints, four books of his work, T-shirts, coffee mugs, and other assorted merchandise.

One suspects that much of the vitriol directed at Williams, a onetime underground cartoonist and former art director for Kustom Kulture maven Ed "Big Daddy" Roth, stems not from the bizarre, quasi-obscene subject matter depicted in his paintings, but from the fact that Williams paints in a representational style. And he paints his blackly funny, nightmarish visions extremely well, to the point of showing off. So, in a time when talentless fine art hacks like Mark Kostabi and Robert Ryman are lionized by the critics from the *New York Times* and *Time* magazine, Williams is faulted for being too much of a storyteller and too much of a craftsman. You figure it out.

But enough about his work; what's Robert Williams the man like? In all my dealings with Williams, I've found him to be unfailingly professional, courteous, and highly intelligent. He's a unique combination of redneck gear-head and intellectual aesthete. He's one hell of a painter, a man who works fourteen to sixteen hours a day, seven days a week. He also loves to go tooling down the highway in his own handmade hot rod. Read on and learn why Robert Williams paints what he does, and why he's damned if he'll change to suit anybody's preconceived notions of what art should be.

Steve Ringgenberg: Where and when were you born, and where did you grow up?

Robert Williams: I was born in Albuquerque, New Mexico, in 1943, on March 2nd, 1943. I was the child of a father that was in the military during and after the Second World War, so there was a lot of traveling.

I lived in Indianapolis, Indiana; Fort Walton Beach, Florida; Montgomery, Alabama; and Albuquerque, New Mexico. My father was in the Army Air Force, and he was in charge of training pilots for the glider program, which was a tremendous failure. Probably more people died when the things landed than were killed in combat, but it was originally started by the Nazis, the Germans, and the British, and the Americans followed suit. My dad was very instrumental in the use of gliders. He was a very important person in the Second World War, as far as that glider program went. It was his responsibility to train pilots. He was in charge of over a hundred thousand men.

Ringgenberg: What was your father's name?

Williams: It was Robert W. Williams.

Ringgenberg: So are you a Robert Williams Junior?

Williams: No, I'm named after my grandfather . . . My father was quite a character. He's still alive, and he lives in the South. He was very, very good friends with Hank Williams.

Ringgenberg: The Hank Williams?

Williams: Yes, *the* Hank Williams. In fact, there's just been a German documentary made on Hank Williams, and my father was extensively interviewed in this.

Ringgenberg: Are you a fan of Hank's work?

Williams: Well, I was always a big fan of Hank Williams, but when I was young, when I knew Hank Williams, he was just a skinny, emaciated guy that would come over to the house, and my parents would run me off, so I was just a little child. He died in '53. I was ten years old. I really didn't have a hell of a lot to say to him.

Ringgenberg: How did you finally wind up in California?

Williams: Well, I was living in Albuquerque, New Mexico, and I was twenty years old. I had been in a lot of trouble with the police . . . and I was obviously going to get in a lot of trouble if I stayed in Albuquerque. I was trying to get an art education in New Mexico, and the University of New Mexico would not take me. There wasn't much opportunity, so I came to Los Angeles to enroll in a junior college. The tuition was only $6.50 a semester. So I came out to Los Angeles in '63. I'd been out to Los Angeles in '55 for a small period of time, living with an aunt and uncle, so I was familiar with the place. There was a tremendous romance in Los Angeles other than just the movie industry. There was hot rod mystique about Los Angeles. I'm sure a lot or people did come out here because of that, and I was one of them. You know, my interest was getting into a career and associating myself with this hot rod karma that I'd read about for years in car magazines.

Ringgenberg: What kind of scrapes were you getting in with the cops?

Williams: Well, I had been involved in a tremendous amount of truancy and gang involvement, and it was apparent that coming up on the horizon was going to be a lot of drug problems. I had a lot of aggravated assault arrests and public drunkenness arrests. and I was . . .

Ringgenberg: Were you pretty tough when you were a young man?

Williams: Well, I had a knack for finding fights. And I had been in a tremendous amount of fights, and I think I was the winner of very, very few.

Ringgenberg: Why did you get in so many fights?

Williams: I ran around with what was called the wrong crowd. The right crowd was so fucking boring. You know, they were football players with their letterman's jackets and the girls that followed that group. It was just so fucking square and predictable and unimaginative, and there wasn't a real bohemian society in Albuquerque for me to follow. There was something in that style that hung around the college that were drug addicts and stuff, and then there were gangs. And I found myself running around with a lot of criminals because they were the more interesting people. I had a propensity for being a bohemian, and the only people that would fit that bill were criminals, nonconformists.

Ringgenberg: So you were hanging around with the guys in the leather jackets? Bikers, people like that?

Williams: That's right, I remember wearing a motorcycle jacket about 1955 and having about ten or fifteen Latinos just work me over, because I had that motorcycle jacket on, because I looked like a poseur, a pretender, I looked arrogant in it. That was a common thing. If you wore a motorcycle jacket, you had to be able to back up wearing it. And now, today, it's just a common fashion.

Ringgenberg: So you came to LA to go to college, and that was what time?

Williams: It was '63. I went to Los Angeles City College, the same school that Ed "Big Daddy" Roth went to earlier, and it was a pretty famous school.

Ringgenberg: And how long did you stay there?

Williams: I stayed there a couple of years, and then I went to Chouinard Art Institute for a little while, and then I could no longer afford that.

Ringgenberg: What kind of training did you get in these schools?

Williams: I got all the beginning classes, and I got a very good, broad base of an education, an appreciation, all history, painting, drawing, sculpture, lettering, layout, and three-dimensional design.

Ringgenberg: Did they teach you oil painting there?

Williams: Well, I oil painted there. I guess I must have picked up something, but I was pretty good at oil painting before I entered that school. In '63 all the schools were predominantly occupied with abstract expressionism, where you could just slap it and dab it on there and it was a matter of just using earth colors and maybe blue and it wasn't really that challenging. I mean there was no technical ability to it. That period of abstract expressionism predominated art school up until just ten years ago.

Ringgenberg: So you were always more interested in some type of representational art?

Williams: Yeah, and consequently my peer group brought a lot of pressure on me because I took a chauvinist's amount of pride in craftsmanship, and it was obvious that I was showing off and that I had a predilection for cartoons. I set myself up in the eyes of others of looking like an illustrator, and that was what I was referred to as.

Ringgenberg: Was that a term of derision in the crowd you hung with?

Williams: Yes, very much so.

Ringgenberg: Were you always interested in art, even as a child?

Williams: Yeah. From the very beginning, as long as I can remember. I remember in the 1940s, just a little baby with crayons, putting down a big piece of butcher paper and just drawing all over the floor, and drawing a red skeleton and naming it "Red Skeleton" after the comedian [the popular radio and television host Red Skelton].

Ringgenberg: What about your interest in cars? That seems to have been a big factor in shaping your tastes.

Williams: Well, yeah. That was a pretty common thing with people my age back in the 1940s and '50s. If you were mechanically inclined, that would be a natural thing.

Ringgenberg: What was your first car?

Williams: I was eleven or twelve years old, and my dad bought me a car that I had wanted for a long time: a '34 Ford, five-window coupe. It was a beautiful little coupe.

Ringgenberg: And did you turn it into a hot rod?

Williams: Sure.

Ringgenberg: The old 1930s Fords and Chevys were the main cars that were turned into hot rods, weren't they?

Williams: There is a paradox when you look at *Happy Days*, and you look back at what you think of in the 1950s and you think of Chevrolets. Well, Chevrolets were not the hot cars. Chevrolet was a very undesirable car. When Ford came out with that V-8 engine in 1932, and you took that car and you took the fender and the hood off it and got the power to the weight ratio up on it, it was extremely fast. Chevrolet was a little better car in some respects because it had a wood frame in its body that had to be handcrafted, but after a couple of decades that wood would deteriorate and the car would start to fall apart, and it didn't have that flathead V-8. It had an overhead valve six in it, and it just didn't have the power that the Ford had. So, by the time hot rods got started in the late 1930s, '40s, and '50s, the inexpensive car that would really fly would be the early Ford. In the 1950s, it was the Ford flathead V-8 that predominated right up until the very late '50s.

Now, Chevrolet came out with its V-8 in 1955, which was a very fast overhead valve engine. But the average kid, you always see these *Happy Days* kids, driving a '55 or '57 Chevrolet or Corvette. Well, that didn't happen because they couldn't afford these things. Only the rich or well-to-do people could afford to buy new cars in the 1950s. So your average kid sure as hell didn't have a Chevrolet. Toward the end of the 1950s, these real hot Chevrolet engines were starting to hit the wrecking yards, and when they hit the wrecking yards, then kids could buy them and put them into Ford hot rods. The reason they would put them into Ford hot rods was because they couldn't put them in those old Chevy cars of the 1930s, because they had wooden frames in the bodies that were not good.

Ringgenberg: What could you pick up one of those engines for in those days?

Williams: Well, probably forty-five to fifty bucks, but back in the 1950s, that was a lot of money. The hot-rodder thing represents the old blue-collar culture before the Vietnam War. See, that died out in American youth after the Vietnam War. The hippie movement killed that forever. In the 1940s and '50s, the American youth's aspiration was to become a journeyman or to own their own shop. After the Vietnam War, most kids were intellectuals that had to go to college. So that blue-collar aspiration was gone forever, and hot rod-ding represented that blue-collar culture. You know, you had to be able to work with your hands and have an imagination, have a certain amount of ability and skills, and that's a bygone thing now.

Ringgenberg: Getting back to when you were in art school, after you left Chouinard, what did you do?

Williams: Well, I was married, so I had to go out and start bringing home the bacon. So I started taking any job I could. I had to come down to reality and accept that I wasn't going to be the great artist I had intended to be. I had to start looking for practical means of making a living, so I had to depend on jobs from unemployment agencies. And the first job I landed in the art field was art director for *Black Belt* magazine, the karate magazine. They had me lay the magazine out and do some illustrations, and after a while, I wasn't laying the magazine out fast enough, and I was doing too much illustration. So after six months they fired me, and then I was back out on the streets, very des-perate. Through some kind of bizarre connections, I ended up as a container designer for Weyerhaeuser Corporation in Vernon, California, a suburb of LA. I had to wear a tie and a suit and brown shoes and be there early in the morning; it was a junior executive job, but they didn't pay too fucking much.

Ringgenberg: How did you feel about being part of the whole corporate structure, wearing the tie and all?

Williams: Well, I hated that, but this was about the time I discovered LSD. This was like about '64.

Ringgenberg: What kind of effect did LSD have on you?

Williams: It had a tremendous effect, because if you have a mind that enjoys abstraction as mine does, God, you can just sit back and ride out a tremendous mental roller coaster; your mind just opens up, new tributaries of thought in all directions. Your mind protracts in all directions. One unfor-tunate thing about LSD is that while you're taking it, you have delusions of grandeur and think that everything you write down is great, and then after-ward, when you look at what the fuck you wrote down, it looks like some idiot wrote it. That was a major drawback. [*Laughter*] So it took me a long while to realize that I wasn't getting a lot of good out of psychedelic drugs. I got some degree of inspiration, about as much inspiration out of it as Rick Griffin and the rest of the psychedelic artists did.

Ringgenberg: What did you do after the Weyerhaeuser Corporation fired you?

Williams: I went back down to the unemployment agency with no hope in hell. And you know, when you're an artist and you go down to an unemployment agency, you're looking for something intelligent and interesting. Because "everybody's an artist," the chances of getting a job as an artist there are really not very good.

So I went in there, and I told them that I was looking for work because I'd been in there six months earlier to get the last job, and he says, "Well, we just don't have anything right now, but we do have this one thing that people keep coming back from—they say the conditions are just too dirty, and one thing or another." And I say, "Well, what is it?" And he says, "Well, they're looking for an art director down at this place called Ed 'Big Daddy' Roth," and I said, "Well, that sounds like it was just made for me."

Ringgenberg: Were you aware of Roth at the time?

Williams: I'd met Roth at car shows. He didn't remember me. You know, he'd gone all over to different car shows around the country, and I rubbed elbows with him a lot. He was a hero of mine. I went down to his shop, and he looked in my portfolio and said, "Well, if I knew you existed, I'd have hunted you up."

Ringgenberg: That must have made you feel good.

Williams: Oh, yeah, because one minute I'm in this desperate deal of being a container designer for this fucked-up fascist corporation, and the next minute here I'm a person, twenty-two years old, and treated with all the dignity that I could ever hope for, and I was just making tons of money working for Roth.

Ringgenberg: What kind of stuff were you doing for him?

Williams: Well . . . initially, it was what I did the whole time, you know—helping him design T-shirts, and I was an idea man, and I was in charge of getting his advertising out.

Ringgenberg: By this time, Roth had already developed his style, right? With the Rat Finks and the bugged-out eyes.

Williams: He had always employed different artists, and he kind of picked up Basil Wolverton's style with the bug eyes. And then the Rat Fink body was kind of a cartoon nebbish. Ed Roth styled himself after a hot rod artist named Von Dutch, a beatnik flute player and machinist and gunsmith, a remarkable human being who invented flame painting and pinstriping and flying eyeballs and Salvador Dalí kind of biomorphic amoebic monsters.

Ringgenberg: He sounds like a really interesting character. What can you tell me about him?

Williams: Well, Von Dutch died about three weeks ago.

Ringgenberg: I'm sorry to hear that.

Williams: Well, it's not that bad, because he was kind of hard to get along with.

Ringgenberg: Was he a real eccentric?

Williams: Well, he was a genius, and to say "eccentric" would be putting it lightly . . . He was just a punk rocker about thirty or forty years before its time. He loved violence. He was a real beatnik. He played the jazz flute. He was good friends with Lord Buckley . . . And when he would pick up women, he would go into this Lord Buckley riff and start imitating Lord Buckley. I remember him doing this on a number of occasions.

Ringgenberg: It sounds like you knew him pretty well.

Williams: Well, I knew him . . . Yeah, I guess I knew him damn well. He'd come over to my house, and we'd bullshit and drink until the sun came up, talking about mechanics and art and one thing or another. But he was very mentally disturbed, and he'd get very violent, and he would do an about-face on you, and . . .

Ringgenberg: Was he one of those people who would turn mean when he drank?

Williams: Yeah, and it didn't always take drinking to do it, but he was a tremendous alcoholic, and he died here just a while back of chronic alcoholism. His liver went out on him.

Ringgenberg: How long did you work for Big Daddy Roth?

Williams: I worked for Roth for about five years, 'til he went out of business. That was about '70.

Ringgenberg: When did you start doing underground comics?

Williams: I started doing underground comics in '68. The whole time I was working for Roth, and the whole time I was doing this other stuff before I was continually attempting to do oil paintings. When I was working for Roth, I had the time to do oil paintings in the evenings.

Ringgenberg: Do you still have any of those early paintings?

Williams: No, they sold. They sold for a lot of money back in their day. For a bunch of them, I think I got ten thousand dollars a piece, and that was in 1970. That would be sixty-thousand to one hundred thousand dollars now; it was unbelievable. You know, I went for a long time on those sales.

Ringgenberg: You had a day job . . . Were you producing many canvases, or was it just a few over a year?

Williams: Just a few, but they were very intense paintings with a lot of detail.

Ringgenberg: When you were working for Ed Roth, were you doing cartoon strips for any of the car zines, or just illustrations?

Williams: I think after I was working for Roth, I did a few things for *Cartoon Magazine* and *Cycletoons*.

Ringgenberg: How did you get to work for *Zap*? How did that happen?

Williams: Well, I was doing these paintings we were talking about, and I knew Stanley Mouse, Alton Kelley, Rick Griffin, and other people who were doing psychedelic posters, but I was working for Roth, and he was giving me a pretty free hand. He was giving me just about as much of a free hand as Kelley and Mouse and those guys [who] were doing rock posters. Both were commercial, pretty much commercial, but as free for commercial as you could do. I'd always wanted to be a painter, so I was working on these paintings, and I went to the Monterey Pop Festival in '67, and I noticed that Mouse had a display there of artwork, and I figured there was going to be another Monterey Pop Festival next year, so I started working on this real big oil painting of this eye. Of course, there never was another Monterey Pop Festival, but I did finish this painting, and it was like super-psychedelic, so I'd gotten in touch with the Print Mint that was printing *Zap*.

The first *Zap* I saw was the number zero, which Crumb did, and I wanted to know, since they distribute prints, if they would publish one of my paintings. They kind of encouraged me for a while and kind of led me on, and then I guess they backed out or something, but they'd mentioned that they wanted me in their comic *Yellow Dog*, which was a competitor with *Zap*. It was probably the second or third *Yellow Dog* to ever come out. So I did some work for that, and then Gilbert Shelton contacted me and said that they wanted me in *Zap*. And they wanted me in *Zap* because they needed what was called a slick artist because Rick was the slick artist before, but Rick Griffin was off on one of his artistic hiatuses. He was kind of undependable, and they wanted to keep the comic going really fast, so I filled the bill. I came in on *Zap* #4.

Ringgenberg: How many issues did you appear in?

Williams: Well, it's gone to #12, and I came in at #4, so that means I've done eight . . .

Ringgenberg: What else were you doing besides the *Zap* work?

Williams: Well, I was doing other comic book work, too. I can't remember right off. You know. I was doing covers and stories and one thing or another . . . I remember when I started in underground comics, there were maybe about eight or nine of us, you see. There were the seven artists in *Zap*, and then there was a guy named Jack Jackson, and then there was Jay Lynch, and I think that was it. That was it. Period.

I had been working for Roth as kind of an underground artist, but you know, getting in a lot of trouble, getting rejected, so I know I was the first underground comic book artist in Southern California. I wasn't the first underground cartoonist—that was Ron Cobb—but I was one of the first underground comic book artists.

Robert Williams, Cover for *Zap Comix* #5, 1970.

Ringgenberg: How long was it before you actually met guys like Shelton and Crumb personally?

Williams: '68 . . . somewhere like that. See, before *Zap*, Gilbert did a thing called *Wonder Warthog*, which was a comic book that was a spring-off of a car magazine by Pete Millar.

Ringgenberg: Didn't he do some *Wonder Warthogs* for some of the car mags?

Williams: Yeah, he cartoons for independent newspapers, and even before that, when he was in college in Texas, so you know, it would be very easy to say that Gilbert Shelton was probably the first underground cartoonist . . . I don't want to take away from Robert Crumb, but he has so gigantically overshadowed everybody else that Gilbert and these other people are just kind of lost in the smoke.

Ringgenberg: Do you like Shelton's work?

Williams: Sure, yeah. He's one of my favorites.

Ringgenberg: What underground cartoonists do you like?

Williams: Gosh, there's an awful lot of them I do like, you know. Greg Irons and Jack Jackson and the *Zap* artists and a lot of the artists, a tremendous amount of the artists that are in *Raw*. Gary Panter . . . there's just an awful lot of them I like. I'm not . . . you know, there's stuff that, it's not that I don't like it, it's just that—it's stuff that don't interest me, you know what I mean?

There was an awful lot of crap that came out, and I was going to say, it started out with about nine of us, and inside two years there were more than two thousand underground cartoon artists, you know. About '71 there were more underground cartoon artists than you'd ever believe, and the economical boat was starting to sink under the weight. You had an awful lot of people that had no fucking skill putting out underground comics, and their justification was that they're more intellectually into the literary end of it than the old shitty physical drawing of it. So you had a lot of bohemian crap hitting the market, and . . .

Ringgenberg: A lot of poseurs?

Williams: Yeah, and you had two factions even with *Zap*. There was the graphic faction that was me, Wilson, Griffin, and Moscoso, and that was in mild opposition to the literary end of it, which was Gilbert, Crumb, and maybe Spain. It wasn't a definitive demarcation, because Crumb is very graphic. He's a brilliant draftsman, and Spain is a tremendous draftsman, but it was obvious that there were two schools of thought, and when you got away from *Zap* and you got into these other comics, it was very defined. You had a few remarkable draftsmen and a lot of shitty geniuses that couldn't draw, you know what I'm saying?

Ringgenberg: How did you get involved with *Felch Comics*?

Williams: Well, we did *Snatch*, and *Zap* started getting stronger and stronger in its material, and a few of the other comics got stronger and stronger in their material, and all of us were thinking that we were going to get arrested. We just thought that we were all going to get arrested somewhere down the line because there'd never been material like this. Remember, 1969 is when the first adult magazines ever came out that showed pussy and asshole—and this was just flipped, to actually have this in a printed magazine that went through a printing press. You know anything before that was just some secret thing. I don't know if you're old enough to realize this, but I remember the first time I saw, in '69, a magazine that showed assholes and pussies, I thought, "Man! How are these people doing this?"

This was in the middle of the Vietnam War, and I knew that I was on the FBI's list because of my draft record and my association with Roth, who was continually investigated by the FBI, and I knew I was down because of *Zap* comics and my political association. In 1969, 1970, and 1971, there was a very, very solid and plausible fear of the government going extremely right-wing and starting to round people up. In fact, the internment camps were being refurbished at this time, and there was photographic evidence that these internment camps were being reconditioned.

Ringgenberg: The same ones the government used to confine the Japanese Americans during World War II?

Williams: That's right. So we were like really scared when we were doing this. We knew that we were cutting new territory. You look back at it now, it's just a silly nothing. An underground comic is a silly nothing now, but in 1968, '69, and '70, we were really cutting new territory . . . We had gone pretty damn far in *Zap*, and we had penetration in our comics, and that was the real forbidden fruit to show sexual penetration. That's what none of the magazines would dare do. So anyway, *Snatch* came out. And *Jiz* came out, and Rory Hayes had *Cunt*. I was talking at one of our little meetings up in Northern California with the *Zap* artists, and S. Clay Wilson mentioned to me that he had talked to Ken Weaver of the Fugs, and Ken Weaver had this real curious word called "felch" that meant sucking the sperm out of someone's rectum after they'd been cornholed, and that was so flipped, man. That there was a word for such a far-out act. And so I said, "Hey, that's got to be the name of our next comic." So I became the de facto editor of the situation. Since I liked it, it was my responsibility to get all the artwork put together to do that *Felch* comic. So I did the cover. Once you get a cover going, then that's the criteria to pull in pages, see? So, gosh, everybody wanted a share of it, you know? Crumb and everybody.

Ringgenberg: Did most of the people write their own material?

Williams: Yeah, well, back then everybody wrote their own material, you know. There was almost no similarity between overground comics and underground comics. Very little similarity.

Ringgenberg: So did anything ever happen as far as being prosecuted for *Felch* comics?

Williams: No. Surprisingly, it went on for a long time, and nothing came down. Now, with *Zap* and a couple of other comics in '69 and '70, I think there was some real heavy court problems. I think about seventy-five or one hundred newsstand dealers were arrested in New York, and about seventy-five in San Francisco, and some amount in Los Angeles, if I'm not mistaken. When it got to court, I think it was *Zap* #4 that had big busts, but *Zap* #4, they got Crumb for. Oh, what the hell story was it? It was that family story. You remember the family? And they also got Spain for his story. My story was a lot ruder than Spain's, but they got his and said there was actually no social redeeming value in Spain's story.

So anyway, *Felch* came out in '72, and about '74 or '75 an incident did happen. Now, there's a fellow down here in Los Angeles named George DiCaprio, who's the underground distributor for Southern California, and he related this story to me: there was a bust at a psychedelic shop or a bookstore in Long Beach, and the police came in there and they just rounded up all the underground comics and threw them in a box and arrested the clerk on duty. That's the way they do it—the poor bastard working the cash register is the guy they always arrest, see? So he said that all his sales, all over town, just stopped because they wanted to see how the court verdict was going to be on this one case.

The word had just got around that there's a bust, see. So he had to go to court, or the hearing, with the owner of the bookstore and the clerk that got busted, and the lawyer. And it was a real nervous affair. So they were sitting outside the judge's office or something like that, and the prosecuting attorney was in there with the judge, and they were all sitting outside the office where they can hear, and the judge and the prosecuting attorney are digging through this box of comics, and apparently what had happened was that the police and the prosecutor figured that they'd base their whole case on *Felch*. They figured no one was going to miss this little fucking thing, and they took it. So when it came time to present this before the judge at the hearing, they're going through this box, and they can't find that goddamn little comic. So George DiCaprio and his lawyer and the bookstore owner and the clerk are sitting' outside, and all they can hear is the judge and the prosecuting attorney in there yelling at the top of their lungs, "Where the *Felch*? What happened to the *Felch*?" [*Laughter*]

Ringgenberg: So, in the end, the *Felch* case got thrown out of court?

Williams: Yeah.

Ringgenberg: You're pretty fearless about what you paint, and I was wondering, is there anything that you can think of that you wouldn't depict in a painting? Where do you draw the line?

Williams: I certainly wouldn't touch racial situations. I would not paint anything that would directly cause harm to somebody.

Ringgenberg: You wouldn't use a really extreme racial stereotype like a Stepin Fetchit?

Williams: No. No, I wouldn't touch anything like that. There have been some examples in underground comics that have backfired from that. One example of that is there used to be an underground magazine that was a competitor with *High Times* called *Flash Back* in the mid-1970s, and it went to two or three or four issues, and for the fourth or fifth issue, they decided they were going to do a story about how Blacks had been stereotyped as drug addicts and sexual deviates, and they made the mistake on the cover of representing a Black man snorting cocaine while he ran down the road towing a white woman by her hair. There were no newsdealers in the United States that would take this, and that magazine immediately went out of business.

The second example of something like this happening was when we did a comic with Rick Griffin called *Tales from the Tube*, and Crumb was very sensitive to how the Blacks had been completely denied out of the surfing circles, see? He did a back cover story about this Black guy walking up and down the beach dragging his surfboard and not being accepted on the beach, not fitting in. Now, to most everybody, they understood that he just brought up a very obvious paradox: how Blacks were not incorporated into the surf scene, you know, and maybe it's time to change that. The criticisms and the mail that came in on that were gigantic. So it was just obvious that some of these situations you just cannot do right.

Ringgenberg: Do you ever feel your work is exploiting women's bodies in the way you depict them?

Williams: Well, of course, I bear that in my mind. But, on the other hand, it's a situation that's so inbred on being a living creature that you're attracted to these sexual characteristics of the opposite sex that I think it transcends being prohibited. I certainly wouldn't do a certain woman's face that's a woman that really is, and then make a sexual fool out of her. I would never do anything like that.

Ringgenberg: Are all your women generally composites?

Williams: I use models sometimes, but by and large they are composites.

Ringgenberg: Do you ever work from photos?

Williams: I never copy photos, you know, though I've never really had a dislike for that. What I do is, I'll get four or five photos of the same person in different positions, and then I'll come up with a completely different position for them.

Ringgenberg: When you're working with a live model, are you actually working on your canvas while you look at her, or do you take photos?

Williams: I'll use sketches and then get her back to make corrections.

Ringgenberg: Have you used live models throughout your career, or is this a recent development?

Williams: Well, it's just a matter of convenience and expense. Is it convenient to do this? Is it a point of foreshortening that I ought to get a model to look at or something? By and large, my stuff is hand-drawn out of my head, and it's got mistakes because it has to go through my head . . . You know, there's the vast majority of artists today, especially illustrators, who will just lucigraph photos. Norman Rockwell did that for three-quarters of his life.

Ringgenberg: Could you describe how you work up a painting from the idea stage to doing the finished canvas?

Williams: I sit down with drawing paper and a pencil and a thesaurus and a dictionary and encyclopedias and all the books I need for reference. And then there's the matter of coming up with the idea, and for the food for the idea. I pick things that interest me tremendously, and then I pick things that I don't like, and I pick things that I have reactions to, and try to find things that are related to things that I have an interest in that might lead to something. In other words, I'll take something like a pencil or a yo-yo or something and figure out, how is this made, and who uses it, what kind of wood is it made of, how long has it been around, are there any substitutes for this thing? If this thing's a pencil, what's an anti-, no-pencil? Is there an abstract idea of something that's a not-thing? I work through a bunch of systems of imagination. The one thing I never want to do is do something that someone else has already done. I'm continually trying to screen myself from picking up ideas from other people, so I'm always trying to maintain a certain amount of pride and originality. Part of that's sure as hell not using photographs, not lucigraphing photos.

Ringgenberg: How did you develop the style that you're currently using, where you have multilayered images?

Williams: Well, the painting has got so much into it because it's telling a story, and it's actually like doing a comic strip and then pulling the panel edge. You don't see things defined in a panel, but there's the multiplicity of stories there. It's trying to tell a story with a lot of different images, a pictographic language. What's been really missing from art for the past forty or fifty years is that the pictorial language has been allowed to atrophy. With the exception of comic books, a form of graphic language that's advanced tremendously in the last thirty or forty years, while the visual arts, fine art, has just become a bunch of shit. It's just no language at all, there's no . . . The artists that call themselves painters today have no graphic vocabulary.

Ringgenberg: I take it you don't have a high opinion of the current fine art scene?

Williams: Well, being part of it, I have to subscribe to the code of absolute freedom, you understand. But I have my philosophy that art is a language. And it's a language that's better than thirty thousand years old. Scratchings on the Lascaux caves are an indication that there was a striving for a language. I think that something that even comic books have lacked is trying to develop this language into a form of abstraction on its own. They've done it to a certain extent, but no one's actually, purposely, attempted to do it. And I think this is still a very large field for fine arts artists and cartoonists and illustrators as well.

Ringgenberg: Are there any contemporary cartoonists you look at? You mentioned the *Raw* staff and contributors . . .

Williams: Well, gosh, I don't know. I'm sure there is a lot . . .

Ringgenberg: For instance, have you ever seen *Love and Rockets*?

Williams: Well, sure . . .

Ringgenberg: Does that stuff appeal to you?

Williams: I don't think those guys particularly have any interest in my artwork, but . . .

Ringgenberg: I thought you said you liked Gary Panter . . .

Williams: Well, you know, Gary Panter . . . Gary Panter is a paradox, like Crumb is. Robert Crumb is brilliant. He's a genius, but one thing that he's really good at is making really incredible, involved artwork look extremely simple. And he's got a hand vibe into his line work that makes it look like it was dashed out. So a lot of people can relate to Crumb because they think that they can do that, too. There's a vicarious enjoyment looking at Crumb's stuff because people think, "Oh, I could do that, too. Look at this scratchy little thing here." And Gary Panter has this, too. Gary Panter is a fairly good draftsman, and he's very, very intelligent, and he knows what the hell he's doing. But his language has got this scratchiness to it, it has this vibrance and this . . . what the hell, what's the musical word I'm trying to think of? It's . . . a resonance. His work has got a resonance that no one can duplicate. But when people look at it and they see these chicken scratches, they think, "Gosh, this is, like, modern and happening and I can do this, too." But they can't. And this is what separates a really brilliant, capable person, from the fucking person that's just trying to pose for a minute or two in a situation that he's not going to be able to stand up in.

Ringgenberg: It's funny you should mention that about Panter. I always got the impression that his work had the feel of something that you might see in a high school student's notebook, some guy who was a good artist in high school.

Williams: Yeah, that's right, but after you see a lot of Gary's artwork, then you'll start noticing in the similarity a kind of resonance. In other words, he has a natural knack for these things, you know, it's very hard to define it. Fortunately, it's hard to define it, or it would be worn out by now. But there is a structure that's only unique to him in these things. It's the same way with Crumb . . . Robert Crumb does not bandy around the idea that he's a great draftsman, and probably one of the best of this century.

Crumb can draw anything he can think up. He's an absolute genius. I've always worried that Crumb was picked up by so many fucking fanboys that praise him, and they always praise him for the wrong goddamn stuff, you know. An example of that was the praise he got for *Fritz the Cat*. Granted he did it at nineteen years old, but it was one of the silliest fucking things I'd ever seen. And the accolades that were heaped upon him for that fucking thing, it was just embarrassing, you know what I mean?

Ringgenberg: Oh, yeah, compared to how great so much of his later work was. I think one thing about Crumb that's so amazing is that not only is he such a brilliant draftsman, but I think he's an equally good writer. His work is really funny, it's penetrating . . .

Williams: Of course, of course. Perceptive and intuitive.

Ringgenberg: Your writing always seemed more stream of consciousness. It was like what was popping into your head . . . I don't get the feeling you wrote the same way Robert Crumb wrote.

Williams: No, no. no. Crumb can work out little nuances of mannerisms, see, and I don't pursue that. I'm putting on a pictorial stage show, see? Everything of mine is overstylized. Now, one thing that I do that really shuts a lot of people off is that I don't exhibit humility in my work. I'm very proud of every little brushstroke. I'm very chauvinistic about this, and this is the wrong time to do this in history. This is a period of equality, and even the smallest situation is equal to the mass, so what I do comes off as the work of someone who can do something really slick and shows off. In a lot of cases, it turns people off before they can see the substance in what I do. It shuts a lot of people off. They see it and they don't like it. It's too challenging, and it's just obvious that I'm showing off, which I am. That is the virtue of it. I am actually fucking showing off and I'm posing. That is part of the beauty of the goddamn art, you know; it's like a beautiful woman showing her tits or something.

Ringgenberg: There was a period, around the mid-1980s or so, when your work had heavier brushstrokes.

Williams: Well, yeah, because I had to compete against people like Gary Panter, Bob Zolen, and Ray Zone, these punk rock artists who were just whipping this stuff out.

Ringgenberg: Was that a conscious choice on your part?

Williams: Oh, yeah. I was whipping these things out, too; I was turning out a painting every three days, a nice oil painting out every three days. That was slow.

Ringgenberg: That's incredible to me that you could do a painting as detailed as your stuff in three days.

Williams: Well, those paintings you're talking about back in the early 1980s weren't as detailed as the stuff I do now. I had to incorporate shock value in there and make stuff rough, and I was utilizing some skills that I never thought I'd have to bring to the forefront.

Ringgenberg: Now, looking at your current work, the paintings that were at the Bess Cutler show, you've gone back to a slicker rendering style.

Williams: Yeah, but it's not like the real slick stuff I used to do in the 1960s and '70s. You know, that stuff in the '60s and '70s was like Vermeer or something. It was like some Dutch master. And the old stuff used to be done in three layers, and everything I've done since the '80s has been alla prima: one coat. But the interesting thing is that artists like me that have attempted to do comic paintings now, cartoon paintings are starting to meet with a damn good amount of success.

Ringgenberg: You can also look at the success of someone like Roy Lichtenstein enjoyed with cartoon subject matter.

Williams: Well, yeah. Pop art seemed to open the door for a return to representational art, but there's other artists like me, you know. There's a fella named Todd Schorr, there is Bob Armstrong, up in Northern California doing paintings, Spain Rodriguez does some paintings . . . There's an artist on the East Coast named XNO, a young fella that's doing *Raw*-style monster paintings. There's a guy named R. K. Sloane, and there's a fella named the Pizz that's just really taking off . . . There's a number of artists that are doing cartoon paintings who are doing pretty good: Paul Mavrides . . .

Ringgenberg: Do you feel any affinities for any of the earlier artistic movements, like the pop artists, or . . .

Williams: Well, abstract expressionism had been around ten years before pop art came along, and it was a very domineering thing, and it just upset the hell out of me. I just really didn't like that movement at all. And when pop art came, the first name pop art had was neorealism. It meant a new objectivity, and then later they called it pop art. That was its proper name. And when that came out in '62 and '63, man, to me it was a fantastic revelation and some chance of hope for the art world. So I've always got a real warm spot in my heart for pop art.

Ringgenberg: If you were trying to describe your painting style to somebody who'd never seen it before, what kind of label would you give it?

Williams: Well, I would describe it as morose cartoons, cartoons that are oil paintings. Cartoons that are presenting themselves and trying to pass themselves off as fine art, but the subject matter is so heady and so overdramatic. Now, cartoons have a big problem, and the big problem of cartoons is getting drama across. So you have to use a couple of devices. There's four or five devices open to you to load a cartoon up with drama. One of them is gratuitous violence . . . another is sex. Another is the subject matter in it which doesn't seem to have a logical justifying end to it. In other words, some atrocity or some situation happening that you can't reconcile in your mind.

Now, since it is being done in a cartoon style, you tend to want to make the story that's happening before your eyes as simple as the cartoon work itself. Well, if you twist that a little bit, if it's immediately logical, then you can start edging toward drama. And, of course, the use of color. You have a few options open to get in there and work up drama in a cartoon. Another problem cartoons have is that they're immediately associated with humor, and this is a big mistake, a real big fucking mistake. And if you look back into Egyptian hieroglyphics and pictographs and other real ancient and prehistoric art, and art of the Middle Ages, it's just obviously going to look like cartoons, like Bible illuminations and stuff, but they weren't meant to be cartoons. The thing about humor is people think things are either serious or they're silly and humorous. Humor is actually a form of abstract thought, and if that abstract thought is altered but not meant to be silly, you can get people to think in that direction, that you're looking at something that has got irony to it but isn't silly and isn't funny. In other words, what I'm groping for is another form of language to direct this comic imagery in, see? A form of abstract thought that has a certain dignity to it.

Ringgenberg: In a lot of your paintings, are you trying to express the ambiguity you feel about something? Could it be funny and horrible at the same time?

Williams: That's right. And that things are not always as logical as they seem, although I've painted you a picture of a story here that seems to have all kinds of directions you can follow. The virtue and the answer to it isn't sitting right there with it. Here's all the elements, and here you can see how all the elements are associated, but what are you trying to shove down my throat? You're used to having a moral to a vision, you know? Just like a dream doesn't have a moral.

Ringgenberg: Do you ever get ideas for your paintings in a dream?

Williams: Well, I've searched out my dreams, and I've got volumes of different dream books and one thing or another, and you know, there's nothing in the world . . . there's no drugs, there's no booze, there's no dreams, there's nothing like just having to sit down and force yourself to come up with a good old fucking thought, to come up with your own thought conclusions. If you can perceive something in a dream as being artistically usable, then you can perceive a very similar or better notion in total consciousness. I remember when I was young and I used to paint, I'd come home at night and start painting, and I'd do a couple joints and I'd be painting and painting, and I'd realize, I'm painting the same thing over and over again and not getting it right. And I'd do it night after night, the same strokes, and not getting it right. And I was realizing that I was causing myself an impediment here by trying to look for a device to give me imagination and capability. When you do artwork, the best artwork is done when you approach it like a graphic athlete.

I don't live a very colorful life. I live this very pathetic, monastic life. You know, I get up at 4:20 in the morning, and I paint twelve or fourteen hours a day, seven days a week, get the work fucking done. It's a very unfulfilling thing as far as bringing pleasure to my life. Now, the satisfaction is having it done. I just filled a gallery in New York with thirty oil paintings that took me nineteen months to do. That was tremendously satisfying. I went to a town, I went to the world capital of art. It's now on its knees because of the economy. Half the galleries have gone out of business. They're just really dying. I went there with a sold-out show, see. The show was sold out the day before the doors opened . . . thirty oil paintings! It caused a tremendous stir in New York.

Ringgenberg: Have you seen the reviews for your show?

Williams: Well, they're starting to come in, little by little. I got the "Pick of the Week" in the *Village Voice* last week. I got mentioned in *Details* magazine and a couple of other magazines in New York. I'm getting a review in the top European art magazine coming up, and I just heard the other day that *Artforum* is going to review the show, and then I heard *Art in America* is going to do a little article on it. So this is starting to happen . . .

Ringgenberg: Before the show, you had said that you felt like the art establishment had their knives sharpened for you.

Williams: Well, I thought they did. But when I got to New York, I realized that they're so damn desperate, they're just sitting there observing me. Now, this may yet come to happen because if what I do leaves an example for them, they're either going to have to make some adjustments for me or figure out how to make it on their own. And I don't think they're going to make some adjustments for me. If they start having to change forms of art, it's going to affect even the structure of the museums. I mean, the art world you're looking at now isn't just some new thing. It's a thing that's slowly evolved over thirty or forty years of back-scratching and politics and ass sucking and every form of ability except being capable. The museums are manipulated by big money, and the galleries are in there trying to slip their artists into museums, and big buyers that control corporation buying want to make sure that certain artists get into the museums, and so the art has always got to be kept very trite and boring and very large and useless, and subtly dynamic, and that's what the art world has come to—big, useless fucking things that are put together shitty. And these things have fallen down and lost 90 percent of their value in the last year and a half. There are people that have invested vast fortunes in this junk, and it's starting to dawn on them in the last six months that there ain't no way they're ever going to get even a fraction of their money out of this shit.

So, anyway. I have done very well. It's my fourth sold-out show. I've got a waiting list of buyers, about 250 buyers with ready deposits, see. It's just a matter of me painting them.

Ringgenberg: Your work is selling well now?

Williams: Yeah, it's selling well. My next three or four shows are sold out if I don't raise the prices ridiculously.

Ringgenberg: What does one of your canvases go for?

Williams: Well, my average painting goes for nine thousand dollars, and you can take that painting out on the sidewalk and get twelve thousand dollars for it. You can make three thousand dollars as soon as you buy it. But the fact is, there's a waiting list, see? There's two hundred, three hundred people on this waiting list, so you just don't immediately get that painting. The average painting takes nine to twelve days and that's getting up at 4:20 in the morning and hammering twelve hours a day for seven days a week.

Ringgenberg: In your recent interview in *Gauntlet*, you said you were the victim of de facto censorship.

Williams: Yeah.

Ringgenberg: What did you mean by that, exactly?

Williams: I think the basis of that is: I'm no longer feeling any pressure from the right, but I'm getting it from my comrades on the left. In the early 1960s, I was a liberal young artist—I still am a liberal young artist. Later on, when I got involved in underground comics, I immediately started feeling pressure from the United States government and the local officials, dealing with underground comics, and censoring them.

Ringgenberg: When you were doing the undergrounds, were there any specific instances where your work was censored?

Williams: Many, many times. Many times.

Ringgenberg: What are some examples?

Williams: Well, almost all the *Zaps*. I think all the *Zaps* felt a lot of persecution. The thing is, I've always fancied myself something of a liberal, and what's happened is that I've pretty much followed the same road of ethics and ideals all along my life, but the world has changed around me to a certain extent. And the people that are liberal now look at me like I am some archaic stick-in-the-mud who's an adversary of theirs. In other words, I have gained the dislike of feminists. I am obviously a target of the feminists. I am an out-and-out adversary in neon to these people, when, in reality, I'm very sympathetic to their movement. And now I've discovered that there's some elements of the gay movement that I've offended. And this is a whole new thing to me. This happened at the show, the MOCA show, *Helter Skelter*, two months ago, here in LA. That was a real important art show. And one of the important facts about this art show was that more than half of the subject matter in the show was cartoon related, you see. Now the critics cut this fucking show to pieces, all across the country. This thing was written up in every major newspaper in the United States, and some in Europe and Canada. It was on CNN, PBS, and a lot of stations on the networks, and they cut this thing to pieces. It had the largest attendance of any art show in Los Angeles. It was loved by the public, but the officials hated it.

Two groups that didn't like this were the feminists, who were lying in wait for me, and I happened to have a painting in there of Oscar Wilde that was, in reality, pro–Oscar Wilde, but some subtleties in it were misconstrued, and members of the gay community made a big issue out of this and said that I was a gay basher. So now I've got these people against me, gnawing on me like a bone. I'm being shoved out of my own world, you know, but I'm sure as hell not going to react to these people and become right-wing, you know what I'm saying? So I'm wondering. I saw this happen to Thomas Hart Benton. This same thing happened to Thomas Hart Benton and the gays. A coalition of gays started working on him and didn't like him, but he was a little more active in disliking the gays. I'm not against gays. He tended to irritate them. But they railroaded him.

Ringgenberg: What do you think it was in the Wilde painting that specifically offended the gays?

Williams: It was a painting about Oscar Wilde, and I've always been a big fan of Oscar Wilde, and one thing that really stuck out in my mind about Oscar Wilde was when he visited the United States in 1882. He got off the beaten track of his lecture circuit, and while giving a lecture in Denver, a mine owner from Leadville, Colorado, went up and saw him and said, "Come down to Leadville and lecture our miners." And at this time, in 1882, Leadville, Colorado, was one of the meanest towns in the world, period. The rate of murder and crime was gigantic. So they talked him into going down to the little opera house down there, in Leadville, and lecturing on Botticelli and aesthetics to this roughneck bunch of miners and cowboys and cutthroats.

Me, in my mind, this was the most incredible thing to visualize . . . him on a stage dressed in these Edwardian tights, lecturing about beauty to these people. So I rendered this in a very large oil painting. And I researched the hell out of this and learned everything I could about Leadville, Colorado, especially that period of time, the people involved. And when I wrote the titles, I wrote it in kind of an air of negativity toward Oscar Wilde, so you'd get the sense of tension of him standing up there on the stage, confronting all these roughnecks and cowboys and prostitutes and miners and gunslingers, see? Well, he got up there on the stage. He was a big Irishman with a deep voice, and he got up there and won them. He absolutely won these people over! He started to open up to these people, and to have something in common with them when he was talking about aesthetics, he started talking about Cellini the goldsmith, because Leadville was a silver mining town. He thought this would open them up to him. After he started talking about Cellini, one of the miners jumped up and said, "Well, where is this fellow? How come you didn't bring him?" And Oscar Wilde said, "Well, Cellini's dead." And then another guy jumps up, pulls out his pistol, and he says, "Well, who shot him? I'll kill the son of a bitch!" And then the guy turns around and runs out to look for this guy that shot Cellini. So this is the kind of situation he was in.

The night before he went onstage, he went into a bar, and there was a sign over the piano, and I'm sure you're familiar with this term: "Don't shoot the piano player, he's the only one we've got." And Oscar Wilde's comment to this was, it was the first time he'd ever seen capital punishment meted out for bad art. So I did a painting that I'm very proud of on this subject. But in the title, I used the language that was used against Oscar Wilde when he faced trial in England for sodomy, you see? Which was real rough on him. You know, it referred to him as a syphilitic and one thing or another, and I used these kind of remarks in the title. So when these sensitive gay people came in and they heard about this, they immediately flipped out as me being a gay basher, see? Well, consequently I've been written up in a couple of papers defending this thing, just like I've done to you right now, so I've got the thing kind of calmed back. I've always had a pretty big gay following, and I don't know how much this has hurt me or not. But I'm finding myself worrying more about my political correctness these days than I'm worried about fucking GI Joe or the government getting me, you know?

I think the best thing that ever fucking happened in this goddamned country was old Jesse Helms blowing it like he did. Look at all the stimulation he created. I mean, that guy did so much to get American artists in an aggressive stance like they should be. But I remember I was in a showdown at Lace five years ago—Lace is a local little art museum. It's publicly funded, downtown. I was in a group show there, and I had a bunch of my *Zombie Mystery Paintings* there that had nekkid women with big tits. And one painting depicted two lesbians fighting each other over a prostitute, and it was predominantly gay women that run this museum, and I caught hell. They wouldn't take my books in their bookstore, and they just really come down hard on me.

Ringgenberg: Were people coming up and verbally abusing you, that sort of thing?

Williams: Well, I would hear snide remarks. It never got to that point, but it was obvious that I was being de facto censored. But later, when the Jesse Helms thing came out, Lace became the center of the fight against censorship, see? Three years later, they're the hard core of the fight against censorship, and I remember they wouldn't even let me put my fucking books in their bookstore when five or ten years before I'm one of the forefighters of the goddamned liberal underground. So I would rather fight Jesse Helms and [Edwin] Meese and people like that, people I really don't fucking like. But these people, my liberal cohorts here, need a handle to attack, and I, at some times, make myself the easy handle for them to grab . . . So that's what I meant by that.

Ringgenberg: Did the controversy over the *Appetite for Destruction* painting help your career or hurt you, ultimately?

Williams: Well, anytime your name's spread around, it always helps you, you know, I guess, unless it's if you're a child molester or a serial murderer. But it wasn't an ideal context for me. It made me look like I was a lackey in the hire of Guns N' Roses, and that was just not the case. It did get me in front of millions of people. I think fourteen million copies of that record sold, and each one of them either had the image on the cover or on a sleeve inside. There were many T-shirts put out. I think they made over a million dollars on the T-shirts, and I never saw a penny of it, see. It was a very sad matter for me.

Ringgenberg: Oh, that's unfortunate . . .

Williams: Well, life is like that, you know. It was a hell of a controversy. You know, I had . . . There were six or seven women's groups picketing up north over that thing, weekend after weekend after weekend. That was a real stink!

Ringgenberg: Besides that painting, has any of your other work been picketed?

Williams: Well, the only thing that rivals that problem in size was the MOCA show. They picketed me outside there.

Ringgenberg: Was that women's groups, gay groups, or both?

Williams: A women's group called PIGS: Politically Involved Girlfriends. A large women's group down here. And then the gay group Queer Nation said they were going to picket, but then they backed out. I guess they realized that maybe I wasn't fair game, maybe I wasn't a legitimate problem . . . I don't know. But I've gotten a lot of criticism from them.

Ringgenberg: You said the MOCA show was panned by a lot of the critics in the major media. Did you get any good write-ups?

Williams: Yeah, there were a couple of good write-ups. The fellow at the *Washington Post*, he had the insight to say, when he wrote about it, that it was incredible to go into a real art museum and see *Zap Comix* art hanging on the wall, meaning my paintings. And lots of small publications that didn't matter were supportive of me. They realized that it meant a turning point, that comic book art has now got a real foothold in the art world. The show ran for three months, and in the first couple of months, a couple of papers came out with it, and then the rest of the papers watched how it was slowly being written up, and then they jumped in and followed suit and cut it to pieces. And Robert Hughes was the last one to cut it to pieces in *Time* magazine, and he really butchered it. But he sat back very comfortably and watched what the major consensus was going to be among the intellectuals, and the intelligentsia, what their take was going to be on it. So they all played it very safe, you know what I mean?

Ringgenberg: So, even with the greater exposure, I guess you don't think your work is getting much more respect from the critics?

Williams: Well, no. It seems like I'll never succeed in that world. I'm out. The only thing that's going to happen is . . . If I'm going to be any matter of success, it'll have to be in a new regime, apparently.

Ringgenberg: How many paintings a year do you do?

Williams: I average about twenty to twenty-five paintings a year. It depends on how many big ones are in there. If I do a big one, it really knocks the time back.

Ringgenberg: How long does an average-size canvas take you to paint?

Williams: An average-size canvas takes me from nine to eleven days. That's 30 × 36. That's conceiving it and everything.

Ringgenberg: How would you describe your audience? You say you've got a waiting list for your paintings . . .

Williams: Yeah.

Ringgenberg: Who are these people?

Williams: These are people that basically like the images, and they're the kind of people that like comic books, like movie posters, like science fiction, like carnival midway art, like tattoos, like hot rods, motorcycles, skateboards, surfing, psychedelic art, people that have a visual hunger to search things out—the exact same thing that's been denied by the art world for the last thirty fucking years, you understand what I'm saying?

Ringgenberg: I think I know what you're driving at.

Williams: When you go into a museum and here's two railroad ties chained together and sprayed Day-Glo, and it's titled "Untitled Number Fourteen," and it sells for $250,000, and you're looking at this fucking thing, and it is about as interesting as watching paint dry . . . that's what the art world is. Now, being an artist, I have to follow the noble code of absolute freedom, see? And the problem there is, modern art came up through a series of revolutions that started in the 1870s, and 1880s. And it had an academy that dominated to resist against. And art from the 1870s to shortly after the First World War was a legitimate revolution against an academy . . . But then in the late 1920s and '30s, the academy was dead, and then you were left with the revolution just rehashing itself. There was no longer the adversary there to dominate it, to resist against, in other words, your artists before the First World War that were abstract artists, artists that were capable draftsmen to begin with, had resisted academic pressure.

Afterward, up to World War II, you're starting to get artists that couldn't even fucking draw that were abstract artists, and they're passing on their inability through becoming teachers because most of them can't support themselves with art. You've got teacher after teacher teaching generation after generation how not to be able to do something, see? And it's all in the name of artistic freedom and modern art. So consequently, in the middle of all this, you've still got a strain of human beings that are evolving that are alive that, in their DNA, clear back to the Lascaux caves, have a hankering to draw and paint, see? So this crew of people is up doing commercial art, illustration, comic books, movie posters, and things like that, see? But they're relegated, off to the side, as some secondary kind of hobby or something while this main bunch of so-called revolutionaries have copped all the laurels for the last five, ten generations. But I can live with these people. I'm not out there to crush the established art world. What I want is to live with the damn art world, do you understand what I'm saying?

Ringgenberg: Yes. Peaceful coexistence.

Williams: Yeah. I'm not interested in taking the people's bundles of sticks away from them and saying, "Look, this is just a fucking bundle of sticks and you can't do a goddamn thing but these sticks," and "you need to read a twenty-page fucking manifesto to even understand the sticks." I'm not trying to deny these people their right, but I want my fucking league, you know? I want to be able to circulate in the world of art, too. That sums it up.

Ringgenberg: I noticed a repeated motif in your work, which is pairing women up with food, like a nude woman reclining on a cheeseburger or a plate of enchiladas. Why were you using that particular imagery?

Williams: Well, because the food makes your mouth water, and the female irritates your prostate . . . So you've got these two wants working against each other, you know, and it causes anxiety. Do you understand? The picture doesn't exist for your approval, it exists for your reaction.

Ringgenberg: That brings me around to something you said in the earlier interview in *Gauntlet*. You said that when you paint, you want to "mentally get a hold of people."

Williams: Right.

Ringgenberg: Can you explain what you mean by that?

Williams: You know, liking something and having a taste for something is . . . that might be relative, that might be saying, "Well, I like chocolate bars,

Robert Williams, *Pecos Fiona and Her One-Woman Range War against Troglodytic Hipsters*, 1987. Oil on canvas, 122 x 244 cm. Private collection.

but the guy's holding a pistol to my head, and I have to eat seventy-five choc-olate bars," and by the time you eat twenty chocolate bars, the acid in the chocolate has come to be the dominating taste feature. Just eating concen-trated acid from the chocolate is terrible. So "likes" are relative, see? It's like your relationship with a woman. She just happened to be there in your space-time continuum . . . maybe that ain't your true fucking love, but she got you by your nuts some way, you know? Some way that's the one there for you. That's the situation as it exists for you. That's in your space-time continuum. That's just like the painting. The painting wasn't designed for you; the paint-ing was designed to work on human beings' anxieties to hold them there, to lock in their memory, to activate their imagination, and hold them there long enough to have a few ingredients happen. Then, when they walk off from the fucking painting, these ingredients are still gnawing in their fucking cerebel-lum, in their fucking head. It's starting to work on them. What the fuck is going on, you know . . . They'll come back to their painting, or they'll look for more paintings like that. They'll say, "I hate that fucking painting," and they'll look for more paintings like that to hate while their appetite's developing for them. That's the formula I'm using to gain an audience. And it has seemed to have worked for me.

Ringgenberg: So do you see some of your work as a sort of psychic time bomb?

Williams: Yeah, but it won't be a big explosion, it'll just be a satisfaction over a period of time.

Ringgenberg: Is that one reason why you layer the images? You'll have three different scenes overlaid in the main scene of some of your paintings.

Williams: Well, there's two or three reasons for that. One reason is to keep you there as long as I possibly can to win your attention . . . And there's a part of the human mind that sees more than is there. That's how a guy can sell you that bundle of sticks, because you can stand there in front of that bundle of sticks and read some depth into it. You can sell a person their own imagination. Now, there's another very basic reason that any other artist wouldn't admit to. But it's my weakness or compulsion to overdo the fucking things, see? We can sit here and talk about philosophy till we're blue in the fucking face, but the bottom line is, a human being as an animal has a compulsion to fucking do these things. Do you know what I mean? There's a neurosis in these things, of overdoing them, see?

Ringgenberg: Well, I've noticed that your work has stayed really detailed over the years, but your rendering style seems to have gotten simpler . . .

Williams: I'm always trying to be simpler and fresher, but this thing takes over in me, and I'm drawn into more convolution in it. It's just like Celtic art or something; it just gets more convoluted. It's like when they started digging up stone tools from cavemen; they noticed that [when] they went through the very first ones two million years ago, they were just rocks with the side knocked off them for sharpness. Then they got to the Neanderthals, and they actually made points. Then they got into the Cro-Magnons, which are us, and they started noticing that as tools they were beautifully done. And then they started finding real long lance points, spear points, that were done beautifully. They were so perfect and delicate that they could have never been used for spears. They found lots of these, and they believe that this was just an egotistic artistic attempt. They'd taken their science to its last inch. So there is a compulsion in human beings to do that.

Ringgenberg: That sort of quest for perfection?

Williams: That's right, a compulsion to fucking do these things. You know there's a drive in there that makes people . . . people. You understand what I'm saying?

Ringgenberg: Absolutely.

Williams: It makes a fine machinist; it makes a fine painter. You know, it makes a good craftsman who can make a beautiful hot rod.

Ringgenberg: Or, by the same token, it makes the unpublished artist or writer keep doing what they're doing just because they love it.

Williams: That's right. You got it. You got it. Fucking compulsion, like wiggling your tail.

Ringgenberg: One other thing I wanted to bring up is, in some of your paintings, I've noticed a tendency to objectify women. By that, I mean reducing them down to a pair of breasts or buttocks. What are you driving for when you do that?

Williams: Well . . . I like naked ladies, and I vicariously experience a woman by rendering her, you know what I mean? And I'm sure I do these things in very bad taste. I am a big admirer of women. I worship women. I'm not a religious person, and I don't believe in deities after death, and I don't believe in ghosts or things that go bump in the night, but the closest thing that I would come to worshipping is females. And they're like little magic creatures . . . I'm a rational person, and I see that they're just another mammal like me, but there's something in me that says, "Naw, these aren't just something, these are special, these are just fucking special things." Without them, I would probably shoot myself. There's nothing to live for but to watch a woman cat or walk across a room, or cuss me out, or tell me I'm a sexist. I mean, in my twisted mind, a woman can do no fucking wrong, even when she attacks me. Even lesbians that come up and drive me nuts and hate my guts. I seek fucking virtue in them, see?

Ringgenberg: Well, is objectifying women that way one of the things that feminists find particularly objectionable?

Williams: Yes, they do. They certainly do. They relate it to someone rendering Uncle Toms and Stepin Fetchits, see? . . . And to a certain degree, I have to agree with them, but I don't agree with them fully, and if women decided to render men like that, I would have no objection to it. A few female artists have attempted to do this with men's images, and it just doesn't seem to work, drawing goofy men with big dicks, it just doesn't seem to work.

Ringgenberg: Sometimes in your paintings, you employ stereotypical caricatures, like Aunt Jemima–looking characters and things like that. Is your source for those images things like old advertising?

Williams: Yeah. Well, Aunt Jemima wouldn't be a good example. I've kind of stayed away from Blacks. That's too touchy a situation, really. Rendering women is another thing because I've got a compulsion about that; I've just got a fucking dirty compulsion about rendering naked ladies. And I'm not that big on big breasts, but for some reason, to express a breast, they always seem to come out a little bigger than they should be.

Ringgenberg: In your art, there are echoes of old tattoo designs, and old-time, under-the-counter pornography, and things like that.

Williams: Yeah, that's right. You're right there.

Ringgenberg: Because a lot of your work, despite the modern eclecticism, really does seem to harken back to American pop culture of the 1940s on up. What are some of your influences as an artist? Where does your imagery come from?

Williams: Well, a lot of my influences are out of EC comics. Those were the comic books the Kefauver Committee pretty much outlawed. That was a remarkable set of comic books. The Kefauver Committee was right. It poisoned the youth, and I was one of them. And I'm just doing it in turn, so . . .

Ringgenberg: Were you a fan of the horror comics?

Williams: Oh, yeah, yeah. EC was the best. I remember all the rest, and EC was head and shoulders above all of them . . . There were other comic books I liked, but EC was just it. They were adult comic books. They were for eighteen years old and older. They were very intelligent, well-written comic books.

Ringgenberg: Did you do the *Crimes against the Eye* paintings specifically for the card set, or was that just a spin-off?

Williams: Well, I think all those cards came out of my book *Visual Addiction*. I'm pretty sure they did, yeah . . . that was my last book.

Ringgenberg: How have the books gone over?

Williams: Well . . . when they started . . . I'm the first underground painter to come out with a book, so I pretty much started that whole style of publication . . . My first book was *The Lowbrow Art of Robert Williams*, which was half underground comics and half paintings, so it did pretty good because it already had the comics in it, and it would go through that underground network of comic books . . . But my second book, *Zombie Mystery Paintings*, was just paintings. I was off on thin ice all by myself, for the first time, and that took off slow, but now it's really kicking ass. It's been reprinted and reprinted and reprinted. It's really doing good now, and now with my third book, *Visual Addiction*, it is really kicking ass, too.

My next book, my fourth book, it's got a very large, ready market for it. I've kind of established a thing here. And this is open for other artists to do, too, see? Before long you'll have a whole bunch of these different paintings, underground painting books like that.

Ringgenberg: Do you have other ideas for marketing your work, like more card sets, or T-shirts?

Williams: Well, I got T-shirts and mugs and all kinds of odd stuff like that. My primary interest in marketing right now is the prints of the paintings. That way I can get the images to a lot of people, and they don't have to pay very much, and they come in different degrees of value. There's some of them as little as ten dollars, and there's some expensive silk screens as high as four hundred dollars. So there's an investment market there, too . . . for the people that can't afford my paintings. I'm really concentrating on my print sales because when I get older, I'm not going to be as prolific with these paintings and want to be able to depend on the print market.

Ringgenberg: I think as painters go, you're incredibly prolific now.

Williams: Well, I'm burning out too. I'm almost fifty years old, you know, and I'm not going to be able to hang on to this much longer.

Motor Mouths

NICOLAS CAGE / 1994

From *Mouth 2 Mouth*, Sept.–Oct. 1994. Reprinted by permission of Robert Williams.

Nicolas Cage: Robert, would you say cartoon imagery is to fine art what rock 'n' roll is to classical music?

Robert Williams: There's like two art worlds, Nicolas, the one I belong to, and the formal art world. The formal art world won't accept me, so I have to run around with the bandits, the outlaws, and the underground cartoonists. Fifty years from now, when you look back, you'll see the good music of this century wasn't the classical music. It was rock and roll. And the graphics, the visual imagery, will be cartoons.

Cage: It seems like I've had kind of hallucinations where everything became very cartoonlike. Is there another dimension, a cartoon dimension so to speak, that we're all getting closer to? There's a theory that we're actually the hallucinations of chimpanzees, that we've kind of become the psilocybin mushroom of the chimp hallucination.

Williams: Most people do think in cartoons because they're the visual language of our time.

Cage: Do you think we might be turning into cartoons in some weird way? Is happiness subjective, like art? Some can get happiness out of a rumble; others can get it out of a daisy. Have you ever painted something with the notion that you're going to try to get pure happiness on the canvas?

Williams: Sure.

Cage: As you know, I collect your art, and unlike formal art, your painting has always been uncompromising in the face of society. It's never conformed to the lowest common denominator, what I call hotel room art, and yet, ironically, you've become wildly successful and are considered to be extremely commercial.

Williams: You've got one thing wrong there: I'm not commercial.

Cage: You might not be *intentionally* commercial, Robert, but your paintings sell.

Williams: Look at it this way, one problem with art today is that it's got to compete with television, movies, rock 'n' roll, and computer art, so there's got to be so much energy pulled out of the canvas to compete with these things that you have to go to extremes. You need attention-getting devices that generate emotional energy. This doesn't exist in the formal art world, which is just getting more boring. There is an attitude or snobbery against illustration or comic book art.

Cage: We have to go further and further to wake people up, to shock the system. I tried to do that in *Vampire's Kiss*, where I felt that if I ate a live cockroach, it would wake them up and they would see the movie. I had to lower myself to the standard of a geek to get any attention. Now, when you paint, do you actually think, "I'm going to shock them," or does it just come out of you and shock people in spite of itself?

Williams: It's more like a science of finding something that will disturb people to the point that they're not scared off. It works on their minds.

Cage: Like an aftertaste?

Williams: They might not like it, but they'll look at the next painting . . . and the next. Before they know it, they've developed a fascination, and they're going to keep coming back.

Cage: That's what happened to me. I'd seen your work at these two galleries, and then one day I walk into another gallery, and it was just like an explosion went off in my head. I had to get one of your paintings. You know, you talked about movies today, and painting competing with movies. Do you believe in some ways that paintings are kind of like the first movies?

Williams: Certainly, movies are a high art form.

Cage: There's a tragedy that's happening with the overstimulation of movies. I went to the *Back to the Future* ride at Universal, which is so intensely mind-boggling that I can't imagine an eight-year-old child going through that and then looking at a work of art and saying, "Wow! this is really stimulating!" Because the ride was so overstimulating, I felt completely nauseated afterwards, which got me to thinking about the line between great and not-great art. I've come to the conclusion that what it boils down to is whether or not it's pure—be it purely evil, or purely good, or purely beautiful. To me, your art seems pure and doesn't have the stink of mass marketing that *The Flintstones* movie has.

Williams: Well, the first thing about movies is that people associate emotionally with them, so you have to consider where you pull the audience in.

That's why morality plays such an important part. The bad guy has to be killed at the end, because everyone who watches the movie is so emotionally associated, vicariously. In my paintings, I can go off on any kind of abstract tangent and pull people in without them associating with the picture. They don't have to make a value judgment along the lines of "Well, that isn't what I would do."

Cage: My liking your art isn't a sign of what I'm like, nor does the art show something that I'd believe in doing, but it does evoke powerful images. There are a lot of things about your paintings that are singular, mainly that they have sound. I can really hear *Death on the Boards*. When I look at your paintings, I hear the explosions. When you paint, do you say, "You're gonna hear this," or does it just happen to do that to me? It's the strangest thing.

Williams: Sound is part of the action.

Cage: What do you think about virtual reality? Would you be interested in programming some of the imagery?

Williams: Sure, it would be no problem. I'd love to get into something like that, but I'm still obsessed with hand workmanship. There's a virtuosity in doing something with your hands. It's really played down. It's considered in really bad taste in the formal art world to take a great deal of pride in draftsmanship. They say it's not intellectual. It's a cheap trick. I say it's because they're trying to get as many people in the art world as they possibly can, so they lower the standards and open the doors.

Cage: I have a genuine appreciation of handmade things. I bought a handmade car, and it meant a lot to me to think that, as I was going 140 mph, the leather on my steering wheel was hand stitched. I don't know why, it just did. They say you built a car when you were twelve?

Williams: My father got me my first car when I was twelve, a '34 Ford five-window coupe, and I made a hot rod out of it. Now I've got a '32 Ford roadster, and I just got another '32 Ford, a three-window coupe, but they're both rust. I've always liked half-assed, half-finished hot rods. That's kind of a symbol of not being able to finish the cars—having the primer on it. If you paint them, you're finished. I've never gotten to that point because as soon as the car got painted, it would be so precise, you couldn't drive it around anymore. Someone would throw a beer bottle against it, or kids would walk on the fenders. That'd really cramp the style of being independent and free with it. It'd be what's called, in hot rod lingo, a garage queen—a hot rod that's never driven.

Cage: I drive a 1967 Corvette. It's not a hot rod. It's very stock, but the feeling of that car is like an old Spitfire. I put my old bomber jacket on. I drive it. I love the sound, the smell of the oil . . . the whole bit.

Williams: You'd enjoy riding in a hot rod.

Cage: I know. I've been looking for a chop Mercury.

Williams: You'll defeat yourself with a chop Merc. It's too big and bulky. It's beautiful, but it's hard to park. You can't see out of it. It's a heavy car. It's not nimble.

Cage: It doesn't perform like a hot rod?

Williams: A hot rod will go where you aim it.

Cartoon Surrealism

CARLO McCORMICK / 1995

From *Grand Street*, no. 52 (Spring 1994): 47–57. Reprinted by permission of Robert Williams.

Carlo McCormick: It seems as if the decadence of lowbrow, which your art has come to epitomize, had its genesis in the rise of the American leisure class in the 1950s.

Robert Williams: I think you're right. You look back at the fifties as Mr. and Mrs. Idyllic America: the housewife in the apron, the man in the business suit. There were all these standards set up to revolt against, all these ideologies to knock down one by one.

McCormick: A dominant outlet of youth play in the fifties in which you participated, a seminal landmark in the then-emergent genre of subcultural art, was car culture.

Williams: Hot rods were a mechanical-spiritual thing. There were a lot of old cars from the thirties lying around then. People realized that if you took the hood, fenders, and running boards off and put in a new engine, they could outrun any contemporary car. There was a romance to messing with the spirit of the car. There was also a machismo. From car culture, a form of art and graphics developed: pinstriping, flames, scallop paint jobs, metallic and metal flakes, pearlescent, and candy colors. It also involved a sophisticated form of metal craft, welding, grinding, polishing, and chrome plating. There hadn't been anything like this in the art world before.

McCormick: The next evolutionary step in this history was the eruption of the underground comix scene in the sixties.

Williams: Comic book history played a dominant role in my development. In the fifties, there were Senate subcommittee hearings on the effect of comics on violence and crime. A lot of great comic books fell under the axe at that time, especially the titles from Entertainment Comics. One title that stayed around was *Mad*, later [stylized as] *MAD* magazine, and its effect was tremendous—on me, Robert Crumb, Rick Griffin, and the rest of American culture. It inspired the kind of humor and sarcasm you found in comedians like Ernie Kovacs and Steve Allen (who were both involved with *Mad* at one time). When all those great comic books disappeared, every kid felt a little revenge, a retaliation, coming on. It came decades later with the undergrounds. We did things that not only violated the Comics Code but violated every code possible, including laws on pornography. Nineteen sixty-three was just like 1952. The bohemian movement had advanced some, but the Vietnam War caused such a change. Before then, your average kid wanted a high school diploma, maybe a year or two in college, and then a blue-collar job. The war stirred an intellectuality, a social consciousness. The white-collar ethic developed. No one wanted to get their hands dirty. The buying market became youth controlled, and the youth movement was born.

McCormick: Your art has graced more than a few rock albums, and you've been known and collected by a slew of bands over the years. How does rock 'n' roll play into this history?

Williams: Rock 'n' roll in the fifties wasn't taken seriously at all. The Vietnam War made it very serious. It was no longer a nuisance like comics had been. Then it started getting sweeter, more formal, formulaic, and smooth. Punk was a revolution against that. And a lot of people who were doing punk were also going to art school, so a whole shock wave of art came along with the music. It was like the fifties, when abstract expressionism accompanied free jazz. Punk art was sloppy with a lot of Day-Glo colors. I was pulled into the energy of that, but I was too much of a draftsman by that point to feel completely comfortable with it. That's when I did my *Zombie Mystery Paintings*—rough, crude, and fast.

McCormick: The emergence of new visual languages and art forms is not so much about play as it is about how the playful and serious coexist and interact.

Williams: Exactly. Cartoons are a form of mental abstraction, the pictographic language of our time. They have all the earmarks of something that's supposed to be funny, but they aren't necessarily: they can depict tragedy, rape, and scenes of extreme vulgarity. You prepare yourself to laugh at something, and then it can be heinous. There's a huge middle ground between humor and seriousness, a vast region of abstract thought. Cartoon graphics have been evolving since the Lascaux caves, Egyptian hieroglyphics, and illuminated manuscripts, and there has been a backlash of people trying to get back to those forms. This is my prediction: people will look at the twentieth century and say rock was the music of the age and comics were the art.

Best Intentions: New Work by Robert Williams

CARLO McCORMICK / 2001

From *Juxtapoz* 9, no. 1 (Jan.–Feb. 2001): 59–67. Reprinted by permission of High Speed Productions Inc. and Gwynned Vitello.

Having known Robert Williams, both personally and professionally, over the course of the eighties and nineties, it strikes me now how fundamental he has been to the evolution of my own ideas, sensibilities, and aesthetics. This duration may constitute but a small slice of his life's work, but as this writer savors the last dregs of his thirties, two decades of dialogue mark a significant segment of formative development. Our relationship has certainly had a few rough spots (always my fault, be assured), but to write about Robert's work now has a certain security, a bit of liberty that familiarity and friendship allow, that is rare between the critic and artist. However, to do this for *Juxtapoz*, a publication that bears Williams's imprint even more surely than I, is so akin to a fan's preaching to the already converted that it borders on gratuitous redundancy, if not nepotistic back-patting. But in light of the fact that most every other article, review, and interview we've done on Robert Williams has had to dedicate the majority of its energies to explaining just who the hell he is to an indifferent art world or defending his work to its detractors—those legions of political correctness and cultural higher ground for whom this painter is the epitome of bad art—this conversation afforded another possibility.

What if we assume that everyone reading this not only already knows all about the art of Robert Williams but also likes it? Furthermore, what if the reader, like the subject himself, is sure enough about my being firmly in his corner that I can adopt a more aggressive manner of inquiry without the impunity of a hostile witness? Decades of prolific creativity had already established Williams's vision long before I came to champion it, but the inverse is certainly not the case for me. At a point now in my life where Robert was on his own when we first made acquaintance, what this conversation entails, then, is a chance to question my maker. His art has certainly evolved over the time I have been writing about it, but at its basis, there is no radical change between his paintings of the early eighties and those he is showing this winter at Tony Shafrazi Gallery in New York. What has changed is me.

As each of us must periodically examine our most primary assumptions and beliefs regarding art and culture to ensure a continued vitality, the issues I posed to Robert are really the questions I ask of myself. Unlike just about everyone in the arts today, and supremely funny about his difference, Williams is an easy story for this writer to hype. What we tried to cover here is, to my way of thinking, extremely difficult. Apologizing for the tone before we began, I told Robert that if he felt somehow ambushed by his own troops in his own backyard, we could start anew on more friendly and familiar ground. As you are now reading this, we can only assume Robert Williams is not the pedagogue he might easily be.

Carlo McCormick: I want to start with the assumption that everyone reading *Juxtapoz* somehow knows your work, that we don't need to explain Ed "Big Daddy" Roth, Kustom Kulture, Robert Crumb, and *Zap Comix*, your relationship with the LA rock scene, *Appetite for Destruction*, or, for that matter, what your pictures look like and what kind of art you champion with this magazine.

Robert Williams: I'll try not to discuss all that, Carlo, but I can only go so far in avoiding my history.

McCormick: You can talk about whatever you want, but don't you yourself expect a familiarity with your work here?

Williams: Yeah, that's fair.

McCormick: Let's start with your audience. Be it *Juxtapoz* or the "art world," it seems to me that you're keenly aware of them, that your art directly addresses viewers and the contexts of their perspectives. Many artists would insist that they make their work strictly for themselves, without an audience in mind. I trust you have no such delusions.

Williams: That's a good question. It's awful hard for me to believe that any artist does work that's not directed at any one person or group of people. When I was at *Zap Comix*, we didn't know who our readers were or what they were like. So we kind of imagined that we were doing our comics for a young, hip intelligentsia. In reality, when we started to do comic conventions and got to be face-to-face with large masses of what our audience was, it was a shocking disappointment. We just saw these reclusive, self-conscious individuals who sat alone in their bedrooms reading comic books. They had pimples on their faces and couldn't interact socially with other people very well. So the intellectual, young, dashing "new Turks" that we dreamed we were doing this work for didn't really pan out. But the audience was gigantic and affected our future and, in turn, a tremendous amount of other things. Underground comics certainly affected movies, for instance.

McCormick: But the nature of the beast is such that whenever you gather obsessive collectors together, it's always geeks.

Williams: Yeah, but you've gone to so many art openings in New York that you know exactly what an art audience is—you could organize one for central casting. When [my wife] Suzanne and I went to an art show in Australia, and one in Lima, Peru, we swore that somebody just sent the same people around to be the art connoisseurs. The basic makeup for an art audience is a just-above-middle-class individual with a fairly good education who is extremely liberal and wants to be involved in the humanities. It's a caring kind of person, but one who falls victim to political correctness. I'm coming from left field here, from a rather insensitive, brutal, underground, and hot rod crowd that wants to concentrate more on the emotional reaction of the work itself than on caring sensitively about what effect it's going to have on a large group of people or what its relationship to mankind is.

McCormick: I feel you pay special heed to this notion of "audience" because you've developed an adversarial relationship with segments of "art world" discourse, such as politically correct thought police. Is it easier to have some sort of hypothetical enemy, a high-art cultural elite, for instance, to still make work decades into your career?

Williams: Let me see if I can encompass this. I certainly am aggressively pushing work against people who are entrenched in abstract expressionism, minimalism, conceptualism, and, to a certain extent, pop art. But I'm not adversarial in the sense that I'd like to dominate and run them out, as pop did to expressionism. The problem is that there's got to be room for all the "isms." There's not a right or wrong; it's all made up of opinion, a matter of taste. I'm sure that if abstract expressionism fell on the worst hard times, I'd have to come and champion it. The same goes for minimalism, of which I'm so intolerant because it's diametrically opposed to what people call my work: maximalism. There's got to be a provision made to tolerate and protect all these "isms" so that the whole thing keeps its vitality. Does that answer the question?

McCormick: Yeah, it's just that I think this relationship to some imaginary adversary is, in many ways, what gets a lot of people.

Williams: Well, you're right, and it's very obviously in me that I'm resisting what has already been established. I'll go into a big museum on a very expensive piece of real estate, and there's this big white room. Now, it took a lot of politics to get this artist in there, and he's just got this one big thing that reeks of his complete indifference to how he manufactured it. In that same place, I could put on one hell of a graphic performance, and I've waited my whole life to do just that. Of course, I have to not only tolerate it but also endorse it, because it's the same thing I want to do.

McCormick: The triple threat of your painting titles has this form of multiplicity that takes into account such a status quo. Is it purely wordplay for you?

Williams: It's me being loquacious and trying to overexplain. The paintings are overdrawn and over-rendered because they want to draw you in and make you more cognizant of everything. It's just like talking too much. The titles do the same thing. They put you in three different positions of observation. Maybe that's a vice of mine.

McCormick: In making such a distinction between high and low, an intelligentsia and a common-speak, as two sides of the same coin, do you mean to ridicule the academy?

Williams: A little bit. Now, I say this with all due respect to you, but the majority of your colleagues are failed artists who have learned how to work their way into art publications. They've developed a lean toward literature and really polished up "art-speak" until it's almost a dialogue unto itself. I've seen writers take shows where there was almost nothing and work them over again to breathe life into them. But I've put so much effort into my paintings and had art critics just come to a dead end with my stuff.

McCormick: Language isn't simply an indicator of education; it is a very specific manifestation of class. When you hear expressions like "lowbrow" or think about your work in relation to the kinds of art you see walking around galleries, do you ever regard this in terms of class?

Williams: There is obviously a class distinction. I've ensconced myself tight enough in the art world to see the makeup of the young, "nouveaux riches" entrepreneurs who have decided to be art connoisseurs. They can wield power, and there's no doubt about its being class based. What's more pronounced than that, however, is that artists generally follow the dogma that goes along most closely with what they can do physically. If you can't draw, you sure as hell aren't going to start endorsing tight representation; you're going to become a conceptualist. One of the real underlying motivations of art is compulsion. You can intellectualize it until you're blue in the face, but it's like trying to intellectualize jerking off. I have this compulsion to choke up that little sable brush and make it sing poetry. Other people who like to paint from the shoulder may see me as some kind of anally inhibited character with a squeaky pencil. They would tend to intellectualize that, rather than face the fact that it's a matter of metabolism and compulsion.

McCormick: I believe people's aesthetics determine their skills, rather than the inverse.

Williams: What art schools do now is find what the majority of students are capable of, and that's what the curriculum will be. A long time ago, they tried to force students to be tight draftsmen and learn composition. But they would lose students who were not interested in that, and the schools would suffer. So now what the art schools do is follow what the students want to do—which is as little as possible.

McCormick: Again, my ideas may differ from yours here. But I just happen to be reading this oral history of the American art world from '62 to '74 (at the dawn of *Artforum*) called *Challenging Art*. Here it is; this is from Mel Bochner, the noted artist and critic, on precisely such a rift:

> I graduated art school in '62. Carnegie Mellon. It was called Carnegie Institute of Technology then. It was an interesting education, because although it was very provincial it was, starting in '58, a kind of clash between the modernists—who were infiltrating the provinces at that time—and the old beaux arts system. . . . There was an intense competition between these two ideologies to dominate the future of art education.

McCormick: Of course, the modernists won.

Williams: Without a doubt. Another aspect no one seems to want to mention is that people are trying to force a tremendous equality into art. A hundred years ago, if you could draw or paint, people would say you had the gift of God. Now, the philosophy seems to be that if you're such a rare and singular individual, you're hurting others who can't draw or paint but want to be artists. It was Timothy Leary who pointed this out to me. He told me that we're not going to leave art in the hands of an elite few who actually have dexterity. I agree with him, but are you going to make everyone an artist? Why not? I don't know.

McCormick: Neither do I. But while you espouse this "dexterity," or what is, in effect, a technical formalism, how much are you willing to conversely embrace this construct of the underground? I'd still like to believe in a creative community outside the mainstream, as well as the possibility of still being transgressive toward official culture, but it does seem a bit of a fallacy at this point, doesn't it?

Williams: Carlo, you know what the underground is: a large amount of disenfranchised artists who do not have the same work directions or ethics as the majority of successful artists—the junta that rules now. You know exactly what is going to happen. A few underground artists will succeed, a few will become compromisers, and the rest will wash out with time. But overall, it will have an effect on a little bit of every thing. What you don't want is artists like me and my ilk to become all-powerful and start running everything, because that would be an academy that would have to be revolted against.

McCormick: Beyond this very general notion of disenfranchised artists on the margins of the mainstream, you must have a clearer definition of the underground.

Williams: My definition would include artists a little bit older who were around to see the Kefauver Committee bring down comic books in the early fifties, get rid of EC [Comics], and clamp down on the world until the Vietnam War and a young bunch of artists came up to resist with psychedelic rock posters, underground comics, hot rod, drug, and surfer art forms. This underground comes into being when they could develop themselves to become sophisticated enough to form an artists' bloc to directly confront the real art world. That's my ideal, but it's not everyone's. A lot of illustrator types have jumped on this as a way to exhibit and sell their work, in the same way that Dalí jumped on the radical leftist movement of surrealism. He's one of my favorite artists, but nonetheless his ethics weren't too far from a used-car salesman's.

McCormick: If we do accept the "underground" faith that we can still be radical, that there is a dominant culture to oppose, and that we are collectively part of that confrontation, how do we maintain our difference?

Williams: You've made an observation that I think is mistaken. You cannot ask, "how can we still be radical?" when in the art world you can do anything already. You can cut animals into sections and display them, you can preserve your shit, you can harm yourself, and pretty much any perversion you can dream of is open to art now. Being radical is over. The thing now is to go to the next step, to come up with some kind of language or thought pattern that goes off on its own radical tangents. Evolution always moves through mistakes.

McCormick: I suppose I meant this in more relativistic terms: the prospect of being subversive rather than any tired modernist agenda of novelty.

Williams: Yes, that is possible, but it's self-defeating. That is what's been done throughout the twentieth century. The problem with that is each generation ends up reacting to the previous one. If you react to everything that is established, you're a slave to everything around you.

McCormick: You've taken the visual tropes of surrealism and even gone so far as to call your work comic surrealism. My basic problem with that is that surrealism was process-oriented art. Deeply influenced by the then relatively new disciplines of psychology and psychoanalysis, the surrealists invented such practices as automatic writing and the exquisite corpse as a way to tap directly into the subconscious. I don't think that's what you're doing. Your work is meticulously planned out beforehand.

Williams: First, let me say that the surrealist movement got diffused and watered down by things like advertising before it really finished its life. What I profess to practice is taking imagery that has been neglected for four or five decades and picking up where it left off. In the same way, I'm going back to representation—which began with cave painting and hieroglyphics—as a way of telling stories. The process never really died; it just sidestepped itself in comic books, movie storyboards, and stuff like that. When you're dealing with a cartoon or comic book, you're dealing with that old pictorial and symbolic language that was sidestepped by the fine arts. No one has sat down and asked, "What can we do with the language itself? How can we take pictures, symbols, designs, and coded sequences to try to make them compound and abstract themselves into some new form of thought?"

McCormick: Really, Robert, isn't that what art has always been about?

Williams: To a certain extent, you can pull that in there. But no, you're not going to have me bow down to that.

McCormick: As for this imagery, you're very much an American artist. In this far more international age, I wonder if your iconography, from hot rods to hot dogs, is not infused with a deep sense of nostalgia.

Williams: We're far more comfortable dealing with hindsight than foresight. And looking back has an element of romance to it. Another thing I would like to mention, in regard to cartoons, is that they are, unfortunately, forever locked into the world of humor. Well, what in the hell is humor? It's taking a situation that is distorted for your pleasure. Humor is a form of abstraction. We separate drama and humor, but in reality, there should be some kind of bridging logic between the stark drama and the butthole silly. That's what I try to do in my art.

McCormick: I suppose it's really my job, but can you look over the past two decades of paintings and see a clear evolution in your work? Can you say what is different between these paintings in the new millennium and your work from the eighties?

Williams: The paintings are getting tighter, not only technically but also in terms of content and thought. A lot more forethought goes into my paintings now. It's obvious that I'm going to have to start simplifying, to drop the three-title thing, and start painting from the shoulder. I'm getting older, and I just can't continue to work with the same obsessive detail much longer. Sometimes I think I'm painting for an audience that doesn't exist anymore.

McCormick: I find it hard to honestly answer whether the unwillingness to compromise is the liability of stubbornness or the persistence of vision. One issue you have been adamant about is the maintenance of a collectors' waiting list where people interested in your work sign up. I understand it was a very democratic and natural response to the fact that lots of people wanted to buy work directly out of the studio when you wanted very much to publicly show each body of paintings together. There has, from my perspective, been a gradual strain in this system as you are now able to produce enough work to satisfy your market. To me, it seems a little bit artificial at this point, as if your ego cannot handle doing a show that is not sold out.

Williams: I can demand a much higher price for my paintings, but I wouldn't have sold-out shows. I'm not a big shot, and I've never tried to present myself as one who has a whole bunch of sold-out shows. I do what other artists don't have the gall to do: I don't reach for the highest price I can jerk out of somebody's pocket. Almost every artist I know figures if they can get one hundred thousand dollars for a painting, then it's a one-hundred-thousand-dollar painting. That just ain't so. All it means is you found an idiot who will pay that. Everyone's telling me to hike my prices up; Shafrazi's begging me to charge more.

McCormick: There are those who would say that it is not creatively healthy for an artist to pay such attention to the market forces surrounding their work. How would you respond to these criticisms?

Williams: No one's going to wipe your ass but yourself. You have to be rational about this. I'm sure that Tony Shafrazi wouldn't take me if I wasn't selling artwork. I'd still be selling out of my garage if I hadn't followed the formula I developed. You're right in that the sales part of the art market is disturbing. I've tried to be as honest and credible as I can. The bottom line is that your integrity does show up in how you deal with money, and integrity is an awfully important part of being an artist.

McCormick: And when they argue that there are such things as aesthetic criteria, that beauty and the sublime are aesthetically quantifiable truths, I feel a bit ashamed. What I mean is, in this cultural war we've waged to include more lowbrow, democratic, or even vulgar forms of representation and expression, do we really want to subvert this hierarchical authority to such a debased level where truth, beauty, and the sublime are forever forfeited?

Williams: I think about that all the time. We are animals with animal purposes. To my way of thinking, and maybe this is crass, the most beautiful thing in the world is a woman's ass. You can even look through a powerful telescope at the dynamic miracles of the Orion Nebula or the incomprehensible beauty of the Andromeda Galaxy, but a woman's ass will subdue it. For all the intellectual appreciation we may have toward something, that is nothing compared to our emotional animal responses. So where would you put the truth?

Ed "Big Daddy" Roth

GWYNNED VITELLO / 2009

From *Juxtapoz* 16, no. 11 (Nov. 2009): 50–62. Reprinted by permission of High Speed Productions Inc. and Gwynned Vitello.

Walt drew a pleasingly plump, smiling mouse and built a home for him in Disneyland, the happiest place on Earth. Ed "Big Daddy" Roth created a sweaty-palmed, bloodshot-orbed rodent who looked like he frequented the seedier side of the Golden State. Fittingly, Ed Roth ended up spending the sunset days of his career at Knott's Berry Farm, which was known for shoot-'em-up tableaux and way scarier rides. I stopped by Robert and Suzanne's homestead to get a firsthand spin from the flinty-eyed Williams himself.

Gwynned Vitello: In your documentary, he comes off as this real easy-going guy.

Robert Williams: He was. Very sweet, like a big, giant puppy. So the salty stuff you have referenced just reflects how he enjoyed having a great time and innocently got into things. He was a big German, very big. Well, you know, his honesty was a certain virtue, but you could never get the same story out of him twice. Let's use the term "prevarications" instead of "lies."

Vitello: Robert, I have to look that up.

Williams: Prevarication is a nice way to say lies. You'd ask him a story, and someone else asks him the same story three days later, and it's a completely different story.

Vitello: You're saying he perceived things differently depending on the occasion.

Williams: No, it isn't the way he perceived things. He always wanted a sense of promotion and bluster.

Vitello: So that's where his self-described allusion to P. T. Barnum comes from. I wonder how this expansive personality emerged from a strict

German-speaking family, an exacting father, keeping his boys busy with woodwork and all.

Williams: Well, his parents were German immigrants. If I'm not mistaken, Ed was born in Beverly Hills, and his father used to chauffeur Mary Pickford. His father was as German as a son of a bitch could be. Thick accent. The father could not stand me because I had long hair, and he called me "the Girl." The father hated Mary Pickford because she made him haul fertilizer bags in the limousine. A real limousine, I don't mean a town car, a big, long expensive car back in the twenties and thirties. He didn't like that. Anyway, Ed went to Los Angeles City College, as I did many years later.

Vitello: So he predated you?

Williams: Yeah, he was about twelve years older, born in '32, and I was born in '43. He must've always been artistic, because he got a job as a window decorator for Sears. So I guess that's where he learned lettering. Then he got into hot rodding, probably in the late forties or early fifties. He met a guy called the Baron, an old sign painter who had been around so long that he knew pinstriping from touching up cars for used-car lots and whatnot. He was the stepping-stone for Ed. Then Von Dutch came along in '54 and '55 and brought hot rod pinstriping.

Vitello: Tell me when pinstriping came about.

Williams: Pinstriping came about probably in the Middle Ages. It was used on wagons and signs way back in time. You do a bunch of decorations, and you get a line and follow a shape like on the side of a carriage, or on the side of a sign that's outside of the tavern. You get this dagger brush and just run a line, and it makes it look fancy. It was a pretty conservative form of sign painting and decorating until Von Dutch came along and started doing this extravagant stuff. He brought in these wild forms of schizophrenic pinstriping in the mid-fifties, and Ed Roth latched on to it. Dean Jeffries jumped on it, and a number of people jumped on it in the fifties in California. Von Dutch, of course, brought in modern flame painting, which went way back, but he made the real characteristic ones you think of today. Ed Roth pretty much styled himself after Von Dutch. That was his idol, Von Dutch.

Vitello: But he didn't work for him.

Williams: No, they were friends, so Ed got to working down in Lynwood with the Baron and then opened up his own shop in Maywood. Ed got a couple hot rods, one a '32 Ford three-window coupe, and then later, a '31 Model A sedan. There was nothing really distinguishable about them; it was just kind of trendy. He built them, but they were nothing out of the ordinary. Then he started working on this Model A sedan and started doing these fancy hot rod bumpers, pinstriping it up. He started slowly departing from the standard hot rods, and then he built the first fiberglass hot rod.

Vitello: When did fiberglass come into its own?

Williams: Fiberglass had already been popular in Corvettes as early as '63. They started using it on sport cars because it was real light, and you could form it much easier than you could by beating out aluminum or steel. So fiberglass already had a foothold, though it didn't in hot rodding, and Ed picked it up with this wild T-bucket-looking thing called the *Outlaw*. It was originally called *Excalibur* because he got his first wife Sally's grandfather's Confederate officer's saber, broke it in half, and used it for a gearshift lever. He named it *Excalibur*, which was a real stretch of the imagination. Sally hit the roof when he broke that thing in half; it was a beautiful officer's saber, a cavalry saber, and I've never seen one that fancy. It wasn't just a regular trooper's saber; it was a high-ranking officer's saber. He fucked that thing right up, broke it in half, and welded it to the part that goes into the shift tower, so it was a shift lever. The *Outlaw* went over big, really big, because of the style of painting that hit in '57/'58 and '59 called scallops. This is where you just fill the panels with different colors in an abstract suggestion to the shape. He did this on that *Outlaw*; that was just wild.

Vitello: How did that come about, and was that the first thing he built?

Williams: No, the first thing he built was when he screwed up this '32 three-window coupe by channeling it. He told his dad he was going to change the radiator, and he cut the whole floor out and dropped it over the frame for him.

Vitello: Was it his dad's car?

Williams: No, it was his, but he fucked it up. When you channel a car, you drop the body over the frame. That ruins the car; that's what it's going to be from that point on. So, in the beginning, he was just kind of screwing around and experimenting. He was just another hot-rodder, but he really pushed it beyond what most people did, this kind of scalloping. Suzanne and I own one of the molds, and from his molds, a couple bodies were pushed out (we got them in the garage). So, anyway, this blew people's minds, and this got him into the big car shows. This car alone, because it was a total creation from nothing, was the first time a hot rod was created from nothing in this abstract form. This really made him famous overnight. So we opened a shop and did pinstriping and whatnot, and this got him really renowned. He had another car here that he bought from someone; it was called *Tweety Pie*. Someone else built that, and he bought it.

Vitello: So he just bought it and pinstriped it?

Williams: Yeah, but then he came up with this thing; there's a world of difference. This is a Model T body made in a factory; this thing is a total abstract wonderful creation from scratch, a giant step in hot rod culture. This was a turning point. And the next car he made, he went one step further in the same vein. He made the next logical step from that T-bucket-looking thing to a whole world unto itself: The *Beatnik Bandit* with the bubble top. Then, at the car shows, he'd set up a booth with an airbrush and do these custom shirts.

Vitello: Was anyone else doing that?

Williams: Well, he started it. Von Dutch did a few airbrush shirts just for friends. Ed saw this, so he started doing this at car shows at three or four bucks apiece. You tell him what you wanted, he'd do a monster, a goof-eyed guy. They were funky looking too. The next car he did I think was maybe the *Rotar*, which was a hovercraft. It's got two Triumph motorcycle engines in the back, driving propellers. And it's supposed to levitate. Now, nobody in it could levitate. These cars at the shows were connected to electrical equipment. Every fifteen minutes, the thing would start, and the announcement on tape would say, "This is *Rotar*, Ed Roth's great creation." And the motors would fire up and it'd levitate. He had some famous person do the tape, some country-western star or somebody, so it was really a sensation at the time. Now, there was a tragedy at the Detroit Autorama, where this thing started itself up, and the blades blew out of the thing and exploded into the roof. There were about twenty blades per propeller; it flew up to the roof and exploded metal everywhere, and a lot of people were seriously injured. It went into lawsuits like you wouldn't believe. "Propeller snaps at futuristic car show. Five hurt." There were pictures with the police holding the propellers, saying, "see what's left of it." This was an ugly situation. Roth never did like the car again. The next one was a rear engine with a Corvair engine, and it was called the *Road Agent*; the car after that one was one he hated. It was called the *Orbitron*. It had three lights that, in theory, were supposed to meet in the middle and create a white light. All colors made white supposedly; well, that's nonsense. This car has just recently been restored at the cost of half a million dollars; a fella I know bought it. He saw it in pieces in front of an adult bookstore in Mexico. Now it's completely restored beautifully.

Vitello: And when did you get in the picture?

Williams: In late 1965, I started working for him, during the beginning of the Vietnam War. I was looking for jobs in the art field, and I didn't have much luck. But they said, "We have one thing, everybody turns it down, and the conditions aren't very pleasant." All these people went down there, took a look at this shitty hot rod place with bikers and whatnot, and they wouldn't want any part in that, saw no future in that. I showed him my portfolio, and he said, "If I knew you existed, I'd have hunted you up." So my life went from being in a very dire situation to all of a sudden being in the chips. This was around the time that was the height of his career. Life was looking pretty rosy; Suzanne and I were really comfortable in Hollywood. Every day, I'd drive to Maywood and back. Along the line, he hired Suzanne to do a little layout in a motorcycle magazine, too. About this time, he started wearing a top hat and formal tux, but he was also running around with some pretty fast characters. He'd always been friends with bikers and what we would call "one percen-ters" . . . the old definition of the "one percenters." The attorney general said these rabble-rousers were only 1 percent of the population, so don't worry about them. It was an honor to have that patch, and if you weren't given that patch, they'd beat the hell out of you. But I spent four or five years sitting not four or five feet away from him, and I ended up becoming an adviser, becoming very close friends. I was just twenty-two to twenty-three years old, and here's my friend, this guy that was a hot rod influence, talking to me. Anyway, he started running around with these bikers. How did he slip in with them? There was an overlap between the bikers and hot-rodders; their worlds are tightly intertwined from earlier, at Bonneville and stuff. The bikers were enormously right-wing and pro–Vietnam War. You have to remember the war was raging during this period, and the hippie thing was just starting to get big and dumb. But Ed started getting more and more interested in the motor-cycle deal. He really had a thing about manhood and manly things, really big on masculinity, and he saw in these scummy bikers a bravado akin to corsairs and pirates, a real romantic adventurism and "swashbuckleness."

I would tell Ed, "You know, these guys are just fucking felons, I wouldn't run with these guys. They'll stab you in the back while reaching for your wal-let . . ." But he had a kind of innocence. Well, he had this innocence because he was enormous, like an elephant around a tiger. He didn't have anything to worry about. When I worked at Roth Studios, every day was like an adventure. There would be a movie star coming in, or a famous rider. He was very good friends with Tom Wolfe, who wrote that book about him, *The Kandy-Kolored Tangerine-Flake Streamline Baby*, and that guy Remarque who wrote *All Quiet on the Western Front*. There was a cultural thing that slipped in on top of all that crap. So Ed started to really want to promote this motorcycle thing, slip-ping into the chopper thing more and more. You don't see this now, but up to this point, those biker gangs and choppers were outré; they were completely unacceptable. The police would stop a chopper at a minute's notice. Like *Easy Rider*. Well, Ed had already tendered the ground before those guys came along.

Robert Williams, *Confluence between Corsairs*, 2006. Oil on canvas, 91.4 x 76.2 cm. Private collection.

Ed just saw this chopper thing as a coming thing; it was so masculine to him. One day some guys come in from *Time* magazine. The piece comes out, and it's an exposé; they just fucked him. The attorney general sees this, and the government is trying to come up with the RICO Act and make bikers part of this new racketeering act. So [he is] the biggest name they know, and what hits him is the IRS coming for him like he's Capone.

Now, Ed was the most honest prick in the world . . . and the most patriotic. Here come the guys from the IRS to go through his books. This square fucking prick comes in, this churchgoing dork comes in every day in the middle of the cesspool, going through the books for three months, and by the time he's through, he's one of the gang! All the wild women and hot rods—and they couldn't find anything wrong with his books—except he's sloppy! Meanwhile the FBI moves in, so they're coming in twice a week. They're looking for something to tie on Ed Roth, drugs or something. Well, there were drugs in there all the time, but they didn't find any. You'd walk out in the back where the shop was, and there's a hotel down the street, and there's a guy with binoculars every day looking at what's going on in the back. They couldn't pin anything on Roth, and Ed got to be friends with the FBI guy. As soon as they get around Roth, they start loving him. And they never found enough to get him on the RICO Act. And maybe he ingratiated himself so much with them that they didn't want to find anything. I guess he got in these situations and slipped out of them, maybe because he was lucky in some respects. His big headache was he put all his money into a magazine called *Choppers*. It was the first outlaw biker magazine with choppers, so he could not advertise it in the car or motorcycle titles. He was the first guy who started that whole world, that whole world the clowns like Jesse James take for granted and use. There would've never been a Jesse James without an Ed Roth, and there never would have been this whole world that Ed promoted at his own expense. It cost him his business. It cost him his marriage. He kept me on as long as he could, but he just had to cut me loose. Ed was really down in the dumps.

Vitello: Is that when he took up religion?

Williams: What he did was, he felt so down on his luck, was in such a state of depression and remorse that he took religion and went to school to learn to work on semi-tractor trailers. Finally, he got involved with Mormonism and got a job as an art director at Knott's Berry Farm.

Vitello: How did he choose to become a Mormon?

Williams: I don't really know much about the tenets. Well, you take the New Testament and the Old Testament, and you throw them away and you get a DC comic. You just start reading pages out of it and tag Jesus on it; that's about what it is to me, a total redoing of the Christian religion. He sought it out. Everything he thought was hip had hurt him; everything he thought was cool had bitten him. He respected me, and we were very good friends, but he was questioning me as a kind of funky guy. Until the day he died, I still talked filth in front of him; he wouldn't let anyone else, but I knew him in the old days.

Vitello: So he moved to Utah?

Williams: Yeah, to this little town in Utah where they had this giant white cathedral made out of white stone. He got deeper and deeper into the religion, although a nostalgia thing started coming back, and he got really big. In fact, when he died, his obituary was in *Time* magazine and the *LA Times*; his obit was bigger than Salvador Dalí's, it was unbelievable.

Vitello: And what was your last memory of him?

Williams: The real enjoyment he had was when he was painting a Rat Fink at a convention, and there would be twenty kids around him. He loved that. Last time, he was at a pinstriping thing in North Hollywood. He's got all these kids gathered, and I'm watching, too. He's painting this green flesh on the Rat Fink; it had some bumps on it. He says, "Well, I don't know what to call flesh like this. Bob, what do you call this?" I wasn't going to stand for this religious bullshit because I knew him from an earlier time. I said, "I don't know, but I got that same texture on my scrotum." And that's the last thing I said to him. He just died too soon.

Robert Williams Interview

ED HARDY / 2012

From *Juxtapoz* 19, no. 4 (April 2012): 60–79. Reprinted by permission of High Speed Productions Inc. and Gwynned Vitello.

One of the most interesting things about Robert Williams to me is the role he has played in influencing visual culture as we know it today. He continually seduces and knocks people out of their minds. Robert came from a secret surf spot universe, an underground artist with a hard-core, passionate following.

I've known him since 1982, when he was working on *Zombie Mystery Paintings*, but I was also well acquainted with his work in underground comics, especially noteworthy for his work with Big Daddy Roth and Psychedelic Solution in New York. Robert commanded such authority, but the masses really felt his impact when he cooked up *Juxtapoz*. The magazine solidified Robert's reputation for having his finger on the pulse of visual expression taking place outside the accepted highbrow vehicles. What often gets overlooked is Robert's writing, one of the most important features of his legacy as an icon of contemporary art. He became the leading person to formalize underground art into a context of real, deep, historical perspective, creating an intellectual viewpoint on this oft-dismissed scene. His writing is never snotty, academic, or stuck-up but succeeds in clarifying people's perception of what his contemporaries' work was all about. I have always thought that there can be a terrific velocity established with very intelligent writing about art, not just pompous bullshit made to confuse people or make them feel they aren't rich enough to afford puffed-up theoretical paintings or conceptual constructs. Robert always pushes the boundaries by the radical act of telling the truth. In anticipation of his opening at Tony Shafrazi Gallery in New York City, featuring half a decade of new works, I spoke with Robert Williams about the past, present, the show, new attitudes toward *Juxtapoz*, and the craft of taking apart the establishment.

Ed Hardy: We should discuss the new work that you're doing and every-thing that has gone on over the years.

Robert Williams: I don't know if I was the right person at the right time, but you have a lot of the same influences that I do, comic books, B movies, and a lot of salacious material that never really fit into the fine arts world. I was stuck in the art world in the early 1960s when abstract expressionism dominated, and representational art was considered the worst thing in the world—the product of morons who didn't have the capability to think of abstraction or to think in two dimensions. So that's pretty much the world that you and I were in. But I was fortunate enough to get tied in with Roth, where I could do representational work, and through Roth, I met some under-ground cartoonists like Rick Griffin and Stanley Mouse, who later got me tied in with Crumb and S. Clay Wilson. When I got involved with the underground comic world, I realized that these guys also faced the same prejudices in art school. They were taught that they had to paint from the shoulder and not the wrist, and just use earth colors, the sloppier the better, and the more emo-tional the better. Any kind of self-discipline was a sign of weakness.

Being involved in comics was a wonderful and free situation, but nobody seemed to want to venture into that fine arts world. I kind of struggled along, pretending I was like somebody important doing representational paintings, and the thing was, the only thing I could find, the only group that I could relate to or that would tolerate me, was this peer group of punk rock artists.

That fostered *Zombie Mystery Paintings* that led on and on, especially in Los Angeles, also in San Francisco, and New York, but especially in LA. The book just slowly started a firestorm, and more and more artists joined. But time went on, and more people jumped on the bandwagon, losing that under-ground ethic. I miss that really outlaw esprit de corps, that daring to do.

Hardy: When you and I both came along, I didn't particularly have a great agenda or game plan. I went for something that seemed really cool to me and seemed to have as much relevance and potential as any other kind of visual. That was my trip with tattoos. I was ten years old, and I'm on the pike in Long Beach, and I just thought, "Tattoos are the coolest fucking thing ever seen." Both of us came out of this thing of rough-and-tumble street culture, a passion for a sensibility of things that connected to our everyday lives that weren't theoretically based.

I mean, art history is all right, and it is great to look back. For myself, I find great comfort in dipping into what I see as this chain of eccentric and malcon-tent artists. And you look at some of these people—and maybe they weren't

Robert Williams, *Robt. Williams' Graphic Influences*, 1987. Originally appeared in a catalog for the *Bad Influences* show, Otis Art Institute, Los Angeles.

the Rembrandts or the Michelangelos of their day—and those guys are okay, too, but it's the weirdo ones that really light my fire the most.

Williams: That's right, for me, too.

Hardy: And you with cars and me with surfing, all these things coming out of the West, this kind of artificial environment . . . I think California is enormously important on a global scale, with the beach, LSD, music, the whole deal. And you got into that with the underground comics. I'll never forget the first time I saw a *Zap* comic, it was like, "Wait a minute, man," as if the earth moved. It was the finesse of draftsmanship and sophisticated graphic and conceptual capabilities mixed with these wild flights of story lines and invented universes that didn't exist anywhere else. It grew to global proportions.

Williams: I wanted this stuff to look down-to-earth, but on the other hand, I wanted it to look intelligent. As salacious and lurid as this stuff is, it has a certain conceived intelligence. If you just look at it and think, I can't show this to the grandkids, and write it off, you're losing the pleasure you could have if you took some time with it.

The art world enjoys the pretension of intellectuality. And you look at some of these goddamn things, and it looks as if they've been secreted anally or something. How emotional and intelligent can I be to try and understand this thing? That's always been a problem with me; I've had a very difficult time trying to get any kind of academic acceptance. And then other people say, "Well, why do you want academic acceptance?" Because, unfortunately, that's the only goddamn game in town.

Hardy: When we got into this thing of expressing ourselves in a way that wasn't mainstream, we both came into it from a total underdog thing, and we were looked down upon for it. It's why I've been on this fucking crusade about tattooing. I don't give a shit if people get tattoos. I don't even know why people get them. My stance was I shouldn't get looked down on as some subhuman piece of shit because I wear tattoos or want to do them. It just burns our ass that we have to be relegated to the other circles of dirty because we aren't in the "anointed realm." It's such bullshit. I think we've had the last laugh in a lot of ways. Thank god my mentor told me, "Don't get stuck in this academic thing." That's what switched me into going back to tattooing. Buddies of mine who are now firmly entrenched in academia are department heads at fine universities, but they're pretty much miserable and trapped. You and I are truly independent. Maybe we missed out on some of this stuff, but I think overall it's been a more interesting ride.

Williams: My first remark here is kind of a joke, but eventually I'm going to be completely run over and forgotten by the people who paint big-eyed children, and I'm going to be smeared into a footnote. Unfortunately for you, I think you're going to be run over by people wanting to get piercings and whatnot. You're probably going to end up being a fucking footnote, too.

Seriously, though, I look at this screwy fucking art world, and I'm thinking, "Well, how screwy can the goddamn situation get?" I mean these people are talking about millions and millions of dollars, serious businessmen that handle these deals. And I'm thinking somewhere down the line someone is going to kick the underpinning out of all of this stuff, and it's just going to collapse. I looked at abstract expressionism, and I used to hate those sons of a bitches. And then I look and see what the younger generation is coming up with, and I discovered in some respects I'm more comfortable with these idiots that were abstract expressionists, because at least those assholes drank wine, wore sandals, were bohemians, and screwed each other's wives. There was a color to those fools.

Hardy: It's so dry now. When I was a teenager, I wanted to save the world with art and was really won over by the idea of nobility and you could do things that mattered. It's good to have ideals when you're young and to try to reach some shred of them in some form. It used to piss me off about abstract work, and then I started looking at it, even analyzing it. Most of them were alcoholics, and a lot of them, like Rothko, committed suicide, and they drank themselves to death. I think they wheeled themselves into a boxed canyon where they were pursuing the absolute purity of "we got to get away from any subject matter." It's impure if it's recognizable, and it's a losing game.

What's a Robert Williams painting? Well, you have alternate forms that are taking you off into this insane mental space, but really these are pure paintings. They can be enjoyed on all these levels. It's like going through a mirror, man. You can be in that world and contemplate, "How the fuck did he think this up," but what does this imply with the way these things fracture and disseminate? It's crazy! But then they are so beautifully painted and intentionally bringing these emotions about. The work is just so much more sublime than so much stuff there is. Now, who knows what's going on in the art world? There's obviously this tidal wave that you created, and no matter how much it might get warped or misunderstood, there's purity.

Williams: I'd hate to see a Robert Williams Art School develop. I could get tired of this stuff really quick. The art is good as long as it's on this climb and it's fighting for life, but when it gets on top, when any art gets on top, it gets stale. The art world doesn't ever seem to be able to have about fifteen or twenty "isms" existing at one time. It can only deal with about three, and they dominate.

Hardy: Back to our initial question, your show at Tony Shafrazi Gallery. I don't know how the swing is going to go, but the art market is in an interesting spot. We're definitely in a situation worse than you and I have ever seen before, probably as bad as the Great Depression.

Williams: Right. You know that the only upside to this is that it peels off a lot of the slag. It's an ugly way to look at it, but that's the truth.

Hardy: It's going to clear all the shit out that was just hanging on there that maybe didn't have a rightful place anyways.

Williams: Let me see if I can run off with the ball here with my new show. I've been in LA since 1963, and when I came to LA, trying to be an artist and going to art school, there was an art philosophy already established here since the 1950s. It was an abstract expressionist philosophy that art had to express a truth. In other words, if you painted with paint, it had to look like paint; if you carved in wood, it had to be gnarly. If you used metal, it had to be all burnt up with a cutting torch. You had to be true to your medium. I was real facile and tight and wanted to defy the teachers and the mediums. I wanted to do ice sculptures out of dry ice, do the impossible with materials, which really went against the grain. I remember I was in an art lecture in a large auditorium full of students, and the teacher had some slides up on the wall. He had a big slide up there of Rubens's famous painting *The Descent from the Cross*. He exclaims to the class, "This isn't a painting, this is a colored-in drawing!" I knew right then I was in deep shit; I knew I had a problem.

Later, I went to Chouinard Art Institute and took a class in lithographing stones. I did this dynamic picture of a person standing in a spotlight with his arms up in the air and an arch of lightning going from one hand to the other, and the teacher said, "This is illustration." From that point on, I realized, gee, I've always figured I was a little slow, but I tried to do abstract work, but it just didn't interest me. It couldn't breathe. It wasn't like giving birth to something. Then, later, it dawned on me what the situation really was: in reality, you have to get a lot of people interested in art; and to get people interested in art, they have to relate to art; and to relate to art, they have to think of themselves as an artist.

The majority of art is marketed on the fact that you're the genius, too; you just haven't discovered it for yourself. So if you have some kind of real tight technique that's popular, man, you're losing like 85 percent of the people. If you got some cute whimsical kind of thing that anyone could do, people say, "Oh, I could have thought of that. I could have made a couple of blobs like that! This guy is a genius because he came up with it first." That was the backbone of art since the 1950s, getting people to vicariously join in. So it's just been an uphill fight since then.

You've got comic books and all this wonderful stuff that came out during the 1950s that just had no chance at being "art," or couldn't be tied in with art. And you saw these very talented people that would never get any higher recognition. Wallace Wood committed suicide. Harvey Kurtzman died a nobody, and Basil Wolverton was just an insignificant character. All these people with all this rich imagination were just born at the wrong time.

Hardy: They were ahead of their time.

Williams: One thing that really hung me up early on, and you had a lot to do with me recognizing this, but I probably had a glance into it before I met you, was the power of tattoos and how they were emblematic. They were like heraldry. And when you put on a tattoo, you made one hell of a commitment; that was your coat of arms. And I've seen some of these back pieces, just incredible. Nevertheless, some of the splash panels out of comic books, stuff out of girly magazines. If I'm depressed or if I don't feel good or something, I can pop a *Hustler* magazine open, and my fucking heart rate goes up and my eyes dilate. It's just like having coffee or something.

Hardy: I still think tattooing is the most loaded kind of medium, because of course it's tied into the whole thing about mortality and social conditioning. People think, "Oh my God, it's on you forever and you're marked," and blah-blah-blah. Tattoos have that thing that no other inanimate art does. It isn't better or worse, just a fact of it.

But it's just a medium, an innocent medium, inert as oil paint lying there. Until the paint gets laid on by a human, it's just paint. But it's the power that these images evoke. I just kicked the bucket over in a very small way compared to all these young geniuses now that are buzzing all this stuff all over the fucking globe. It blows my mind. I always tell people when they ask what I think about the enormous popularity of tattoos. I go, "Well, fuck, that's what I was doing when I was twenty-two, thirty, or eighteen." It's a visceral hit, something that can really open people's eyes.

That's probably the most important thing you've done, trying to get people to see things in a different way and appreciate stuff and not have to feel guilty about stuff that turns them on that's part of their gut-level culture. To meet someone and talk with them, and they say, "Well, I've got this back piece," and you look at them and figure, well, this is kind of just an average blue-collar Joe. Then he takes his shirt off, and you see something on his back, like the historic first ascension of a French hot-air balloon, you know, some incredible goddamn thing, and you think, "How did this guy even know about this?" It's just a remarkable situation. Someone would dare for the rest of their lives to enshrine this idea, this instant; it's just really inspiring. I used to be judgmental about the things that people would want for tattoos. This was early on when I started tattooing, so there were marines, and I was trying to get people interested in trying to choose something unique or commission something different. Later I realized, who am I to criticize someone's tattoo? What makes a good tattoo? I said, "Man, a good tattoo is if it makes somebody feel better about themselves, and they're happy with it, and it adds a little spark to their lives, a little mystery, or a little exoticism," which it is for a lot of these people.

A lot of the early guys that I was putting epic things on thirty to forty years ago were very corporate guys. They loved the fact that they were in the boardroom, with the suits, and they are all up in there with their fucking agendas to rule the world and they had some insane piece under their suit, forever. It's pretty cool.

Williams: Let me discuss longevity here, since we brought that up. I've been selling paintings for an awfully long time and dealt with a lot of people, and it's interesting to see what people think of a painting and how they tolerate a painting, and what they think the intentions of a painting are. Paintings have the big problem of always being an auxiliary form of interior decorating. Now, I can have books laying on my coffee table . . . *Moby-Dick, A Tale of Two Cities, Two Years before the Mast,* or some real dramatic, classic novel. But if I take that book and I start painting pictures of it and put it on the walls, people are going to shit. It's going to be too dramatic, and it will scare the children and whatnot, so right out of the shoot, art has denigrated itself to literature.

You have that problem. The grandparents are going to come in, and they aren't going to be comfortable with the grandchildren when they see the stomach on that wall. I've always tried to ignore or violate that concept or try to get people to think beyond it. That's been a downfall of mine.

Another thing is when people buy art, I sell best when people are in a buying frenzy like they're shopping at Walmart. Now that's unfortunate, but it's true. Even as intellectual as I can be, getting people excited seems to be the best way to sell art. I discovered that I get these collectors that worship me, and some collectors have reservations, and some collectors start to exploit me financially right from the beginning. But I find that there's an average of about an eight-year turnover on them.

First, they have a romance with me, and they start showing all the stuff off to people, and they start to get a lot of people saying, "that's great." After a while, they've accumulated enough negative responses that they start reevaluating the paintings. Then, after a while, they're tired of it, and that's about the eight-year cycle. For some people, it's been shorter, and for a lot of people it's been twenty years. But watching the psychology of people dealing with what I do and dealing with art, in general, is kind of a sad thing. I've seen people buy paintings because they had the number five in them. I've seen people buy something because it was purple! I try to foster in people the thing that this isn't part of your environment; this painting is an entity in itself. In reality, the fucking house should be built around the painting, but that's impossible to explain to people.

People get into collector frenzies, and they aren't very intelligent, and what they'll do is buy about eight or ten pieces from me and a few other artists, and then they'll fill the wall and that's it. The idea of collecting and putting the pieces up in rotation is completely foreign to them. When they fill the walls up, they're over with. Sometimes I feel at the mercy not only of the academic world but these fucking collectors that are so shortsighted.

Hardy: That's the downside of it. I found that sometimes people see things in the work that I never would have thought of. To know that it turns a switch on for them, that's pretty cool. But it does have to be grounded in a passion and obviously something more than just "this is the flavor of the month or decade." It's an object out there in the world that will function somehow with a life of its own.

It blows my mind when you're in museums and you see stuff from centuries back, whether it's something from Egypt or ancient China or something from the nineteenth century. It makes you think this work of art survived and went through these numbers of hands and it's generating this signal or aura to continuing generations. I think that's a very cool thing.

Williams: That's culture in its truest form. But you have the situation where the art is interpreted, misinterpreted, and interpreted by others to the artist's benefit and whatnot, and you know how shaky and floaty that is. When I was a young artist, I had an idea that there was about a 40 percent chance that I would reach the idea that I was mentally thinking about. Then I realized that other artists must be like that, too. As I got older and I became a more seasoned journeyman in this trade, I could do about 80 percent. When I have an idea, and I think of it in my head with the color scheme and the staging of the characters, I can maybe hit 80 percent of what I intended. And I see artists and their work and think, Jesus Christ, these guys look like they're working at about 5 percent or 10 percent of their intention.

You never know, and you sure as hell never let the buyer know how far off you are on these things. They've got to believe that you're a genius and that every stroke was divine providence. You got to keep the bugs flying high on the tent. You know it, much like I do, that the term "art" is kind of like a fucking joke. When people ask what you do, you say, "I'm an artist," and it's kind of hard to keep a straight face. Usually I'll say technical illustrator and get a little more respect. I've always had the philosophy that I've been in trouble with the police, never graduated from high school, always been a fuckup, always been slow, hard learning, dyslexic at one thing or another, but I figured I'll just stick with it at ground level being a fuckup and see where I could go from there. I can always rely on one constant: I'm a fuckup, and I can just take it from that point on.

Robert Williams in Conversation with Kenny Scharf

KENNY SCHARF / 2013

From *Juxtapoz* 20, no. 7 (July 2013): 66–75. Reprinted by permission of High Speed Productions Inc. and Gwynned Vitello.

In the rare occurrences, when wisdom has the ability to evolve, exceptional things happen. Five years ago, Robert Williams had the vision to make his already experiential, immersive paintings emerge from the confines of canvas and into a 360-degree physical experience. Teaming with the technologies and like-minded engineers at Gentle Giant Studios, Williams produced exceptional sculptures that premiered at his last solo show in New York City at Tony Shafrazi in 2009. For this year's Comic-Con International, Robert has once again partnered with Gentle Giant for another remarkable foray into the physical stuff, with new sculptures and collectibles on the offering. Williams recently sat down in Burbank, California, to discuss the history of the form with fellow painter Kenny Scharf, another artist who transformed his paintings into sculpture in the studios of Gentle Giant for a recent exhibition at Paul Kasmin in New York City.

Kenny Scharf: I want to hear what you have to say about your sculptures.

Robert Williams: You know, Michelangelo used to say that he doesn't carve the sculptures; he frees them from the stone. That's just a really great thing to say.

Scharf: He liberates them!

Williams: The sculptures are there. He just frees them. I took sculpture at Los Angeles City College in 1963–64 and made straight As. I did very well in sculpture. I made a number of things, female statues and whatnot.

Scharf: Out of clay?

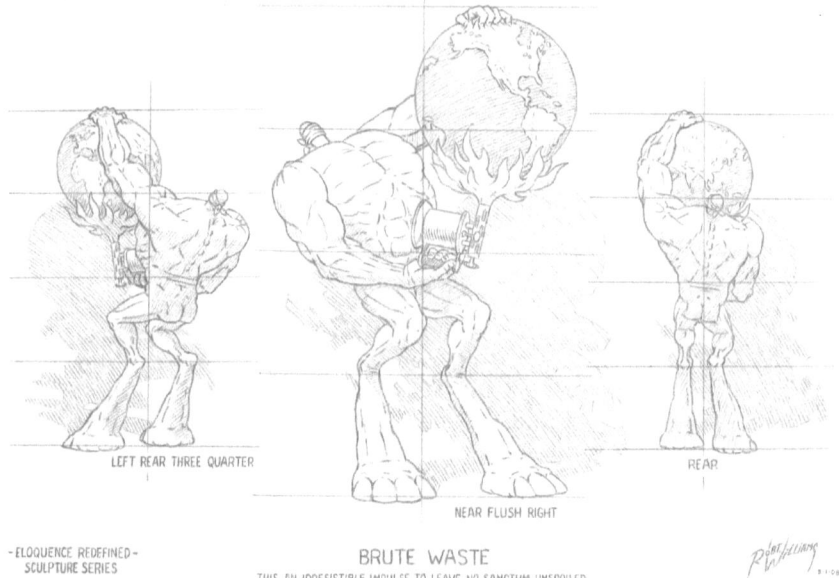

LEFT REAR THREE QUARTER

NEAR FLUSH RIGHT

REAR

- ELOQUENCE REDEFINED -
SCULPTURE SERIES

BRUTE WASTE
THIS, AN IRRESISTIBLE IMPULSE TO LEAVE NO SANCTUM UNSPOILED

Robert Williams, *Design Concept for Brute Waste Sculpture*, 2006. Ink drawing on illustration board, 61 x 41 cm.

Williams: One carved out of wood, one thing out of terra-cotta. I've always had a fundamental understanding of carving things out. Here's how that kind of Michelangelo quote pertains: To be an artist, you are locked in a matrix, just like the rock that houses the sculpture. That matrix is your capability to make the sculpture, the capability to find an audience that will tolerate and buy what you do, and the galleries and museum system that will tolerate it. Even so, with paintings, you are locked in a matrix of circumstance with your art, so you are not really free. You have to think, "What will make these people think about this?"

Scharf: It's so limiting to concern yourself with what people think.

Williams: The people that run the museums and galleries are failed artists. And probably the reason they failed was they lacked inspiration and imagination. So when you come along with it, they can't quite digest what you're doing. It doesn't take very much to exceed your audience.

Scharf: Without being ahead of your time?

Williams: Well, right up until about the 1860s, anything that was considered abhorrent or fantasy was a sign of mental illness. People were very rational during the Victorian period. Very, very rational. And one sign of mental illness was when someone was talking of things that did not pertain to the issues and the functions of the right now. This was why Lewis Carroll would use children as a medium to do nutty stuff.

If you come up with a really good idea that is stimulating, and you start to do it and start talking to people, well, there's a good chance you'll lose 60 or 80 percent of the people because they are brought up to be practical. Something that really helped us out in the last thirty or forty years is that our adversaries, the conceptualists, put thinking above productivity. And that's our mutual intent, to be able to think freely.

In the 1980s, they said painting was dead. I would say 80 to 85 percent of the people that go to museums and enjoy art, and maybe just the general public, see art as decoration. The painting should be nice on the wall; it should be presentable so that the grandfather can bring the grandchildren and share it with them. And it should lend itself to integrating with the architecture and the decor, you know? Getting people to think beyond "art as a fucking decoration," the only allies we've really had in that world are the conceptualists, who've gone way overboard, writing eight-page theses on a pile of sand.

Both you and I have that comic book and B-movie influence and a certain amount of pornography, adventure-action, pulp magazine covers, and all this stuff that doesn't lend itself to what you would call "sophistication." Artists have strived, have always strived, to set themselves aside or ahead of society by pushing sophistication. Well, I really lack it. You lack it. Once you set sophistication aside, you have a whole giant arena to play in, with all these possibilities.

Scharf: Never-ending. But when you reference sophistication, I, in a way, disagree. I see what you do as very sophisticated. It may not be what someone might think of as sophisticated subject matter, but I mean, no one can paint the way you do. I love when I go to your studio and at first glance think, "Oh my god, this is crazy, what is going on here?" There's an immense sophistication and elegance to your craft.

Williams: Well, I think you are confusing the word sophistication with intelligence and virtuosity.

Scharf: Maybe I am.

Williams: I hope that's the way it's coming off. Sophistication is being dry and boring and snotty and aloof.

Scharf: Can't you be sophisticated about crap culture?

Williams: Well, every time that you say sophisticated, there's another word to describe it. Like part of being sophisticated is not shitting your pants. But I would say that's good hygiene and respect for the people around you.

Scharf: But if you shit your pants and turn those shitten pants into an incredible piece of art, there is some sophistication in that. Or is that completely wrong?

Williams: You have way exceeded your audience! But the reason why I am avoiding it is because I want to attack it. I want my art to confront Richard Serra, modernists, and conceptualists. I want to knock the underpinnings out of what they promoted. I wanted to do these sculptures, but I knew there was no chance in hell that I would ever find underwriters to do them. I thought, why don't I sit down and do a set of four drawings of what would be possible to do as sculptures, that would be really liberating and wild. I called the series *Eloquence Redefined*. You really have to stretch elegance, stretch the word, like putting a prophylactic over the mouth of a mason jar.

Scharf: What do you think it is about eyeballs and teeth?

Williams: They are biomorphic. We relate to ourselves.

Scharf: We can't get away from them. No matter what.

Williams: The thing about eyeballs is, when a predator sets its eyes on you, you know you're in danger. So that's one thing you look out for. The second thing, in that same predator, is when you see its teeth; it's like how chimpanzees hate when you smile at them because they think you're aggressive.

Scharf: You have made such amazing paintings for all these years, and they're all depictions of these scenes in your head. And there are obviously 3D elements everywhere. What is it about sculpture that you wanted to achieve that's not in painting?

Williams: The thing about sculpture that's negative is you can't sculpt a blue sky. But the shortcomings of a painting are that you can't walk around it. When you can walk around something, you emotionally comprehend it to a point of satisfaction. Men judge flavor by shape. It's the shape of something that stimulates your mind, and when you look at something, you say, "Well, I don't quite believe what I'm looking at!" When you walk around it, your mind starts putting in vectors of mathematics, and you start calculating, storing that, and verifying what you see. It's like massaging your brain. A real satisfaction.

I'm fairly well versed in sculptural history. I'm familiar with Alexander Calder and his father, who very few people know about. His father was a remarkable sculptor, and one of his most important sculptures was a fountain that was in the Panama-Pacific International Exposition in 1915 in San Francisco. It was Victorian art, but it was really good. I went clear through fucking art school and never heard of Antoni Gaudí. And then I found out about him and thought, "Oh, man, this is the fucking best!"

Gentle Giant Studios (photograph), Robert Williams with *Brute Waste*, 2010. Sculpture made of fiberglass and enamel paint; photograph.

Scharf: Psychedelic!

Williams: This is emotion, warmth, depth, which is what the Bauhaus cut out.

Scharf: So both of us love emotion. We were talking about minimal art at the beginning and the whole idea of art as severed from emotion. It's like, okay, this is an unemotional object, we can look at it, and it's basic and all the way to its basic-basic-basicness, and without the frills. Well, what's wrong with the frills? We want the frills.

Williams: Kenny, our world is coming around to us. I'm seventy years old, and it's coming back to a warmth and feeling, and a humanity.

Scharf: Like the touch of the person who actually did it gives you, the viewer, something that you can't get from an unemotional block.

Williams: The thing is, if you do art and you take the Thomas Kinkade philosophy of "I have to find out what the people want," and stay within the bounds of what their emotions want, you're in this little box. But the idea is to expand that son of a bitch really large and do things that bring out excitement, that play with the id and the libido. People are very much against violence. I hate violence. I really hate violence. I dodged the draft. When I was kid, I was always in fights. I hate violence. I can smell it coming.

Scharf: Yeah, who wants to get hurt?

Williams: But it's part of the human emotional panoply. From, you know, the mother caring for the baby to fighting for your life. Part of the drama. That's the pathos of existing. And to completely take that away from the art world . . . that's not right. A good example is that you could not show Géricault's *The Raft of the Medusa* today. The suffering on that raft, the starving and suffering and drowning of those people, you couldn't show that big, beautiful, wonderful painting today. People couldn't tolerate it because we've cultivated an anemic art world, so politically correct and whiny . . .

Scharf: You have been working all these years, and you understand the modes of the art world, what is in, what is out, what is accepted, what is not. Yet you decided, "Screw that, I'm going to do what I love to do. And I might be hated." And we were talking about not being worried about the reaction of the audience.

Williams: You are exactly right. Here's my turning point. I went to art school, I tried to be a good artist, I tried to use discretion, I tried to be a little out there, sometimes, but then . . .

Scharf: Terrible! Robert Williams using discretion? Keep going . . .

Williams: When I got involved with underground comics, all the stops were pulled. My influence was S. Clay Wilson, because I couldn't believe anyone was this fucking daring and this disrespectful to the people that read his comic books. The thing about underground comics, this was a learning thing for me; they were not made for the general public, they were made for a small arcane audience. This stuff wasn't shoved on them; they had to hunt it up.

I realized the best things in life you have to hunt up! They're not coming to your fucking door. Disney ain't bringing the best shit to you. You got to go out! And all the better when you get it. The really good things in life have got to be ferreted out. And when I got involved in underground comics, I was with six other wild, anarchist, communist-crazy fucking guys that hated the government, hated the war, liked drugs, liked pussy. I just went wild in the underground comic book scene; it was like someone opened the door on imagination and said, "You can't think far enough out. You can't go far enough out." I thought to do that and yet still have enough technical virtuosity to show that I am serious.

Scharf: I'm right there with you. I hate to use the word, but we're talking sophistication in the execution. High sophistication. I come to you; I call you the professor because you know lots of stuff, technical things that artists don't talk about anymore. But I have a hunger, and I love that you have that kind of knowledge; it's almost like you've taken this professorial approach to wildness.

Williams: When I started looking at art at school in 1959 and went to college in the early sixties, I read everything I could about art history, and I saw everywhere that I didn't fit in. I have to be objective and not turn my back on this; these people are not stupid, and this is an academic world that knows what they're doing. They are in an abstract world.

Scharf: Back to sculpture, when you are working on [a] large scale, it not only costs money, but it also takes up space, and somebody's going to have to pay money to store. There is some responsibility for what you're putting out, but at the same time, I don't think you want to think too much about that.

Williams: There's the romantic aspect of it, but it gets out of your hands, and you pass on, and this thing falls into disrepair; then in another thirty or forty years, people find pieces of this thing and restore it. An example was the giant horse that Leonardo da Vinci made. He got it up in clay, but before he could cast it, there was an invasion, and they used it for target practice. So people have been lamenting all this time, "Oh, that must have been a wonderful horse!"

Scharf: I'm looking at this sculpture you are doing now, watching it being made, and I'm in awe. This is so nuts, I can't believe that it exists in 3D, and I can't wait to see it colored. With your wealth of imagery, what makes you decide the one you are going to make?

Williams: Because there's a lot more at stake. I have to select something that is a unit in and of itself, something you can walk around and has an appeal.

Scharf: But I see that in a lot of your paintings, a lot of units you could pull out and make it into a sculpture.

Williams: I just have to think of it as a single unit designed as a sculpture and not something that is going to have to be aided with a story behind it, with a blue sky and a mountain range. Then I think about what effect it is going to have, how much I consider it architecturally, with the single end itself going into an architectural surrounding.

Scharf: You and I have both worked with Gentle Giant on our sculptures, and to take this imagery and make it 3D is a new thing. I think that's a *very* exciting thing to be able to do.

Williams: It's opened up so many doors and possibilities. I think we are just right on the threshold, right on the cusp of this busting wide open. There should be some really flipped-out art coming out of sculptures.

Scharf: Anything you could possibly think of, you can make. You can make it exist.

Williams: It's remarkable. This process originally started out about six or seven years ago when I did a series of drawings on the Tower of Pisa falling over, with different ideas on how to catch it, and how to shore it up to make it look like it really isn't falling but leaning on purpose. It had all these different elements, and it was done in a proper Renaissance style. After that show, I thought, well, maybe I'd do something else like that, maybe a series of improbable sculptures. Well, these things will be so improbable, I should call them *Eloquence Redefined*, because these things are never going to get fucking made. So I showed them to Tony Shafrazi and said: "These are perspectives on sculpture; what do you think of them actually being made?"

He took me over to a place in Hollywood that did movie props, and they got real cold with *me* but said, "Well, you need to go over to Gentle Giant." And I thought, "Well . . . that fucking ended that. I have no money to do this. I can't finance this." But a friend of Karl Meyer of Gentle Giant saw the work and said he would take it over there. So I was sitting at the very table and showing it to them, and Karl says, "These have got to exist." So that's what got the ball started, these people's generosity and faith in me.

Scharf: So now that these are happening, I'm sure you got a multitude of other ideas.

Williams: Well, if these other two work out and warrant others, then I'll sit down and restrain myself to some intelligent, far-out stuff.

Scharf: With teeth and eyeballs, I hope.

Williams: Yeah, it will have a visceral character to it.

Robert Williams: The Master of the Slang Aesthetic

JEFFREY DEITCH / 2015

From *Juxtapoz* 22, no. 3 (March 2015): 49–61. Reprinted by permission of High Speed Productions Inc. and Gwynned Vitello.

In French-toed blue suede shoes, Robert Williams strolls up to the sun-dappled home of art seer and culture maven Jeffrey Deitch, who greets us, not breathless from his morning run, but invigorated and ready for conversation. Contemplating the anticipation of a new body of work from Williams is like anticipating a great collection of short stories while savoring a box of See's Candies, a feast to observe and absorb. On the occasion of *Slang Aesthetics*, his new show at the Los Angeles Municipal Art Gallery in Barnsdall Art Park, Deitch talks to the painter about artistic and political labels, cartoons, and *A Tale of Two Cities*, and how he puts it all on a canvas no frame can contain.

Jeffrey Deitch: Let's start with work formation, because I love that you are, to me, the archetypal American artist.

Robert Williams: You're making it hard for me to keep a straight face here. I started art school and started taking art classes when I was very, very young. I was born in Albuquerque, New Mexico; my father was a right-wing military man, and my mom was a liberal Yankee. And they were married and divorced four times; you couldn't shack up back then. I had the influences of a very strict fundamentalist father and a very liberal mother. So I see any situation through two eyes.

Deitch: That's fascinating, because what makes a work of art strong is tension between two opposite forces. Extraction and figuration, then you go in deeper. Isn't it interesting that a creative statement often comes from that opposition?

Williams: As a young person, I was very involved in comics, especially EC comics. I liked monster B movies, pulp magazines, hot rods, motorcycles, and, especially, females.

Deitch: Very typical of young American men, but for most people with creative aspirations, that's knocked out by school systems and universities.

Williams: Well, I'm coming to that! I learned to be a draftsman really early on, starting art school, coming out to go to Los Angeles City College, and thinking, well, I can draw, I'm going to go over really big, attracting the girls and whatnot. Then I come to realize that I came in the wrong period in history, during abstract expressionism.

Deitch: When did you arrive?

Williams: In 1963, and my art teacher said, "I don't want to see any converging lines because they suggest perspective." I remember being in a lecture, right here at LA City College, where I met my bride, and the teacher was showing slides, modern art, and the old masters and whatnot. He projected Rubens's *The Descent from the Cross* and said, "This is not a painting, this is a colored-in drawing." I knew I was in trouble right then.

Deitch: If Rubens is in trouble with this guy, imagine from your perspective . . .

Williams: If his was no better than an illustration, I knew that I had some problems. My friends who went to Otis and Chouinard (where I later went), all my contemporaries, referred to me as "the Illustrator," and I struggled with this. Of course, Salvador Dalí was an inspiration, but he was frowned upon in the sixties. I really didn't have any place to look to and ended up working for Ed Roth. I wanted to avoid the car culture because I was trying to become a "young intellectual" and get that out of my system, but I ended up working for him at his shop in Maywood, California. I ended up being his art director, made a lot of money, and lived a wonderful life there, dressing any way I wanted—in the middle of a bohemia I couldn't have dreamed of. I still had aspirations of being a painter, so every free moment I had, I painted, thinking, well, there's going to be a turning point. If I'm really good, apply myself, read history, and can carry on a marginally intelligent conversation about art, then I can get some respect and get somewhere. But no gallery would show me. No publication could handle this realism. A magazine called *Avant Garde* that came out in the sixties . . .

Deitch: Sure, that was among my influences. One was *Zap Comix*, and *Avant Garde* magazine was right up there when I was in junior high school.

Williams: There was a painter named Mati Klarwein, a realist and devotee of Dalí, the only one I could find in any of the art books who didn't copy bland stuff like a lot of photorealists. Years later, Mati and I got to be good friends, and I asked, "Mati, why did you quit? What happened?" He says, "I couldn't handle the pressure of New York, so I moved to Mallorca." He just couldn't deal with the abstract expressionists. I said, "You son of a bitch, you were the only one who was holding down the whole East Coast for me." When I met the *Zap* artists through the psychedelic poster artists, then I was at home with a peer group. Every one of these artists from *Zap* faced the same situation: draftsmanship skills in the middle of the abstract expressionist movement. All of them had faced this. I'm not against abstract expressionism; in fact, I support it, but it was so goddamned all-encompassing and dominating.

Deitch: Conceptualism is the new equivalent now.

Williams: And that's wonderful too! But it made everybody who can shake their foot an artist. So, anyway, when I got into *Zap*, all of a sudden I was liberated, and I couldn't believe this!

Deitch: The chronology is interesting.

Williams: I got one more step but still couldn't find painting peers. Then the punk rock movement comes along, and they start having these after-hours, fly-by-night galleries, and I realized if I slopped this stuff up a little bit, and I stuck with gratuitous sex and violence, I'd be a winner here. I could use draftsmanship slowly and started pretty much building back up to realism.

Deitch: When and where did you begin connecting to the underground and comic artists?

Williams: I knew Rick Griffin fairly well, and I knew Stanley Mouse, who was originally a hot rod competitor of Roth's, and he and I hit it off early on. Mouse was one of the guys who went up to San Francisco and started the psychedelic poster movement, which incidentally was much more far-reaching than the poster movement of Toulouse-Lautrec in the late 1890s, though that is heralded in every museum. Through these guys, I ran across an early *Zap* and asked for some pages. They contacted Gilbert Shelton, who talked to Crumb, and I got a call back saying, "We got pages for you." I was maybe the eighth or tenth underground cartoonist, period, before *Zap* got big. I had the antisocial and sociopathic characteristics the others had, wasn't big on the war, and had been in jail a number of times. Gilbert was an out-and-out leftist, still is; Spain Rodriguez was a Stalinist, which is really a rare bird; Crumb moves left. I'm a liberal, so I was in perfect company with these guys. I'd have political arguments with Spain's communism, "Well, if you think your regime is going to get me to go out on weekends to pick vegetables for the common good, you're full of shit." So I was happier with them than I was with society.

Catherine McGann (photographer), members of the *Zap Comix* collective posing for a group portrait at the opening reception of their show at the Psychedelic Solution gallery, New York City, June 8, 1989. *Left to right*: Spain Rodriguez, S. Clay Wilson, Robert Williams, Rick Griffin, Gilbert Shelton, Robert Crumb, and Victor Moscoso.

It was not an affectation to be an underground person; it's just the only place I've ever fit. When I was young, the only people I could run around with, unfortunately, were criminals because they were the only people who defied society. Later I realized there was like a bohemian community, so both my wife, Suzanne, and I were beatniks and listened to progressive jazz and smoked marijuana and went to coffee shops.

Deitch: Tell us about your circle in Los Angeles in the early mid-sixties. Even though you didn't have an exhibition platform, you associated with the major artists.

Williams: No. I knew a lot of artists in LA, a lot were friends, and I drank beer and smoked weed with them, but my art was contradictory to theirs, and they saw me as a novelty. My friends who were abstract expressionists had to make a living, as in production painting. Once they got out of school, the only way they could make money was to go to a factory and paint a sky; they'd do the trees and hand the painting to the next guy. This was pretty big back in the early sixties; it was the way they'd fill motel rooms. Only a small fraction ever went on to do this as a career.

Deitch: It takes tremendous commitment. When I ask people who have been to prestigious art schools about how many colleagues from their MFA programs, ten years later, are full-time working artists, it's only 1 percent.

Williams: You could sit in a classroom of forty students, and if one of them, in ten or fifteen years, makes a living at it, it's a miracle. The only thing worse is poetry. But I had to do it. I was a ditch digger, a truck driver, a forklift operator, a short-order cook, and I worked for a carnival. I've done it all to be an artist and make that work, against a lot of odds.

Deitch: I admire that, as art director for Big Daddy Roth, it wasn't just your day job. You really made a terrific aesthetic contribution.

Williams: I think I did. At night, I'd go home and work on a canvas. All day at Roth, then go home and start pecking on a canvas, with no hope, no hope. This was no hobby.

Deitch: You must have exhibited during that time.

Williams: No, no one would take it. There was no place.

Deitch: That's astonishing. One thing about the art world now: though we know there's a narrow conceptual academy trying to keep everyone in line, there are many opportunities where everyone can find a platform to exhibit.

Williams: Now there is more opportunity than I've ever seen, but I'm concerned this narrow window will pass. I feel responsible for opening the doors and pushing realism. Maybe it's grown because it's time for a change and it's the last change to come about, going back to the language of realism. Our times are very positive. It's a matter of gumption. The art world, in my observation, is a self-contained situation with foundations, galleries, curators, artists, and agents. The important thing is to catch the young nouveaux riches, catch them because they're looking for culture. Catch these young people who have money, educate them, and give them the gratification; they want this thing, to have culture. But you can't snow them with heavy art, so you gotta keep it simple, and the most perfect is pop art. It's already referenceable: you know Marilyn Monroe; you know Elvis Presley and the Campbell's soup can. That's the best thing that's come along, financially, because you're catching the gratification of being a part of this upper world.

Deitch: You have a somewhat cynical view that way. I feel that the audience is still hungry for art that addresses their life experience, which pop art does.

Williams: Yes, but my problem with pop art is the appropriation, that it doesn't do anything for imagination. Instead, that jungle frontier, that deep darkness of imagination to go and mine, is gone with pop art. It's got to be referenceable, so that's my criticism.

Deitch: We've had conversations before about how so much of the high culture is born out of subculture, and I view you as one of the great connectors between the two. In the essay accompanying your new work, you talk about comics, hot rods, punk rock, skateboarding, surfing, graffiti, and all these subcultures that were invented in America, on the West Coast, and how so much of the most exciting and important contemporary art, film, literature, and music comes out of these subcultures.

Williams: When I was young, when boogie-woogie turned to bebop, bebop turned to bop, and bop turned to rock 'n' roll, this music was considered slag, just something to tolerate, not for mature people. You could tap your foot to it. Now, rock 'n' roll is far beyond the level of classical music. And I'm a big fan of classical music, but the social acceptance of rock 'n' roll is not even in question. I'm sure comics are going to eventually be at the top of the visual arts, whether that's right or wrong. The bottom always comes to the top.

Deitch: Your painting has built up over the years, and you've talked about the origins in comics, that kind of vernacular culture; but you go so beyond that. You're in dialogue with great artists of historical periods, so tell us about this evolution.

Williams: When I first started, I was influenced by the surrealists. I tried to do sophisticated surrealist subjects, but I realized I was falling way short. Cartoon imagery kept slipping into my sophistication, so I did a series of paintings in the seventies called *Super Cartoons*. I just faced up to the fact that these are going to be cartoons, and I did them as technically fine as I could. Three layers of paint, isolated with amber varnish, and one hairbrush. I put in a lot of time making them truly fine art, but they were overdone cartoons. One of these ended up on the cover of the Guns N' Roses album *Appetite for Destruction*. When I got involved with the punk rockers, I said to myself, I got to start slinging these things out fast and nasty, and they've got to show energy, they got to show brushstrokes, but look like they're casually done. I knew the old Romantic painters would work hours on end staging the thing and come along with a brush stroke to make it look fast. I started cranking out these cartoon pictures, and my audience was young, drunk, on drugs, and it was one o'clock in the morning. My favorite audience. These paintings were going to be spit on, might be cut or urinated on, so I got to paint them on jute, so if they get stitched up, they'll look even better. This has got to be low-class, really imaginative, it's got to have energy. These things have got to attract you and have a good use of color. I kept wanting to go back to that realism, so I'd have a little background shot in there, a landscape, just a little tableau. As time went by, I expanded that tableau bigger and bigger, and before you knew it, we're back to realistic paintings here. But I could break them up into cartoon panels. The nice thing about having a background is that it has an environment, a suggested depth.

I realized with paintings, in general, that modern art homogenizes and fits well into a modern environment. That's why abstract expressionism went over so big. It's good in bank lobbies, hotel lobbies, and hospitals; there's no denying that. I'm not running it down, but I realized a painting loses its worth integrating that well into an environment. Like literature, if you have a coffee table with a bunch of books, *Moby-Dick* or *A Tale of Two Cities*, it looks good. But you can't open them and show people because there's shit in there that's horrifying. This is making art secondary to literature, and it shouldn't be. In my opinion, one of the greatest paintings was Géricault's *The Raft of the Medusa*, but you can't have that in the presence of children. There are penises, people drowning, and desperation, but it's one of the strongest paintings. I always reflect back on that. So I should not try for this big audience. I should try for a select and intelligent one that has investigative skills and is interested enough in my art to make me a living. That's pretty much the foundation of my logic. Art is a playing field that's as wide as your imagination can make it, and if you pull out all the stops, how far can you actually go in it? How far does imagination go? Where in the hell can we go? Plumb all your sexual factors, your violent factors, anything to get energy. Contrast it with the most trite kitten pictures. Has anyone ever done this?

Deitch: Where did you present these works during that period?

Williams: I had enormous success with the *Zombie Mystery* and punk rock paintings, and I had a waiting list of people wanting them. I finally found a snob gallery on Melrose that dealt in upper-class funky prints, Tamara Bane Gallery. They started giving me shows, and I had some shows at the Psychedelic Solution in New York, which did very well. I sold out shows at Bess Cutler [Gallery] in the early nineties, and Tony Shafrazi came, which is when he got interested in me. He worked me very hard, but he only had one mold to follow, Andy Warhol. And he wanted to make me into a Warhol. We were always at odds, although anyone who deals with Tony is at odds with him. Still, Tony did a whole lot for me, he did. Meeting you was part of it.

About 1992, I was talking to this girl with a tattoo magazine about needing a magazine like the surrealists had back in the 1920s and '30s for just this kind of art. I was trying to get a funnel point for this movement of artists. She called back and said, "I've got you that magazine." *Art? Alternatives*, right out of the shoot, did well, and I was the guy getting the artists. For some reason, they fired her, leaving me and the magazine down the drain. So Greg

Robert Williams, *Runaway Imagination on the Back of a Wild Mare*, 1993. Oil on canvas, 50.8 x 61 cm. Private collection.

Escalante and I got our heads together and went to Fausto Vitello, because I'd already done a couple of covers for *Thrasher* magazine. He said, yeah, we'll start the magazine and come up with our own title. I submitted 120 names; they picked five and took them to a lawyer to check. And the only one that they went for was *Juxtapoz*.

Deitch: Maybe within this whole situation of parallel art worlds where there's *Juxtapoz* and *Artforum*, we come up with a number of others, and that's the new reality. Among the several exhibitions that I'm brewing, there's one I told you about, to be called *Sub Pop*, but I have to get the permission of the people at the record label, and I hope that they'd want to do it. *Sub Pop* would reference all of these subcultures we talked about, how they were the foundation for really great, ambitious art.

Williams: You're the one to do it. You should look at this more seriously; it's coming. I think that's our only option. The art world is so constrained down to its little world that it doesn't open to the much larger factors.

Conceptualism and pop art are the art of today, and they don't want anything else in there.

Deitch: How do you see your situation art historically?

Williams: I'm happier with the extreme surrealist crowd, like Todd Schorr, who is like a brother-in-arms. He has imagination and rich talent, always exploring and daring, and he likes texture and depth to a painting. Though I think academic finery, like Todd Schorr and I do, can be stifling, if it dominates. I'd hate to live in a world where my kind of art is the primary art. I have an appreciation for abstract expressionism and conceptualism, and I would like to see it portrayed in an equal manner. It's very, very hard to put together a show to explain, well, this guy just pissed in the corner, and this guy spent two years on this painting, and they're equal. A senior citizen comes in with grandchildren on a Sunday to see art, it's hard to hit them with a heavy philosophy.

Deitch: What themes are you excited about? What are you working on right now?

Williams: When you come to the picture, there's an entry point you can relate to, then all of a sudden the painting goes pathological, and you realize that this was done by someone that probably wouldn't do well at vacation Bible school.

Evil is as much a part of the art world as good and political correctness. I'm liberal, but I think art in the last seventy years has so deeply involved itself in the humanities that it's left behind this whole colorful part—the suffering of war, all the pathos of the human creature.

Deitch: I had an interesting conversation at Art Basel with a very accomplished businessperson, not a creature of the art world. He says, "I've been here for two days, seen all these booths, and there's not one work that references what's going on in the world today, not a reference to issues confronting people." I actually think he would have found them in the political art where the message is more subtle, but I understood what he was referring to.

Williams: If you deal in subject matter that is poignant to the time, when that time passes, the relevancy in that work tends to slide. In LA, during the Vietnam War, the big main art area here was La Cienega, and all the galleries had a show about their disfavor with the war. A lot of important artists built this assemblage on the vacant lot, but it was so shitty and pathetic, you'd think the finest intellectual minds in Los Angeles put this piece of shit together to show disdain. I hated the war and dodged the draft, but I wouldn't have left that mess up. I like to pick out subjects in history and give an abstract view to pull people in to see certain points in history from another view.

Deitch: Are you still very interested in hot rods?

Williams: I can't get away from them. I've tried. I have run into one or two other people in the arts that are involved in hot rods, and they're much like me and didn't want to admit it, because basically there's a large right-wing contingency in hot rods. My father made enough money with his drive-in restaurant that he had a stable of stock cars, so I was always around these dirt and race tracks, and I picked up this male affectation. There was something romantic about these old cars put back in time, and it was actually pointed out to me that there were teenagers who drove these things on the streets, and they were hot rods, these old 1930s cars, souped up. My little imagination got real excited, so I was twelve years old when I talked my dad into buying me a '34 Ford coupe. I learned to drive it on the back roads and made a hot rod out of it. My parents got divorced for the last time, and I moved to New Mexico with the same proclivity for old cars. Every cent I had went into hot rods, and I had a beautiful fiancée who left me because I wasn't going anywhere, since I was only into hot rods. And then I decided to move out to California, and no more hot rods. I'm going to become a sophisticated gentleman. I come out here and go from job to job to job, and I end up working for Big Daddy Roth. I'm working next to this guy and say, "If you ever come across a '32, '34 roadster let me know," so I slipped right back into it. I started building hot rods again. And I thought, well, this is what I do, I'm not hurting anybody, but I've never lost sight of its significance in art; it has almost no significance.

Deitch: It's interesting that you say that, because one of the key aesthetics of the twentieth century was collage assemblage, and the hot rod is an artistic assemblage.

Williams: It is, making a Frankenstein out of a car. Walter Hopps had this big show of automobiles in 1982 or '83. I went and looked the show over and later told Walter that the most important car of California was not in there— the fucking hot rod. I don't want to be primarily associated with hot rods, but I can't get out of it. It's something you just put over there. I go to a hot rod event, and I am treated like royalty, but I don't aspire to a future in that world. I go to an art show, and it's, "Oh, there's Robert Williams, that guy who was in *Helter Skelter* and caused that problem." I'm just lucky to get in the door in the art world here. I haven't done twelve or fifteen car paintings in my life, but everything is pulling into that hot rod world.

Deitch: The hot rod is part of this American vernacular assemblage aesthetic tradition.

Williams: Well, would you like to go for a ride in a hot ride sometime? They are fun!

Robert Williams: "My Stuff Is Way Kitsch—to an Abstract Level"

CHRIS CAMPION / 2015

From *The Guardian*, April 1, 2015. Reprinted by permission of Guardian News & Media Ltd.

Nonconformity comes as second nature to Robert Williams. Famed as one of the original *Zap Comix* artists alongside Robert Crumb but perhaps best known for his 1979 painting *Appetite for Destruction*, which provided both the title and cover art for Guns N' Roses' debut album, Williams is a West Coast art icon and underground culture legend. His fans revere him for his lurid psychedelic mash-ups of hot rods, hot girls, and bug-eyed men, like a Tex Avery cartoon run riot, with lashings of sex and violence all wrapped in biting sarcasm.

Yet, despite its popularity, Williams's work, currently the subject of a major solo show at the Los Angeles Municipal Art Gallery titled *Slang Aesthetics*, continues to confound the art establishment. He has been critically snubbed and vilified for decades.

"I've gotten a lot of bad write-ups in newspapers over the years, and they like to refer to my stuff as 'kitsch,'" says Williams. "Well, my stuff is way fuckin' kitsch. It's kitsch to an abstract level, you understand. It's fuckin' meretricious."

Born and raised in the American Southwest, Williams talks in a reedy voice that, befitting his reputation as a bad boy of contemporary art, makes everything sound like a sneer. Nevertheless, with his southern ways, he comes across as unfailingly polite and erudite, even when pouring scorn in the most scabrous of terms on those who would underestimate him. At seventy-two, there is little sign he has mellowed or is willing to give ground. The art world at this point, he believes, is little more than a fight for the use of real estate: "If you can get into those big museums, in a big white room, and you've got a pedestal, and you put a dog turd on that pedestal, that thing is going to be sanctified."

Even if he's never been fully accepted, Williams, by his own admission, has always had one foot in the art establishment, whether they like it or not. His work was included in the 2010 Whitney *Biennial*. He was featured in MOCA curator Paul Schimmel's groundbreaking show *Helter Skelter: L.A. Art* in the nineties, alongside Mike Kelley and Paul McCarthy. Williams likes to boast that he was described as the "nadir" of a show that, while a huge hit with the public and now considered hugely influential, was critically reviled at the time. He was also represented for twenty-seven years by gallerist Tony Shafrazi alongside Francis Bacon, Ed Ruscha, and Jean-Michel Basquiat. Shafrazi, according to Williams, saw his charge as the next Andy Warhol. "He realized that I had a certain capability and that could be turned into an acceptable academic direction." But despite his gallerist's best efforts, Williams says he remains "the same asshole I've always been."

Shafrazi's belief in him is not as far-fetched as it may sound. Williams has had an enormous, almost immeasurable impact on the art world not only through his own work but also through *Juxtapoz*, the populist art magazine he cofounded in 1994 that is still going strong today, for which he also provided "direction" during its first couple years. Styled, he says, "in the same flavor of the old surrealist magazines in the 1920s and '30s—*La Revolution Surrealiste* and *Minotaure*," *Juxtapoz* quickly found its place, becoming the biggest-selling art magazine in the world by covering artists that none of the others would touch—artists who had similar concerns as Williams and were unabashed in their love for and inspiration from pop culture. In the process, he says, it "punched a hole in the wall" of the art world that "people could pass through."

CARS AND GIRLS: A FASCINATION

Raised for the most part in Albuquerque, New Mexico, Williams had to create his own way in. Some of his childhood was spent in Montgomery, Alabama, where his father owned a restaurant called the Parkmore, then "the largest drive-in restaurant in the world." There he was first exposed to the two overriding obsessions in his life: cars and girls. The roller-skating waitresses in hot pants who worked at the Parkmore and the girls in bobby socks who frequented it became, says Williams, "a fascination I've never been able to slow down." His father, who had invested proceeds from the restaurant in a fleet of stock cars, bought Williams, then twelve years old, his first car, a 1934 Ford coupe. Soon he would become involved in illegal hot rod road races that became the subject of a 1976 painting.

"I've always been in trouble," he says. "I just socially didn't fit." In the fifties, in the South, he says, "you were a good citizen or a criminal; there was no middle ground there. So I early on related to beatniks, the bohemian world of letters and art."

In the early sixties, he moved to Los Angeles, only to study fine art at the Chouinard Art Institute. At that time, abstract expressionism was in vogue, and despite the fact Walt Disney and his brother Roy had bought Chouinard in 1961 to incorporate it into CalArts, Williams was upbraided for his commitment to draftsmanship and denigrated as an "illustrator." "That was the argument that's always thrown up to me in art school. 'You're not really a painter, you're really an illustrator. You should take up illustration.' Well, yeah. What am I going to do, be a commercial whore? No, my work's as fuckin' valid as anyone else."

A break came working as an art director for Ed "Big Daddy" Roth, the Walt Disney of custom car culture, whose most famous character, Rat Fink, reimagined Mickey Mouse as a syphilitic, thrill-seeking, hot-rod-riding reprobate. After leaving Roth's employ in the late sixties to concentrate on painting, Williams joined the ranks of contributors to Robert Crumb's groundbreaking *Zap Comix* and found fellowship with underground comics artists—like Gilbert Shelton, S. Clay Wilson, and Crumb himself, who had experienced similar discrimination in art school. After a while, Williams says, "the hippie thing started getting so saccharine and so self-righteous." When hippie culture morphed into punk, Williams found himself embraced by a whole new scene in Los Angeles. He exhibited in makeshift galleries and venues in vacant storefronts in Hollywood that used art as a front to sell liquor in the back.

"I *loved* the music," Williams says of the punk scene. "It was just *pure* energy." The musicians, in kind, recognized the same thing in his paintings. Debbie Harry, whom Williams once described as "to the twentieth century what Jenny Lind was to the nineteenth century," confided in him the story of her near abduction by Ted Bundy, which became the subject of a psychological portrait he painted of the singer and her neuroses. And in the mid-eighties, Williams was approached by Axl Rose, the lead singer of a then-unknown Los Angeles rock band, to use one of his paintings on the cover of their debut album. The artwork caused a furor and brought the band instant notoriety. "I knew exactly what kind of trouble they were going to get into," he says. "I laid it all out to them. And it happened just as I said."

From the eighties onward, Williams's oil paintings, while continuing to be rendered in his familiar style, became ever more structurally complex. Recent work, such as *Decline of Sophistication* and *Death by Exasperation* (both featured in the LAMAG show), are a riot of ideas and fantastical imagery, albeit rooted in specific concepts or ideas that Williams wants to express, that follow their own internal (albeit helter-skelter) logic to tell a story. His canvases are, in effect, like pages from a comic book with all the panels removed.

"SOPHISTICATION" A BARRIER TO UNFETTERED CREATIVITY

Williams puts great stock in never having painted the same image twice or basing his work on anybody else's ideas. "I have a great deal of pride in imagination," he says. This at a time when he believes that the virtues of creativity and imagination, along with craftsmanship, virtuosity, even the very "thinking" that conceptual art implies, have all been disregarded and dispensed with by the art world. "They've run out of *everything*," he says. "You've got a crucifix and a bottle of urine and canned feces, and [someone] doing nothing, and a pile of sand in a museum—what is left? The only thing left is wide open use of imagination."

The only barriers to unfettered creativity and imagination, he says, are the highfalutin ideas of "sophistication" demanded by the art world. With the advent of abstract expressionism, New York, the vanguard and the gatekeepers of art in America became the first port of call for all the "canons of sophistication," as Williams terms art movements like impressionism, surrealism, and Dada imported from Europe in the early twentieth century.

By the time those styles crossed the continent and reached the West Coast, though, Williams believes, they had transformed into something else, something peculiarly American. In his view, the West Coast developed its own popular art forms: "If you take into consideration in the last thirty or forty years, the advent of psychedelic art, underground comics, movie posters, B-movie posters, the pornography industry, skateboards, surfing, tattoos, biker art, hot rod art—all of that is the West Coast."

This is the art, and these are the cultures, that have long informed Williams's work, along with things like EC comic books and the golden age of Warner Bros. animated cartoons. "There's no question in my mind that the greatest art of the twentieth century was the cartoon," says Williams. "No other form of art has such a great and giant form of vocabulary than the cartoon."

There's probably a good argument to be made that the cartoon is also one of the most influential art forms of our time. But critical oversight says otherwise. "Everyone has a certain appreciation for cartoons, but no one really wants to think of them as 'fine art,'" he says. "The obstacle that stood in the way of the cartoon is fucking sophistication."

Maybe Williams can have the last laugh after all. The work of once-fashionable artists inevitably fades from view, but decades on, Williams and his dirty, funky, kitschy pictures still feel vital and remain very much in vogue.

Appendix: An Unpublished Interview with Greg Escalante

DARIUS A. SPIETH AND JOSEPH R. GIVENS / 2015

The following, previously unpublished interview with Greg Escalante was conducted by the editors in his home in Huntington Beach, California, in April 2015, two years before Greg tragically took his own life. We decided to include the interview in this volume for two reasons: one, the undeniable importance of Greg Escalante in promoting lowbrow art, especially the art of Robert Williams, from the late 1980s through the mid-2010s; two, because surprisingly little—apart from a sympathetic obituary in the *New York Times* by Neil Genzlinger (September 15, 2017)—has been published about him. One of the original cofounders of *Juxtapoz* magazine, Greg Escalante was a leading collector, supporter, impresario, and, later on, art dealer of the movement. His ability to connect, entertain, and inspire people greatly contributed to making lowbrow art a linchpin of the art scene in Southern California in the late twentieth century and the early twenty-first. Greg never grew tired of reiterating the historical truth that this movement originated with Robert Williams alone and that it had its roots largely in underground comics. He was keenly aware that Williams's work not only defined lowbrow art's aesthetic agenda but also helped inspire the by-now generalized turn toward the figurative in contemporary art today. Greg was unwavering in defending Williams's art and in helping to give a public stage to his idol's ebullient imagination, which ultimately spawned an American art movement of great importance that can rightly claim its place next to the Ashcan school, precisionism, regionalism, abstract expressionism, and pop art.

Darius A. Spieth: Can you tell us a little bit about your family background?

Greg Escalante: I remember back to age five, I think; my parents lived in a trailer because my dad was a traveling salesman. I grew up in Orange County, in Los Alamitos, just across the freeway from here in a place called Rossmoor. I went to high school there and then went to Cal State, Long Beach. I stayed in my parents' house because it was really close to college. But, for nine months, I moved to LA to work in commodities for a broker named Harry Kipper, who's now been married to Bette Midler for like twenty-five years.

Joseph R. Givens: Could you tell us the story about how you got into the surf culture?

Escalante: I was like anyone else up until about the summer after sixth grade. I was on a baseball team with the guy who decided to have his birthday party at the beach. I didn't really want to go, because I hated the beach. I was really thin, and the beach was just cold, windy, and dirty. But when I went to his party, I was like one of two people who didn't get in the water. He kind of felt sorry for me. So he said, "Greg, tell you what, if you go in, I'll let you use my inner tube." I went out on the inner tube, and somehow the wave hit me, and I caught a wave and felt that ride—that sensation of that wave. And I was like Iggy on that show *Taxi* the first time he smoked pot. It was like my life changed right in that moment.

That beat everything at Disneyland, which used to be my favorite place. This was kind of like, once I had that ride on the wave, I never went back to Disneyland. I mean, I did, but it just wasn't the same. At the end of the day, they had to drag me out of the water, because I wouldn't come in. I was on this inner tube, catching wave after wave.

I went back the next day—I made my mom take me back—and I had my own little rubber raft. I saw some guys on these little belly boards, and I had to get me one. I started with the belly board, but a friend said, "If you like riding waves on a belly board, you try standing up on a surfboard." I tried it, and I went surfing every day for the rest of the summer.

This was seventh grade, and I was maybe the smallest kid in the whole school, and in junior high there were all these bullies and stuff. And even the little kids that got picked on, I was their go-to guy that they could bully. I was super thin, but after sixth or seventh grade, I'm starting to surf. Finally, by eighth grade, I'm getting good at surfing. Summer after eighth grade, I enter my first contest.

I had the coolest mom. She took me surfing more than anyone's mom, so I'm going more than anybody, so maybe I get better than anybody. Right before the contest, like all these jocks are holding court, because they surf. They were saying, "Oh, well, you know Bruce is going to probably win," and, like, it's this whole thing. So they didn't even look at me. They didn't know that I took surfing seriously.

After the contest, the first-place person was a guy from Seal Beach, the second-place person was the guy from Seal Beach, and the third-place person is me, the guy from Los Alamitos. I was the only guy from our school who placed in my age division. In 1969, I came back to school in ninth grade, and I had an identity then: I was the hot surfer at school.

Today you can take surfing classes at high school, but back in those days, if you were a surfer, you were kind of an outlaw. Once I discovered the surfing, I got into the counterculture. I subscribed to *Surfing* magazine, *Surfer* magazine; that was when I discovered my favorite artist, Rick Griffin.

I saw his cartoons, and I was like, "Wow! This is art that I like. I can't believe someone drew that." I thought, "This is a guy that I could maybe somehow meet." Then I noticed him in the psychedelic scene with the posters, and then I even later noticed him in the Christian scene because he was the master of those three genres . . . really the best guy of all three. I suppose I first saw Robert Williams comics in a *Zap Comix* in high school. Underground comics . . . I mean this was something you would not want to get caught with. They were totally X-rated back then.

Spieth: Did anybody ever get caught?

Escalante: No. The teachers thought we were reading kids comics, so they didn't bother looking at them. We read these comics so much that we would quote them like the Bible.

Spieth: How did you get these comics?

Escalante: There were people who smuggled them in. One of our friends found a head shop in Long Beach, and they sold them to him even though they shouldn't, because he was in junior high school. So he was the middleman, and he would bring these comics to school and sell and trade them.

Now, we had an interesting high school. It wasn't structured with normal classes. They were in modules of fifteen minutes, thirty minutes, forty-five minutes, and so on, so you would wind up with two or three hours of free time in a day, and if you had a B or over average, you could manipulate it. So we could leave at lunch and go surfing. We could also stay in the ceramics department and just work there the whole time.

Spieth: So you had a ceramics department in high school? Is this how you got into ceramics?

Escalante: Yeah. So all these kids at that school, like me, became prodigies in things like surfing and ceramics. But no one cared about that because some kids were failing. This was only an experiment while we were in high school, and then it went just back to normal, where you have all forty-five-minute classes.

Spieth: In terms of social status, would you say this was middle-class?

Escalante: This was upper-middle class . . . the kind of stereotype Orange County thing. I had the ideal childhood. I mean, my dad got divorced when I was ten years old, but he was responsible. I liked it after he left, because he was kind of the strict disciplinarian guy. My stepdad came in, and he was nice. My dad always took care of us kids and always gave my mom more money than she was supposed to get.

His business was called Superior Outdoor Display Company, and he made and sold signage for business. He had a big factory in Long Beach that was the old Coca-Cola bottling plant. He made custom signs, too. He decorated a lot of streets across the US and Mexico.

Spieth: Did that have an impact on you in some ways, that you became interested in art?

Escalante: It was all those things, and my interest was already there. I even helped design one sign. I had an idea and he liked it and he used it. He had this thing called an Astro, and it had a round bubble circle on it. I said, "You should make that an octagon because then it will look more like a stop sign. When people see that, they will think "stop" and look at it more than the round circle." And so he did it, and it looked so much better. He had another branch called Superior Electrical Advertising. I think that old one disappeared because they made all these sign ordinances—that you couldn't have blinking signs anywhere. So that business went away. My dad was really an entrepreneur, you know?

Spieth: And one thing that strikes me when I'm talking to you is the truly entrepreneurial spirit that is deeply ingrained in you.

Escalante: He totally influenced me that way, and the art thing was there because I would go into his shop and see these artists doing emblematic, bold, gnarly things, not abstracts.

Spieth: Do you have memories of going to the plant where they were made?

Escalante: When I turned sixteen, he gave me what he thought was a really good job there, which was to deliver stuff all over LA. I hated it because I had to drive all over, and I was totally afraid of it and didn't ever want to go to LA. In retrospect, he did give me a better job, but he gave me the job that I hated. He told me whatever I did, I had to work at that job for a month, and I couldn't quit until at least one month went by. After about three days, I tried to quit even though he said not to. It was supposed to be an educational experience.

Spieth: And how about your mother?

Escalante: She was probably married young and had the six kids. She got married when she was nineteen, and she thought we should like go to trade schools and stuff. My dad had a kind of more like "you're all going to college" attitude.

Spieth: If you go back to your family history, Escalante, where is it?

Escalante: The Escalante part is from Mexico. And my mom's last name was O'Reilly, so I think she was half Irish. Some of my mother's family actually came over on the *Mayflower*. There's a house called the Soleil House from the Soleil people that were indentured servants on the *Mayflower* that came over, and they still preserve that house to this day. But she didn't tell me that till I was like forty; I had no idea.

Also, the author Horatio Alger, I'm related to him. This guy wrote all these rags-to-riches stories. There was this saying, "he's a real Horatio Alger story." One of his most famous titles was one called *Ragged Dick*. Maybe things didn't mean the same back then, but maybe they did, because there were these street ragamuffin guys. But when I read the stories, I really liked them because these kids were like my dad and figured out how to become successful out of total poverty just based on their own efforts and intelligence. My dad was really a self-made man.

We didn't see my dad much in our childhood, and when we saw him, he felt he had to really discipline us to make us smarter. But he would go to work before we got up, and he would come back at like midnight.

Givens: You have a big family; there were seven including you. That must have been tough, sharing a house will all those siblings.

Escalante: I loved it. That's why I have roommates now. I like the company. I wanted them to have more kids because every kid was more fun. Everyone added more fun, their friends. There was always something cool going on. Now that's this Catholic family thing, I suppose.

Spieth: That is a stereotypical Catholic family, but did you really grow up in a very religious environment?

Escalante: I did. Yeah. Although I did not have to go to a Catholic school. Most of my brothers and sisters bought into that whole thing, and they're all fanatical Catholics now, except for one other besides me, my oldest sister, who's really a half sister.

Spieth: Perhaps we could move a little bit forward. We were talking about high school and how you were becoming familiar with *Zap Comix*. I'm sure you saw Robert's stuff in there. Did it stand out?

Escalante: No, I didn't like it that much, because it was so cluttered and busy and tight that it actually gave me kind of a headache to deal with it. He didn't hold a candle to Rick Griffin. None of those guys held a candle to Rick Griffin, because Griffin's pictures were beautiful, like every inch, every "like it" was just "like," it was just beautiful. He was like a surfer guy doing this stuff that wasn't all pornos and seedy stuff, you know. I looked at it and thought, "Oh, this guy's like the best artist and the cleanest guy." Although I found out later that Rick did some of the more X-rated stuff, but not very much. Not that that really mattered. That might've made me like him more. My second favorite *Zap* guy besides Rick Griffin was probably Gilbert Shelton.

So there was a black market for underground comics going on at that time. People even got arrested and went to jail for selling that stuff. And most of the people prevailed. It's so weird to think that the new collected *Zap* volume was in the *New York Times*. It is five hundred dollars, and it sold out. I was like, "Did those people read it . . . do they know what it's about?"

Givens: Well, it holds up. Even in this smartphone age of easy-access pornography, that stuff is still shocking.

Escalante: Yeah. It was mostly perverted.

Givens: Thinking back to the late sixties and surf culture. You talked about Rick Griffin and some of the psychedelic culture. You mentioned a relationship between one of the guys that you followed and Timothy Leary. Did you know Ken Kesey or any of his people? They were from the West Coast.

Escalante: I was a clueless surfer, so I knew him because friends of mine were more into drugs. They would hang out at this place, Mystic Arts, which was a hangout for bohemians.

Givens: Was this a place you ever went to?

Escalante: No, no, no. First of all, I totally wasn't into any drug. But some of my friends at that age would go to Laguna to buy their acid, so they probably went to that place. Yeah, I'd watch them have a bad trip on it, which was not motivating for me to try it.

Spieth: Did you meet Rick Griffin when you were younger?

Escalante: Maybe my first year in college, so that would be like '73. There's a record of that meeting because we had a surf art fan club. There was a guy that was in there who wasn't a surfer, but he was an artist, and he saw our *Zap* comics. He liked it so much, he started drawing like Griffin did. He developed these skills and became a cartoonist, and he started getting cartoons that are high school newspapers that are funny.

So I saw these cartoons the next year at college. The guy, Phil Yay, was already in college at Cal State Long Beach. I met him there, and he invited me to the talk, because I was the one who turned him on to Rick Griffin. I was like, "Okay, I'll come for sure, 'cause, you know, all I want to do is meet this guy." I went and met him, and the college newspaper did a story, and I have a copy of the newspaper somewhere.

Givens: What was it like to meet an artist you admired for the first time?

Escalante: It was great . . . and it was also disappointing. I was hoping to meet, like, some charismatic guy, but instead I felt like I was meeting Charles Manson. He looked like Manson, and he was maybe shy. I was just shocked because we'd ask him this big, long question, but he would answer it in one word—we were getting nothing. Finally, we got barely enough to do the story.

A little side note: I had five thousand dollars saved up, and I was going to spend it all on some art piece of his, because . . . I just would do that. I thought maybe they cost ten thousand dollars but was hoping I could make a deal. I told him, "I came here, and I want to buy some art." He said, "I don't have any for sale, but my wife has some; you should buy her art." So I just left. I was just eighteen and didn't know any better back then. He probably thought I had a hundred bucks. Now I know to tell an artist my budget. Like, "Hey, my budget's five thousand dollars." If I would have just said those words back then, I might've gotten a piece.

I also asked him if he would airbrush a surfboard for me. And he said, "Do you have it in the car right now?" He was going to do it, but I didn't have it on me.

Spieth: And so you decided to go to college and study art?

Escalante: Yeah, because the only thing I found that I liked almost as much as surfing was ceramics. Making pots on the wheel was a tactile and addictive thing. That's all I thought about. But they mixed it in with the art department when it could have been an industrial art or wood shop and metal and something. I took art history, drawing classes, and painting classes—all that stuff. So I ended up with an art degree.

Spieth: No business classes, no finance, nothing of that sort?

Escalante: No. Towards the end of college, I thought I should have done that, because I was realizing that it would be easier to make money if I had the business major instead of the art major, but business to me seemed pretty basic, you know. I feel I got a business degree just by watching my dad. I learned how to sell by watching my dad. So when I wound up in sales jobs, you know, I was usually like the best guy because I had just been trained by my whole life.

Spieth: What happened in your private life during those years?

Escalante: I surfed a lot. I met my wife, she was like twenty-one, and I met her at a surf contest. I graduated from college in '80. We hung out for eight years before we got married in '87.

Spieth: After you graduated from college, what did you do then? Did you go straight into finance work?

Escalante: I was a production potter, where I got paid by the piece, and I worked at Pottery Shack as a demonstrator and got paid minimum wage or something like $2.50 an hour. That was the seventies and early eighties. I was also doing the Pottery Shack while I was at school. It was really like a super fun job where you could just kind of make whatever you wanted and do demonstrations and then fire and sell it.

I was making $125 a week at Pottery Shack, and then I would go to the production pottery place and make $125 in one night. So I kind of always had more money than anyone I knew because I worked both those jobs. When I first got into selling commodities, I would sell commodities and then leave and go to the pottery factory and make another hundred dollars.

Spieth: How did you get into the commodities trade?

Escalante: Well, I dislocated my shoulder, and I couldn't make pottery for three months. People said, "Oh, you can go on disability or something." I was thinking, "It's just my arm," so I'll just get a job selling something.

I went looking for jobs on a Saturday, thinking, "Whoever will hire me today is where I'm gonna work." Someone hired me that day—I was selling soccer tickets. There weren't many hours, so I found another job selling scientific glass. When the arm got better, I was only doing scientific glass, 'cause the soccer thing went away with a season or something. I went back to making pottery on the weekends. It was weird because, on the weekend, I worked like, say, all day Saturday, all day Sunday, and I'd make twice as much money as I made all week at the scientific glass. I somehow stumbled across this commodity thing, and it sounded like I could make a lot of money doing that.

So I just applied for a job. I met a guy in Newport Beach, working in commodities, and asked him if he made a lot of money. He goes, "Yeah, that's true." (Most people won't tell you they make a lot of money.) I said, "I read in the LA Times that you can make as much as $400 or $500 a day." He said, "Some days I only make that much." I said, "Well, then, I need to get a job in commodities." He gave me his card. Yeah.

Givens: Do you remember what year this was?

Escalante: I'm going to say like '82.

Spieth: Now, commodities, of course, is a large term, but most people specialize.

Escalante: Yeah, back then, it was gold and silver options mostly. I asked all these people if I should do it or not. Most people thought it sounded like some kind of weird scam, and I shouldn't do it. I called the Better Business Bureau to check them out, and they checked out. They had a business out of Chicago for a long time. My first week in commodities, I made like $750, and then I worked the whole time doing pottery full-time after that job and made another $700, so that was my record-breaking week where I made like $1,500—back then when minimum wage was, like, still not $3 an hour . . . $125 a week.

I ended up being the best guy in that office in the beginning. I bought a Mercedes 450SL. I drove it right to that scientific glass place, where I quit because the guy broke his word to me about the raise he was going to give me. He told me that I would never succeed at anything as good as his job there, so I had to drive back around in the convertible Mercedes and just say "hi" to those guys.

Spieth: Of course, computers then were not what they are today. So were you primarily dealing directly with clients?

Escalante: It was basically a boiler room selling these options with these really high commissions on them. It was, in a way, a legalized scam. It was totally legal, but it was a sales job when it comes down to selling these commodities to private investors. It wasn't like preying on the elderly, like a lot of these things do, and some people did make money, but it was really risky. Most of the people lost money. I was all super optimistic. So, in the beginning, I could do really good because I really believed that they were going to make a ton of money.

Later, I started to realize that most of these people lost all their money that they invested, but not like real commodities, where you can lose even more than you invested, because there were options where you can only lose that much; but at least 90 percent of the people lost all their money. So it was really disheartening to me that no one was getting rich. So, after every year, I made less and less money of the four years because I just—I didn't like it. I didn't believe in it. It was really hard to sell if you don't believe in it. Then I found that the bond business, which I did most of my life, is skewed. In bonds, you make money, like it's impossible to lose money.

Spieth: Was your interest in art also related to the bond business and working in this environment?

Escalante: I got a bunch of people in the bond business interested in art.

Givens: Were you collecting art then?

Escalante: Yeah, so then I was making money. I bought like twenty pieces of Rick Griffin's art from Debi Jacobson at L'Imagerie [Gallery]. I remember I met Griffin a second time at La Luz de Jesus [Gallery] and told him, "I just bought like twenty of your pieces." But it was just like, it wasn't even registering on him.

Spieth: Were you one of her early clients?

Escalante: Probably.

Spieth: Was this your first purchase of this type of art?

Escalante: I'm pretty sure my Robert Williams painting was what started it.

Robert Williams, cover of *Thrasher*, August 1988.

Givens: Which one was that?

Escalante: It was the cover of *Thrasher* . . . the guy holding a half rat. I saw this thing and thought, "Whoa! There is something serious here." And then I look at the pages inside, and it looks like each one seemed to get better than the one before. The girl on the taco and the guy that thinks through the boiler plate glass . . . all these things. I thought, "Wow! I get this."

You know, people say art has to speak to you. That art not only spoke to me; it was shouting at me. It was like, "I'm one of you. I know all this cool stuff, and I can draw well enough to do something really amazing and create a story and a picture that means a lot."

I was sitting there thinking, "This is Salvador Dalí, like, reincarnated into North Hollywood." I looked at it, I saw those pulp magazines, biker magazines, and even the surf art like Griffin. So I just totally got it.

I looked and I saw that the guy who took the picture was the photographer of *Thrasher* magazine, Craig Stecyk, and Lynn Coleman wrote the article.

I knew Craig Stecyk, but I didn't know Lynn Coleman was his wife. I thought, "Maybe I could buy one of these things, because I can't afford a Dalí." This is like the new Dalí.

Givens: You were familiar with his comic work because of *Zap*; did you make that connection?

Escalante: You couldn't. No, no, I didn't even know this was the same guy at all. The style . . . it was so different, and I didn't like his comic art that much. It was later that I put two and two together. I remember telling Robert, "I didn't like it then, but I love it now."

Spieth: So, going back to the purchase of the first Williams painting . . .

Escalante: I called up Bolton Colburn at Laguna Art Museum. He was the registrar there, and I said, "Hey, Stecyk wrote this article on this Robert Williams guy; can you call Stecyk and ask him how much one of these costs, because I just want to know if it was affordable?" So he calls me back, and he goes, "Here's Robert Williams's phone number."

My meeting with Griffin was so weird, and I wasn't interested in meeting Robert. I just wanted to know how much the paintings were. It was one of those things that the number sat at my desk for two weeks. Eventually I picked up the phone and gave him a call.

He was like, just the nicest guy in the world. He took me riding in this hot rod, and we went to the diner by the porn bookstore . . . the one that appears in some of his paintings. Since some of his paintings had hot dogs, we ate chili dogs there. It was a true Robert Williams experience. So then, that's where he explained to me that even though he had all these paintings in his house, I couldn't buy any of them for half price because I had to go and buy them from a gallery in New York called the Psychedelic Solution. That is where they were promised to. I even said, "I'll pay you full price, so you get all the money." Robert said, "I can't even do that, you know, and so you've got to buy it full price from the gallery." He explained that it was important to pay the full price to the gallery, because without the gallery, he was never going to get publicity. An art critic will never come into his garage and write about the paintings, or a curator come in and find them for a museum. There was kind of a wait list, but I called them up, and like the five first choices that I wanted weren't available, but the half rat on the *Thrasher* cover was. I wasn't my first choice, I liked almost every other painting in the article better, but the half rat made a good cover.

So, I thought, well, I can, you know, get something, so I could get the half rat on the cover of the magazine. I'll take that. So that was my first Robert Williams. Then, after I got to be friends with Robert Williams, he's the one that told me about Debi, and he told me, "Whatever you do, don't try to buy it from Rick Griffin directly, 'cause that guy's nutty. He'll tell you it's $500, you'll come back to him with $500, and he will say, 'Now, it's $5,000,' because it's insanity with him. When Debi tells you a price, that's her price."

Givens: Do you remember how much that first painting was?

Escalante: It's kind of hard to remember, but I can get close. It might have been $2,900. Later, I bought another painting from Jim Corcoran for under that price, like $1,800 or something. Or maybe I remember that I bought two paintings from him. I donated one to the Laguna Art Museum. Of course, now, they got a new director who wants to get rid of that thing so quick. I wish somehow I could find out about that. Especially now, because I could just buy it back.

Spieth: How did you discover Sandow Birk?

Escalante: I was a kid. I walked into my brother Joe's room one day and saw a painting. I was like, "Whoa! Who did this?" He goes, "Oh, Dave Birk did it." And there was a mural of a *Starcastle* album cover that he had blown up and did really big on my brother's wall. That was just like this castle in air. It was amazingly good for someone who was in like fourth grade.

Back then, his name was Dave Birk; his middle name was Sandow. Later, in the LA art world, there was two other artists already named Dave Birk, maybe spelled differently, but still Dave Birk. No one was named Sandow.

Spieth: Did you go to high school with him?

Escalante: No, my brother went to high school with him. My brother is nine years younger than me. What happened is my brother didn't really like to surf, but Sandow loved to surf. So I ended up going surfing with Sandow, and we became friends.

Givens: Your brother was in a punk band, the Vandals. Did that have any influence on your tastes, or did you discover any punk art?

Escalante: No, that stuff was so gnarly. It didn't really look that good to me. It wasn't like I saw the Raymond Pettibon thing and it like spoke to me.

I was attracted to the cutout letters, you know, kind of the ransom designs and stuff. But that was cold; I didn't really care about it enough to collect it.

Spieth: Since you were yourself trained as an artist, did that influence your choice or your judgment in any way?

Escalante: Yeah, it was good background. One time, Roy Lichtenstein spoke at our school, and there were so many little paper plates that he did, and you could find one for, I don't know how it works, like one for a dollar or something or $2, but you could buy a whole set of ten for $10. So I bought the ten, and then I saw Roy Lichtenstein in the school art office, and I went in, and I got him to sign all ten of mine. And by about plate number seven, he was starting to make comments about "Hey, you know, is this a business?" Later, like in the late eighties, I saw them for sale for like $1,200 each. So my $10 escalated to like $12,000, theoretically. But they all got lost when I moved out of my old house.

Spieth: Was there any other art that got lost in the process?

Escalante: I hardly had any art. Yeah, there might've been this one or the other one. There was a guy named Bob Downing who was a kind of a semifamous sculptor from Canada. He gave me this print. So I thought, "Oh, wow! I got a famous guy's print . . . I got Lichtenstein plates. You know, I got an art collection started here." Those just disappeared, but I eventually got into the gallery business.

Spieth: How did you get into the gallery business?

Escalante: It was probably around '92 when we started out making Robert Williams prints. I was telling Robert that he should have real silk screen prints done. But Robert was like, "Wasserman won't do those for me." So I go see Wasserman and say, "Why won't you do prints for Williams?" Wasserman said, "Oh, I'd love to do a Williams print. I have a hot rod, I love Williams's art. He's like the best guy. I want to do that print." I said, "Why don't you do it?" He said, "Because we need a publisher, someone to finance the whole thing . . . If you got money, maybe you could be the publisher?" I said, "Okay, I'll do that." So I published a few prints, and I made enough from the first pressing to keep going. Robert Williams introduced me to Doug Nason at a Rat Fink Reunion. That's where the "lowbrow art" big deals were done, at those parties, back then. I got a little booth there.

Givens: How did the Rat Fink Reunion get started?

Escalante: I think the Williamses, both Robert and Suzanne, came up with the first one. I think that was like the first one I went to. I remember it was at Moon Eyes Equipment in Santa Fe Springs, California. I was selling these Robert Williams prints, and Doug Nason bought one. He told me how he loved Williams, but he wasn't as big of an idol as Big Daddy Roth. He wanted to know if I could introduce him to Roth. I said, "If you like him [Roth] so much, why don't you publish his prints, and then that way you're actually in business with the guy and working with him. That's how you really get to know these people. Not by, like, just being a fan; you know, be business partners." So he did exactly what I said. I told him where to go to print them. I told him everything.

Later, after I did my first Williams print, or maybe I did a second one, I realized that I didn't like the accounting for them and keeping track of them. And Nason had more of that type of business background, so we decided to merge his Roth prints and my Williams prints and become Copro and Nason at the time. Nason was like, "We got to have a gallery. We can't just do this publishing." So we had the first gallery in his house, in his garage on the west side of LA, near Culver City. We were like the first art gallery in Culver City, but when the *LA Times* did a whole story on the history of galleries in Culver City, they didn't even mention us. We're so used to that. The *LA Times* never reviewed one of our shows until we did the Odd Nerdrum show, and we paid a publicist who had good connections with the *LA Times* to help make it happen. My friend was the art critic, too.

The gallery was called Copro Nason until Nason decided to leave. I asked Gary Pressman what he wanted to call it, since he had to work there. I had a lot of ideas, but Gary just wanted to call it "Copro Gallery."

Givens: We've talked a lot about this business side of yours, but there's also this patron side where you've spearheaded efforts to get this art into "legitimate" spaces.

Escalante: Yeah, because I believed in it. I always wanted to project the next guy coming up. I think about who I was at eighteen or twenty, and I wanted to make shows that a guy like me would like, instead of all the shows that I had to see as a kid that didn't interest me. When I went to make a magazine, I wanted it to be a magazine about art the eighteen-year-old me would like . . . artists like Rick Griffin and Robert Williams. Robert always says that the art magazine we always wanted is what we made with *Juxtapoz.*

Givens: What was your first attempt at a museum show, and how did that come about?

Escalante: There was different ways, but one possibly great way was to somehow be a trustee on an art museum [board] and just sort of figure out a way to do a show. I did that for the first time for a show that would later be called *Kustom Kulture*. I helped that happen and got all the funding for that show myself. I didn't pay it out of my own money, but I found the people that funded it. The museum didn't find one dime.

Spieth: Who were the sponsors?

Escalante: We had a really good fundraising person at the museum at that time. But it was one of the worst recessions I've ever seen, because it was like the real estate imploded and just wiped out. So much of the wealth around was real estate; this was about '93. Two years before, they start to plan this show.

The ironic thing is they approached like two hundred car-related potential sponsors, and there was zero interest. Some official at General Motors, that like is the president of General Motors now, was all interested in this show, and he came to attend it, but he didn't give a dime. I met the guy that donated money from Ford to the Museum of Contemporary Art (MOCA) for a show, and I told him, "We're doing a show about cars, and the '32 Ford is the number one car in this show, and Ford should donate to this show." I saw that guy after a lecture event at MOCA. He said, "That sounds really good. I'll do it. I'll do it. I'll do it for sure." Typical "Hollywood style," we never could get that guy on the phone again. He never responded to anything. We tried so many people.

So no one would give anything, and the economy was screwed at this time. Somehow I pitched the idea of the show at the board meeting, and this rich lady on the board named Dolores Milhous said, "You want $60,000 . . . for this? I'll put up $30,000, as long as you get Anton Segerstrom to put up the other $30,000." Anton Segerstrom used to be on the board, but he left like the year after I came on, and he's one of the most prominent families in Orange County; their family owns the South Coast Plaza and like ten other prime Orange County properties. They give to the arts like crazy. So I'm in his office, and I'm talking about Milhous and pitching the show, saying, "Milhous said she would put up $30,000 for this show about surf culture and car culture, if you just give the other $30,000." He said, "I'm not giving to that." So I still need $30,000 more to match Milhous.

I go, "Anton, would you do it if I find someone else to match with you?" I was in the jacuzzi with the art collector Stuart Spence and his wife Judy, and they were helping me pitch this sponsorship to Harry Tarnoff. So they're going broke because the real estate market is crashing. They just built this big house designed by Bart Prince, and they spent way more than it's worth. It's just wiping them out. She's a psychiatrist, and he's like a scientist-inventor guy, and if they go bankrupt, it would be the ultimate humiliation. So I'm not pitching to the Spences; I'm pitching to Tarnoff, because they are a big influence on him.

I start telling him the offer: "If you donate to this show, your name would be on and all over the book. It would be this big thing. It's this new art. And Brucker will even throw in; he offered to give the person that donates this show a Robert Williams painting too, *The Venus of Polyethylene*, one of the original supercartoons."

So Harry is like, "Yeah, I could do that." Then the Spences jump in. They go, "Wait a minute, you know, he was asking us first about this, and we were thinking about it, too." Judy says, "Stuart, don't we have that one credit card with the huge credit line?" Stuart said, "Yeah, it's got the high interest rate, but yeah." Then they say, "Okay, we'll do it." So they funded that show with $30,000 off a 29 percent interest credit card.

Talk about investment. Any investment textbook would say, never use borrowed money on that, don't fund an art show on a credit card. But they did just that, because they're passionate. Without their investment, that show wouldn't happen. So it all came together, and that book, it's like amazing. What a good job they did!

Spieth: That was after *Helter Skelter*, right?

Escalante: Yes. That's another story. I went to a meeting at Laguna Art Museum, and the director, Charles Bradley, and his assistant were there. I'm there on a mission to pitch a show about Robert Williams because I'm obsessed with that guy. They said, "We researched it, we hashed it out, and we think he's a genius, but it's just not really art, you know. So we're not going to do it in this museum." And I say, "That's funny that you say that, because MOCA is going to put thirty of his paintings in a show that opens up in a year called *Helter Skelter*." And then Charles, just after he told me he would never do it, said, "Can we do it before theirs?" They turned just like that! And so I said, "I don't think you should, that's MOCA . . . you know. You can't just try and one-up them like that. But we could still do this show after theirs." And he goes, "Okay, let's do it." They changed direction . . . right there!

Spieth: Do you think that the problem with the museums is that a lot of Robert's art fits into the tradition of genre? You know, in the sense of Netherlandish, "lowbrow," "low-life," "peasant art."

Escalante: Well, he really latched onto that term early, but he got sick of it. Like everyone has problems with that term, but I notice . . . the further you go away from here, the LA artists and critics, the more people love the term "lowbrow." So anyway, Williams began to call it "feral art"; then it was "conceptual realism." Others call it "pop surrealism." Maybe because it's had so many different names and never had the right name, it has been harder for it to die out.

Spieth: What I'm saying is, if you look at the history of art, there are many, many instances where folk art really became central to the mainstream. You look at the seventeenth century, you know, some of those things like *The Smokers* by Brouwer, or even early Wassily Kandinsky and his obsession with Russian peasant art. I don't know whether you know that, but even rococo art came out of the popular culture of the eighteenth century.

Escalante: Like impressionism. I mean, it was like the rebellious art at the time. Yeah, it was getting less realistic, but that's where the energy was, and that's where it had to go.

Spieth: From your point of view, where does it stand today? Is it still "outsider"?

Escalante: A lot of people in the art world have never heard of *Juxtapoz* magazine and don't know any of these artists, and they're toeing the line of the whole art world. Mike McGee and Andrea Harris, the head of the Grand Central Arts Center, tried to explain to me this one time that the art world has a huge problem because it's painted itself into a corner and it doesn't know even where it can go. I didn't quite understand them at the time, but I think they were thinking, where was the next place that art can go? I think McGee is in the very beginning stages of maybe opening the first museum of lowbrow art.

He founded the Grand Central Arts Center and showed Robert Williams, Mark Ryden, Sandow Birk, and all those cool shows. Now, Mike knows a guy that has a teapot collection worth over twenty million dollars. It's like, if a famous artist did a teapot, it's in this collection. So he's got this collection that is like a kind of history of art within this kind of a popular culture item. The collector is older and knows that it has to be preserved, so he's going to give this twenty million dollars collection and three million dollars cash to start the museum.

So Mike told me it will need like ten million dollars. Mike is part of Cal State Fullerton, and he built the Grand Central place. He said if it was the old days, he could get Cal State Fullerton to do this museum on campus. Funding works different now, so it may be the city of Santa Ana or another city that's trying to have something cool that distinguishes their city.

So if there were the perfect name for this art movement, you know, like "surrealism" was for surrealism, it would be a different story. Surrealism was such a perfect name. But surrealism died out quicker than any art movement, you know, for different reasons. One, it had the perfect name, the perfect definition of the perfect art room, the perfect group. Two, it was so highly skilled that hardly anyone could do it. So it couldn't last; it had to go back into the abstract and the minimal and all that. So this California movement didn't have the perfect name, you know, so it's always changing. People keep rediscovering it, and that might've helped keep it alive, which is good, because I don't think surrealism lasted long enough to really let it play itself out.

Givens: Do you want to share the story of how *Juxtapoz* came to be?

Escalante: Yeah, Robert's story is probably really similar to mine. He started *Art? Alternatives* with Michelle Delio, who worked for a place called Outlaw Biker Publications that did biker magazines, but they also did a lot of tattoo stuff. So she was a big fan of Williams, like a lot of women are. He said to her, "Why don't you go back and pitch your boss on this idea of doing an art magazine? In the thirties, the surrealists published an art magazine called *Minotaur*, and it was the best art magazine in the world. World War II shut it down, and no other art magazine since then has been nearly as good."

So they made this cool art magazine, and they called it *Art? Alternatives*, with the big question mark after the name. They stumbled around and did like five issues. After about issue 2, they were going to sell it or close it down. Then Williams said to me, "We're going to be out of business." He got me in on it because it was easy for Williams to get his friends, his close friends, into the first issue or two. But after that, he didn't want to cold-call the artists. Also, he didn't know as many artists as I did, because I was out looking at all this art all the time and buying all this different stuff. So I start getting my artists, people I know, like Sandow [Birk], in *Art? Alternatives*.

Anyway, *Outlaw Biker* said that the only way that Michelle Delio could keep her job was if we found someone to buy the magazine. So I said, "Well, I think Fausto Vitello over at *Thrasher* might buy it, because Williams, you were in that magazine. He knows who you are." Williams was like, "Sure, go ahead, but I'm not going to call anybody." So I call up Fausto, who I know but not super well. I had been introduced to him before, and we hung out occasionally. He said, "Yeah, we want to expand titles. We need more titles on the newsstands." I told him it had a 40 percent sell-through rate, which was good.

I hook him up with all the people; he finds out, and he checks his own distributors and finds out. Yeah, I think it sold really good right out of the gate. So he does all his calculations and goes, "It's worth $40,000. I offer him $40,000 for that title." And they come back, "The magazine is worth a million." Of course, we couldn't do that, so we just started our own. Michelle Delio leaves them and comes over to us and does our first issue. Fausto said, "Okay, I'll make Williams owner, you know, like give him a percentage." He gives Stecyk a percentage and gives Kevin Thatcher a percentage. But I had to pay for my percentage because I had money. It's like socialism here, not like, you know, capitalism. So I'm the only one that had to pay money for my percentage. Everyone else got theirs free.

I just could barely pay mine, but I had to. It's one of those things, like the whole time I had this big house on the beach, and it's always like I could just barely somehow get by. Now, maybe if I had a tiny house, it'd be the same thing. You just barely make your mortgage and all your bills, you know? So it's hard to fork out that $5,000.

Givens: Does everyone still have their share?

Escalante: Yeah. Even the guy who quit and Fausto tried to buy back the share from, he wouldn't sell it. I have 10 percent, the Williamses have 20 percent, and then Stecyk got 5 percent, but with the divorce, he has 2.5 percent. Kevin Thatcher probably has 5 percent. Eric Swenson has 30 percent, and Gwynn Vitello has 30 percent. Eric died, so now Linda McKay has that 30 percent share.

Givens: I never knew those details.

Escalante: I usually never tell the percentages, but it's been twenty years, and it seems like, who cares—now it's good to have it documented.

INDEX

References to figures are in **bold**.

ABOUT THE EDITORS

Photo by Terrance Hamm

Joseph R. Givens is an advocate for marginalized artists who specializes in the scholarly investigation of overlooked and neglected art movements. He has presented papers at the International Comics Art Conference in conjunction with Comic-Con International and is a contributing author to Oxford Art Online's *Grove Dictionary of Art*. In 2014, *Juxtapoz* magazine praised Givens's underground art course at Louisiana State University as the only known class in existence where modern and contemporary art from outside the traditional historical canon is thoroughly explored.

Photo by Jean-Claude Figenwald

Darius A. Spieth is an art historian and San Diego Alumni Association Chapter Alumni Professor at Louisiana State University. He is best known for his studies on art markets and French Egyptomania but has also published on many contemporary Californian artists and designers. Major books include *Revolutionary Paris and the Market for Netherlandish Art* and *Napoleon's Sorcerers: The Sophisians*. Spieth has curated exhibitions internationally and collaborated with numerous scholars, art writers, museum professionals, designers, and creators.